Towards Climate Resilience and Neutrality in Latin America and the Caribbean

KEY POLICY PRIORITIES

OECD
BETTER POLICIES FOR BETTER LIVES

Please cite this publication as:
OECD (2023), *Towards Climate Resilience and Neutrality in Latin America and the Caribbean: Key Policy Priorities*, OECD Publishing, Paris, https://doi.org/10.1787/278e52e8-en.

ISBN 978-92-64-80929-1 (print)
ISBN 978-92-64-36745-6 (pdf)
ISBN 978-92-64-81726-5 (HTML)
ISBN 978-92-64-96547-8 (epub)

Photo credits: Cover © Ana Lucía Soto

Corrigenda to OECD publications may be found on line at: www.oecd.org/about/publishing/corrigenda.htm.

Preface

The Latin America and the Caribbean (LAC) region is one of the most biodiverse areas in the world, encompassing a wide range of ecosystems and natural resources. The region is also highly vulnerable to the impacts of climate change, including extreme weather events, rising sea levels and changing precipitation patterns. These climate-related challenges pose significant risks to the region's socio-economic development, natural capital, and the well-being of its population.

In recent years, the COVID-19 crisis has amplified the urgency of addressing the challenges of inequality, climate change and environmental degradation. Economic uncertainties and inflationary pressures caused by Russia's war of aggression against Ukraine have also highlighted the region's vulnerability to external economic shocks, further weakening its green recovery. Climate change is projected to push an additional 5 million people in the region into poverty by 2030, especially vulnerable groups and households with greater dependence on natural resources.

The time for decisive climate action in LAC is now. LAC countries contribute less than 10% of global Green House Gas (GHG) emissions, but in the last two decades the region has seen a significant rise in emissions. Recognising the urgent need to address climate change, many countries in the region have committed to achieving climate neutrality and building resilience. In the wake of the Paris Agreement, LAC governments have committed to reduce GHG emissions in their Nationally Determined Contributions (NDCs) with ambitious emission reduction targets for 2030. At COP26 in Glasgow they made new commitments, especially with respect to climate change adaptation and phasing out fossil fuels to reach climate neutrality by mid-century.

Putting these commitments into effect is therefore imperative for the LAC region. The OECD LAC Regional Programme aims at supporting countries in the region to advance reforms on key priorities such as increasing productivity, enhancing social inclusion, strengthening institutions and governance, and — most recently — in tackling environmental and climate concerns as part of a new Environmental Sustainability priority. It calls for greater focus on effective integration of environmental considerations into Productivity, Social Inclusion and Governance priorities, promotion of a fair and green transition and more sustainable, carbon-neutral development in LAC.

This report, delivered at the first Ministerial on Environmental Sustainability taking place in San Jose Costa Rica on 5 October 2023, highlights the main challenges and actions to address climate change in the region. It provides 40 policy recommendations, presented in the form of an Action Plan, building on policy dialogues among LAC and OECD experts under the OECD LAC Regional Programme. The Action Plan is intended to help support LAC countries meet international commitments such as those under the Paris Agreement, as well as regional and national commitments expressed in the declarations Our Sustainable Green Future and Accelerating the Clean, Sustainable, Renewable, and Just Energy Transition, adopted at the IX Summit of the Americas; the Ibero-American Charter on the Environment, adopted at the XVIII Ibero-American Summit; and the climate and sustainability commitments contained in the third EU-CELAC Summit Declaration.

The report shares policy experiences and good practices from the region, identifies the key policy priorities for climate resilience and neutrality and proposes to adopt integrated approaches in combating emissions and protecting vulnerable populations and ecosystems. The Action Plan presented in this report emphasises, inter alia, the importance of mainstreaming climate change and environmental considerations in sectoral policies, aligning policy priorities and goals with implementation, and ensuring efficient financing mechanisms and rapid green investment.

More effective co-ordination at all levels, nationally and internationally, and partnerships for more coherent and strategic action are also crucial. The OECD LAC Regional Programme's Environmental Sustainability pillar is complemented by the Inclusive Forum on Carbon Mitigation Approaches (IFCMA), another OECD flagship initiative in which eleven LAC countries are already participating, to help optimise the global impact of emissions reduction efforts around the world through better data and information sharing, evidence-based mutual learning and inclusive multilateral dialogue.

We hope this report provides a useful framework to expand that co-operation between the OECD and LAC countries, while ensuring a sound policy basis for climate action that delivers a carbon-neutral, fair and green transition in the region.

Jo Tyndall,
Director,
Environment Directorate, OECD

Andreas Schaal,
Director,
Global Relations and
Co-operation Directorate, OECD

Foreword

This report is one of the main outputs of the *OECD project on Enhancing Green Transition in Latin America and the Caribbean: From Commitments to Action*. It offers governments in the Latin America and the Caribbean (LAC) region recommendations on key policy priorities to advance towards climate resilience and neutrality. The report is not a comprehensive analysis of all existing climate action and related opportunities and challenges across the LAC region, but rather a selection of those that emerged during a series of Regional Policy Dialogues, Expert Workshops and exchanges organised between OECD and LAC country experts over the period of 2022 and 2023. Furthermore, the findings in the report also leverage knowledge-based analysis by OECD and other international organisations on the various topics.

The report was prepared in the context of the OECD Latin America and the Caribbean Regional Programme (LACRP), which supports the LAC region in advancing its reform agenda on key priority areas, such as increasing productivity, enhancing social inclusion and strengthening institutions and governance. In 2022, the LACRP incorporated a new priority on Environmental Sustainability. The report provides a list of 40 key policy recommendations, in the form of an Action Plan, intended to support LAC countries in achieving climate resilience and neutrality, while also integrating environmental sustainability considerations in the other priority areas of the LACRP.

This report represents a collaborative effort between the OECD Environment Directorate (ENV) and the Global Relations and Co-operation Directorate (GRC), under the leadership of Rodolfo Lacy, former Director for Climate Action and Environment for Latin America and Special Envoy to the United Nations. The report was drafted by Dimitra Xynou (Chapters 1 and 2) and Sergio Ampudia (Chapters 3 and 4) of ENV. Eija Kiiskinen (ENV) provided overall guidance and managed the project, overseen by José Antonio Ardavin (GRC).

The preparation of this report, as well as the Regional Policy Dialogues and Expert Workshops that were organised during the drafting process, benefited from the contributions and valuable comments of Aimée Aguilar Jaber, Geraldine Ang, Olof Bystorm, Miguel Cárdenas Rodriguez, Amy Cano Prentice, Joseph Cordonnier, Jane Ellis, Chiara Falduto, Catherine Gamper, Nathalie Girouard, Douglas Herrick, Raphaël Jachnik, Katia Karousakis, Lylah Davies, Nicolina Lamhauge, Xavier Leflaive, Mikael Maes, Florian Mante, Virginie Marchal, Sarah Miet, Mariana Mirabile, Michael Mullan, Daniel Naghtigall, Rodrigo Pizarro, Coline Pouille, Elia Trippel, Klas Wetterberg, Shunta Yamaguchi and Pinhas Zamorano from ENV; Jorge Carbonell and William Thompson (GRC); Peter Haxton, Eva Katzer and Jane Stacey (CFE); Jens Sedemund (DCD); Jonas Teusch and Elena Vidal (ECO); Diana Toledo Figueroa (EDU); and Federico Bonaglia, Luis Cecchi, Olivia Cuq, Juan Larrain and Sebastian Nieto Parra (DEV). Valuable administrative support was provided by Deborah Holmes (ENV). Sofia Blamey, Charlotte Dubald, Daniela Sena and Julie Whitelock (GRC) provided organisational and co-ordination support during the preparatory process. Beth Del Bourgo, Ria Sandilands, Stephanie Simonin-Edwards, Dominique Haleva and Lupita Johanson (ENV) provided publication production support.

Special thanks go to the participants of the Regional Policy Dialogues and Expert Workshops. Their presentations and interventions provided valuable inputs that were later integrated in the report. OECD and LAC members of the LACRP Steering Group that reviewed the Action Plan - an integral part of the report - provided insightful comments and deserve a particular mention. The Action Plan has also benefited from the inputs and comments of the following partner institutions: the Development Bank of Latin America and the Caribbean (CAF), the Inter-American Development Bank (IDB), the International Labour Organization (ILO), the United Nations Economic Commission for Latin America and the Caribbean (UN ECLAC), and the United Nations Environment Programme (UNEP). We appreciate the involvement of Business at OECD (BIAC) and the Trade Union's Advisory Council (TUAC), which also discussed the Action Plan within their communities, providing relevant insights. The Action Plan aims to support countries from LAC in the design and implementation of national strategies for a comprehensive inclusive, sustainable and resilient growth agenda. It does not necessarily reflect the views of any of these institutions.

The report has been produced with the financial assistance of the European Union Facility for Development in Transition. The views herein can in no way be taken to reflect the official position of the European Union nor its Member States.

Table of contents

Tables

Figures

Boxes

Executive Summary

As elsewhere, countries in Latin America and the Caribbean need to take decisive and urgent action on climate change. While many countries in the region have committed to achieving climate neutrality and building resilience, further efforts are needed. This involves, for instance, better management of increasing risks from climate change and climate variability, but also mitigating greenhouse gas (GHG) emissions and promoting innovation and green investments. Achieving these goals requires comprehensive long-term strategic and financial planning, a more integrated and inclusive approach, which better aligns adaptation and mitigation policies and measures across different sectors, albeit at a differentiated level.

The LAC region is highly vulnerable to climate change. Climate events are already impacting ecosystems, food and water security, human health and poverty as well as urban areas, agricultural productivity, hydrological regimes, coastal livelihoods and biodiversity. These vulnerabilities to climate change have a direct impact on national and local economic development and sectors in the region. While adaptation to climate change is a key policy priority for the region, each country's national circumstances, vulnerabilities and needs will require differentiated policy approaches.

Targeted planning for climate adaptation policies is urgently needed to increase countries' climate resilience. Linking climate change adaptation and disaster risk reduction interventions, such as early warning systems and civil protection systems, can improve countries' ability to reduce economic, environmental and social impacts of extreme climate events. Integrating climate considerations in long-term strategic infrastructure planning could support investments in climate-resilient infrastructure. Good water demand management is crucial for the region and requires a combination of water allocation regimes and economic instruments. Combating biodiversity loss can also play a key role in limiting climate change impacts. Addressing climate adaptation and biodiversity challenges, through an integrated approach which mainstreams biodiversity considerations in economic sectors and the wider adoption and implementation of Nature-based Solutions, would be an opportunity for LAC governments to reinforce the policy measures and increase efficiency of responses.

Taking ambitious mitigation actions in economically important sectors, from renewable energy to sustainable transport, urban development and tourism, is vital to combat climate change. Many LAC countries have made significant progress in developing renewable energy markets and diversifying their energy mix to reduce reliance on fossil fuels and enhance their climate resilience. However, more needs to be done to develop and implement energy plans that prioritise the deployment and utilisation of renewable energy sources, phase-out fossil fuel exploration and production, and improve energy efficiency. Action is also needed to promote sustainable transport. High urbanisation rates have resulted in increased demand for transport, particularly using private vehicles, leading to higher GHG emissions, air pollution and traffic congestion. Promoting sustainable tourism development and management presents an ongoing challenge, given the considerable variations in issues and impacts across different destinations, and long-term strategic planning is necessary to contribute to climate-resilient development. Mitigation strategies should be designed to promote equitable outcomes, addressing existing inequalities within the LAC region while creating green jobs. In this context governments should align environmental and health policies to protect the environment and public health, while considering synergies between emission reduction and broader well-being objectives.

LAC countries should align their mitigation and adaptation objectives and measures while considering and addressing potential conflicts, trade-offs, synergies, and co-benefits. Integrated mitigation and adaptation actions can help achieve a coherent and co-ordinated approach to addressing climate change, and create long-term impacts and broad political support. This facilitates the development of common objectives and goals for efficient resource allocation and more effective outcomes. Developing integrated plans that take into account sustainable energy, food security, and bioeconomy that promote the use of renewable energy, sustainable agricultural practices, food waste reduction, and technological innovation with a resilience perspective should help to address the negative effects of climate change in the region.

Climate change is a complex issue that requires creating a knowledge base and engaging citizens. Collecting environmental data and information is necessary to help countries establish clear priorities and targets, make informed policy choices to address the climate change challenges, and follow progress towards achieving their international and national climate commitments. There is also a need to strengthen climate governance (coherent institutional, legal and regulatory policy frameworks) and planning through an increased use of strategic environmental assessments and transparency in decision-making.

Scaling up finance for climate action from a wide array of sources (domestic, international, public and private) is necessary for countries to move towards a net-zero economy and reach their international climate commitments. LAC economies must better use existing domestic resources and mobilise additional public and private resources for investment that help to meet environmental goals. The use of carbon pricing and carbon markets are important approaches in this regard. Ensuring a better use of international climate finance to scale up climate action and better mobilise international private finance could further accelerate the net-zero transition in the region.

Productivity and competitiveness in the LAC region could improve with technology transfer and innovation. The transition towards a resource efficient, circular economy can help improve material use, and environmental, economic and social outcomes. The same applies for implementing policies for a sustainable ocean economy, such as promoting marine spatial planning, expanding marine protected areas, tackling marine plastic pollution and promoting sustainable fishing. Achieving climate resilience and neutrality will not lead to a net-zero economy without social factors that can reduce inequalities and improve productivity, such as green jobs, gender equality and environmental education.

This report captures the outcomes of the OECD project "Enhancing Green Transition in LAC: From Commitments to Action". It identifies LAC countries' main climate change policy priorities, which were discussed through a series of Regional Policy Dialogues and Expert Workshops carried out in 2022-23, and complements these with findings of recent analyses by the OECD and other international partners. The 40 key policy recommendations, in the form of an Action Plan presented in this report, provide a framework for prioritising future climate action by countries in the LAC region, in co-operation with OECD and other actors in the region.

1 Action Plan towards Climate Resilience and Neutrality in Latin America and the Caribbean

Latin America and the Caribbean (LAC) countries have committed to achieving climate neutrality and building resilience. To overcome challenges and grasp the opportunities, an Action Plan towards climate resilience and neutrality is proposed. Through a set of 40 key policy recommendations developed through a series of Regional Policy Dialogues and Workshops, LAC countries can prioritise the most effective sectoral and horizontal actions, define their sequence and move towards implementation.

Identifying climate change priorities in Latin America and the Caribbean

Latin American and Caribbean (LAC) countries are among those committed to achieve climate neutrality and increase climate resilience. This report builds upon the input provided in a series of Regional Policy Dialogues and Expert Workshops, during which experts provided analysis of the challenges and opportunities for achieving climate resilience and neutrality in the LAC region. These Regional Policy Dialogues and Workshops were open to LAC country representatives, as well as representatives of OECD members, international organisations active in the region, academia, private sector and non-governmental organisations. Recent analyses by OECD and other international organisations and further exchanges with experts in the region also contributed to the input provided as background information. During the meetings, discussions focused on maximising the potential of a green transition for greater well-being. From a climate change perspective, participants focused on the following issues:

- **Setting the priorities for climate neutrality and resilience.** Participants exchanged on the need to establish a policy and institutional framework specifically for climate mitigation measures. They highlighted the need to integrate climate change into sectoral policies, as well as to align regional and municipal plans and actions with top-down government policies. On climate change adaptation, a key priority for the LAC region, recognising the value of the local, bottom-up approach to addressing adaptation challenges was considered necessary, in addition to risk reduction efforts and social inclusion (including Indigenous people) and poverty eradication. Nature-based solutions (NbS) were highlighted as central to minimising the impacts of climate change and improving resilience, especially in relation to ecosystems and adaptation solutions in urban areas.
- **Enhancing climate finance and promoting technology transfer.** Participants emphasised the need to reform the policy and regulatory frameworks for climate finance, to create the confidence required to stimulate private sector investments. In parallel, efficient monitoring mechanisms of international financial flows should be developed as well as clear green taxonomies to provide clarity and enable further financial flows to the LAC region. Special focus was given to the need for more and better environmental information and data collection, especially on climate change adaptation, capacity building for an effective use of climate and green financing, and for a set of green incentives to allow for technology transfers in LAC. Countries indicated that more needs to be done on the missing climate adaptation and mitigation linkages and the need to break the silos and align policies to guarantee additionality of the introduced measures. The initiatives on developing green taxonomies in the region and the use of blended finance by development banks were acknowledged, as they could strengthen the private sector's financing activities. Finally, government incentives to support climate change mitigation technology transfers to the LAC region, covering access to finance, creating value for innovation and developing technical capacity, could enhance technology transfer in the whole value chain.
- **Addressing climate adaptation**. Identifying and strengthening policy responses to climate risks through mainstreaming climate adaptation in national, local and sectoral policies was acknowledged as a priority for reaching climate resilience. Participants re-iterated the need to map and develop climate scenarios to identify vulnerabilities and losses, and damages and to exploit the untapped potential for investments in climate adaptation after overcoming challenges. Also, considering the differentiated impact of climate adaptation to local communities, vulnerable groups and women was also emphasised. Biodiversity conservation and NbS can also offer multiple benefits in terms of adaptation.

Enhancing green transition in LAC

The report should not be seen as a stand-alone work. It is one of the deliverables for contextualising the newly introduced "environmental sustainability" priority under the OECD Latin America and the Caribbean Regional Programme (LACRP).

The LACRP, with productivity, social inclusion and governance being the three thematic priority areas agreed by countries, serves as a framework under which the OECD works with LAC countries to facilitate policy dialogue and the dissemination of good practices in areas such as investment, education, inclusiveness and good governance. The new fourth priority on environmental sustainability was introduced in 2022 to complement and interact with these other three priority areas. Intrinsically, the report presents the interlinkages between the four different priority areas of the LACRP, which are especially visible under the analysis on promoting green transition and sectoral integration. This report is one of the main deliverables of the OECD project, with the other two being the 2022 Latin America Economic Outlook, and the 2023 Environment at a Glance in Latin America and the Caribbean: Spotlight on climate change. As such, it is intended to serve as Background Document to support the discussions at the 1st OECD LAC Ministerial on Environmental Sustainability, in San José, Costa Rica, on 5 October 2023.

The LAC Action Plan towards Climate Resilience and Neutrality

The report, through mapping the implementation of climate-related policies and examining their trade-offs and complementarities, proposes a set of policy recommendations which can help LAC countries prioritise the most effective sectoral or horizontal actions, define their sequencing and move towards implementation.

The 40 key policy recommendations are presented below, in the form of an Action Plan for the LAC region. Once again, the Action Plan is not exhaustive nor too prescriptive. It points out key policy recommendations, identified through the Regional Policy Dialogue and Workshop discussions under this Project. Their implementation may vary among and within LAC countries, as their starting points are different, and each country will need to adopt its own approach. However, the policy recommendations identified could serve as benchmarking tools, for measuring progress towards climate resilience and neutrality. The Action Plan can also provide useful framework for identifying priority actions and projects for future co-operation between the LAC countries, the OECD and other international organisations, bilateral donors and stakeholders.

LAC Action Plan towards Climate Resilience and Climate Neutrality

15 Key Policy Priorities for building Climate Resilience

Communities

Reducing Vulnerability

1. Develop and progressively update National Adaptation Plans (NAPs) submitted to the United Nations Framework Convention on Climate Change (UNFCCC), and support their implementation through robust legal and regulatory, institutional and financial frameworks.
2. Align regional and urban planning with NAPs and promote an integrated approach to overcome the risk management, capacity and financing gaps.

Early Warning Systems (EWS)

3. Improve early warning systems to ensure that all people, especially those in communities at greater risk of climate-related extreme weather events in LAC, have access to vital information

in real-time, at the individual level, and that local communities participate in the design and implementation of EWS.

4. Strengthen or create civil protection systems in LAC, which are equipped and prepared with supplies, trained personnel, infrastructure and sufficient funds to provide immediate attention, shelter, and comprehensive medical assistance before, during and after natural disasters.

Climate-Resilient Infrastructure

5. Better align infrastructure planning, development, and investments with short- and long-term low emission, climate-resilient and inclusive development strategies at the national level.
6. Enhance an enabling environment for the development of climate-resilient infrastructure to limit vulnerability to climate damages.

Water

7. Improve water demand management to tackle water scarcity and signal the value of water, through reformed water allocation regimes and better use of economic policy instruments.
8. Review the enabling conditions for water financing and sustainable investments in water security.

Biodiversity and Ecosystems

Biological corridors

9. Enhance connectivity of terrestrial and marine Protected Areas (PAs) as it is vital for the conservation of species.
10. Effectively protect, expand and maintain the biological corridors of Mesoamerica, the Caribbean, the Amazon, the Andes, and Patagonia, among others, to reverse degradation and restore the integrity of their natural ecosystems.

Mainstreaming biodiversity

11. Establish policy instruments that regulate the use and intensity of use of natural resources, respecting the natural cycles and promoting the conservation and sustainable use of biodiversity and ecosystems services. These policies could include objectives of reducing ecosystems vulnerability and greenhouse gas (GHG) emissions, thereby increasing resilience to multiple anthropogenic pressures.

Nature-based Solutions

12. Integrate and upscale the use of Nature-based Solutions in policy instruments that address climate change mitigation, adaptation and ecosystem protection.
13. Properly value ecosystem services to generate economic compensation for the use of nature, particularly, to channel the revenues to entities and communities that protect nature.

Land restoration

14. Prioritise land restoration and climate adaptation policies in agriculture and introduce measures that will transform the food systems and improve the health of land and soil.

Effective control and zero tolerance for illegal trade of species

15. Combat illegal extractive activities and trade of threatened wildlife species by making greater multilateral efforts, co-ordinating between international and national authorities, and supporting local authorities, given the association of this activity with criminal groups.

15 Key Policy Priorities for addressing Climate Neutrality

Energy

Scaling up renewable energy in productive, service and residential sectors

16. Develop and implement energy plans that prioritise the deployment and utilisation of renewable energy sources, while considering expanding affordable and reliable access to electricity.
17. Establish and implement phase-out plans for fossil fuel exploration and production infrastructure, including policies aiming to re-direct public funding towards developing low-carbon alternatives.
18. Adopt low-cost sustainable technologies for clean energy used in electricity production, water heating, cold chains, air conditioning and heating.

Energy efficiency

19. Intensify targeted policies, programmes and institutional frameworks to improve energy efficiency. Apply standards and labelling programmes to deliver energy efficient products such as air conditioning and electric motors.

Green and Low-Carbon Hydrogen

20. Implement policies to create and scale up the necessary demand for green and low-carbon hydrogen as feedstock and alternative fuel, creating a virtuous circle between decarbonisation efforts and sustainable industrial development.

Sustainable mining for the green transition

21. Ensure that the growing demand for critical minerals, used to develop low-carbon energy technologies, along with the region's strategic position, allows for an integral model of sustainable mining, with low environmental impact, well-being for local communities, and linkage in regional value chains that enable their transformation and the production of high-value-added final goods.

Transport

Regional production of zero-emission transport modes

22. Strengthen the application of policy instruments to acquire the industrial capacity needed to promote net-zero emissions modes of transport for 2050, including the local production and use of biofuels and low-carbon synthetic fuels and electric vehicles.

Zero-emission mobility infrastructure

23. Implement public policies aiming to decarbonise freight and passenger transport. Expand non-motorised transport infrastructure such as bike lanes and pedestrian paths.
24. Introduce stringent emission standards and targets for public transport vehicles. Promote clean fuels and common fuel standards that reduce sulphur levels to ultra-low levels. Establish complementary programmes to reduce emissions from older diesel vehicles, focusing on urban fleets.

Cities

Sustainable Construction

25. Establish credible frameworks, standards and policies that promote sustainable buildings and construction practices in cities, thereby recycling materials and reducing GHG emissions associated with construction.

Regulatory frameworks for emission reductions

26. Improve regulatory frameworks for GHG and Short-Lived Climate Pollutants (SLCPs) emissions, with particular attention to methane and f-gases, setting sectoral, national and local targets.
27. Aim for co-benefits of reducing air pollution with regulating climate mitigation by aligning environmental and health policies and diseases associated with environmental risks.

Agriculture, forestry and land-based sectors

28. Develop and implement integrated plans for sustainable energy, food security and bioeconomy, considering the use of renewable energy sources and sustainable practices in agriculture, food waste minimisation, and the promotion of technological innovations with a resilience perspective.

Sustainable Tourism

29. Develop comprehensive long-term strategies for sustainable tourism, supported by action plans. Promote the green tourism transition by leading through governmental example and ensure that all publicly funded or procured tourism infrastructure adheres to the highest environmental standards, contributing to climate-resilient development.
30. Promote the certification of sustainable tourism businesses based on internationally agreed standards, as a tool to mainstream sustainable practices, reduce the negative impact on the environment, meet national sustainable development goals and encourage more sustainable consumer choices and behaviour.

10 Cross-cutting policy priority areas

Climate Governance

31. **Progressively revise and update national regulatory frameworks**. Consider the benefits and challenges of top-down and bottom-up approaches. Updating national laws and regulations aligned with Nationally Determined Contributions (NDCs) updates, as well as the establishment of NAPs and Long-Term Strategies (LTS), are essential to achieving global commitments established in the Sustainable Development Goals (SDGs) and the three UN environmental conventions (climate change, biodiversity, and desertification), while maintaining science-based policy decisions.

Comprehensive planning and strategic environmental assessment (SEA)

32. **Agree on long-term strategies, plans and programmes**. Increase the use of SEAs to promote sustainable decision-making in plans, programmes and policies. Transparency and periodic strategic evaluation will also contribute to compliance regarding Measurement, Reporting and Verification (MRV) commitments established in the UNFCCC instruments.

Environmental Information

33. **Collect more and better information on climate change**. Increase standards in non-statistical offices and establish a robust co-ordination mechanism to capture existing data. Prioritise the development of new data collection efforts especially on climate change vulnerability and biodiversity. Invest in reliable data collection methods and information technologies while creating accurate indicators to assess the complexity of mitigation and adaptation policies.

Carbon Pricing, Climate Finance and Green Investment

34. On carbon pricing, climate finance and green investment:

i. **Adopt green fiscal policies to generate domestic public resources to support climate action and carbon mitigation approaches**. Reform, redirect and progressive eliminate fossil fuel subsidies and establish carbon pricing through taxes and levies, which can also incentivise the net zero transition.

ii. **Align and mobilise private investment support through innovative financing strategies and instruments**, such as blended finance aligned with Environmental, Social and Governance (ESG) objectives, innovative debt instruments, and by developing regional and national green taxonomies for mitigation and adaptation projects. These should respond to local priorities and concerns and be coherent with public and private investment opportunities.

Technology Transfer

35. **Support industrial development and promote innovation**. Undertake a green industrialisation pathway by promoting local production of environmentally friendly clean technologies and innovation. This may include manufacturing electric vehicles, wind turbines, batteries, and solar heaters. It could support the region to reduce public debt, boost economic resilience, create job opportunities, and promote more equitable income distribution.

Green Jobs

36. **Establish investment and policy frameworks that promote the creation of green jobs**. Ensure the implementation of active labour market policies, relying on effective social dialogue, to facilitate the transition of workers into new, formal, high-quality green jobs and strengthen the social security system to support both workers and entrepreneurs in transitioning to a low-carbon economy.

Circular Economy

37. **Advance with sectoral roadmaps**. Achieving a circular economy requires a state policy on Extended Producer Responsibility (EPR) and modification of unsustainable consumption practices. Productive sectors, commerce, and society at large should assume their role in the efficient use of materials and resources through their entire lifecycle, waste minimisation, recycling and re-use as an intrinsic component to market rules.

Sustainable Ocean Economy

38. For a sustainable ocean economy:

i. **Implement policies promoting marine spatial planning and expanding marine protected areas**. These measures can help reconcile ecological, economic, and social objectives. Reach the 2030 marine protected area target of the Global Biodiversity Framework.

ii. **Promote sustainable fishing**. Introduce or further improve sustainable fisheries management and practices to combat illegal fishing activities. Include ocean sustainability as a target in market-based instruments.

Gender Equality

39. **Pursue green growth through gender equality**. Acknowledging the differentiated impact of climate change on women and men, and adopting an integrated policy framework to reach gender equality and empower women, can support achieving a just and green economic transition. Gender equality and women's economic empowerment can be achieved through gender-sensitive and gender-responsive climate policies, instruments and measures, as well as gender-disaggregated environmental information.

Environmental Education

40. **Promote equitable and green education**. Establish an active environmental education strategy, formal and informal, to induce a behavioural change in society, creating awareness, sensitivity and responsibility towards environmental-sustainability and climate change. Education systems, from early childhood, must ensure that future generations shift individual behaviours and preferences away from the current unsustainable methods of production and consumption. Environmental knowledge and green skills should be part of the curricula across all components of the educational systems.

2 Achieving climate resilience in the Latin America and Caribbean region

The Latin America and Caribbean (LAC) region is characterised by its high vulnerability towards extreme weather events and climate disasters, as well as its richness in biodiversity and abundant natural resources. LAC countries have developed and are implementing National Adaptation Plans (NAPs). Yet more needs to be done to manage increasing risks from climate change and climate variability. Based on the discussions in a series of Regional Policy Dialogues and Workshops on these issues among LAC and OECD experts in the context of the OECD LAC Regional Programme (LACRP), this chapter maps challenges to addressing climate change adaptation in the LAC region and presents options on policy initiatives that could be undertaken to this end.

Introduction

The LAC region is highly vulnerable to climate change. It is considered one of the top disaster-prone regions in the world, with the average number of extreme climate-related weather events increasing by 62% in the LAC region during 2001-2022, when compared to the period 1980-2000 (OECD, 2023[1]).

Climate events are already impacting ecosystems, food and water security, human health and poverty as well as urban areas, agricultural productivity, hydrological regimes, coastal livelihoods, and biodiversity (Figure 2.1). LAC countries are facing serious challenges when protecting vulnerable populations and ecosystems. High climate change scenarios – with high levels of uncertainty on the physical impacts of climate change and local adaptation policies – estimate that 5.8 million people will fall into extreme poverty between 2020 and 2030 in the LAC region, increasing the average poverty headcount by more than 300%, when compared to a no climate change scenario (Arga Jafino et al., 2020[2]). Such impacts may vary between LAC countries and sub-regions, as there are large differences on the natural disasters and climate change impacts at the local level, as well as on the impact to the local population.

Figure 2.1. Key socio-economic and environmental impacts in LAC

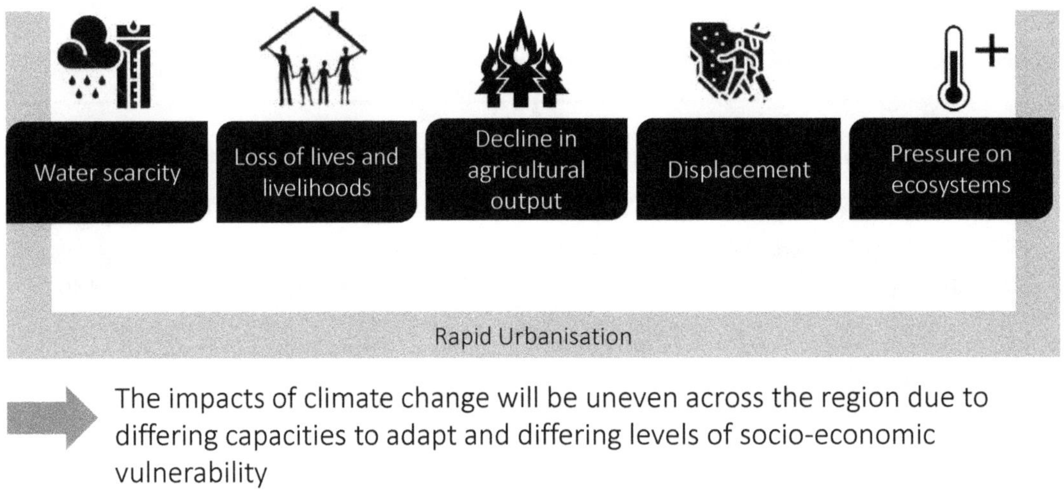

Source : (OECD et al., 2022[3]) ; (IPCC, 2022[4]) ; (WMO, 2023[5]) ; (UNDESA, 2014[6])

Data show that population in the LAC region is increasingly exposed to heat stress from hot summer days (especially in Paraguay and El Salvador), extreme precipitation (such as in Suriname, Guyana and Trinidad and Tobago), droughts (Paraguay, Argentina and Brazil), wildfires (Jamaica, Paraguay, Mexico and El Salvador), wind threats (Caribbean), river flooding (Suriname, Guyana, Argentina) (Figure 2.2; Figure 2.3); (OECD, 2023[1]). The region is also particularly vulnerable to biodiversity loss, as many of the economic activities in LAC are linked to natural resources and the quality of ecosystems, such as tourism and agriculture (OECD, 2023[1]).

Figure 2.2. Climate-related hazards in Latin America and the Caribbean (1/2)

A. Heat stress caused by hot days varies regionally across the LAC region

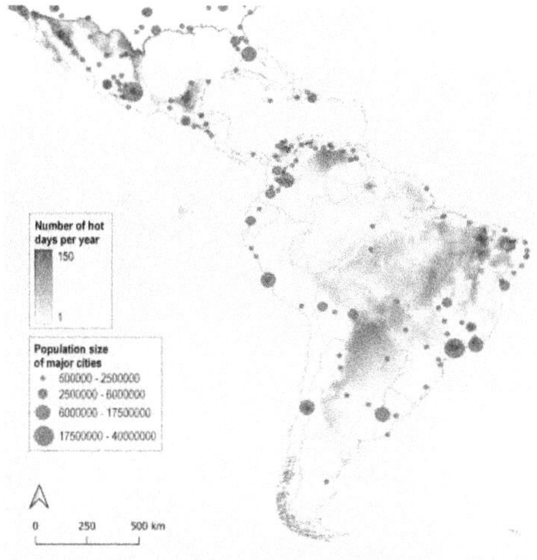

Note: Hot days are defined as days where the daily maximum temperature exceeds 35 °C. Map A shows yearly number of hot days (2017-21 average) and population density across the LAC region.

B. Extreme precipitation affects particularly the tropical LAC regions

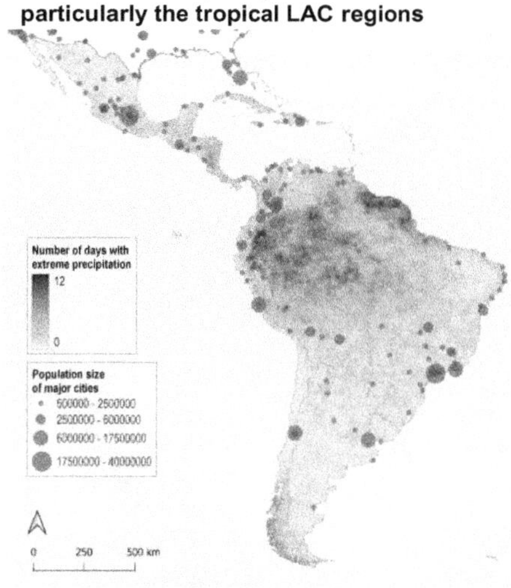

Note: Extreme precipitation events refer to a total daily precipitation that exceeds the 99th percentile value over the reference period 1981-2010. Map B shows yearly number of days with extreme precipitation (2017-21 average) and population density across the LAC region.

C. Large swaths of Central and South America are experiencing droughts

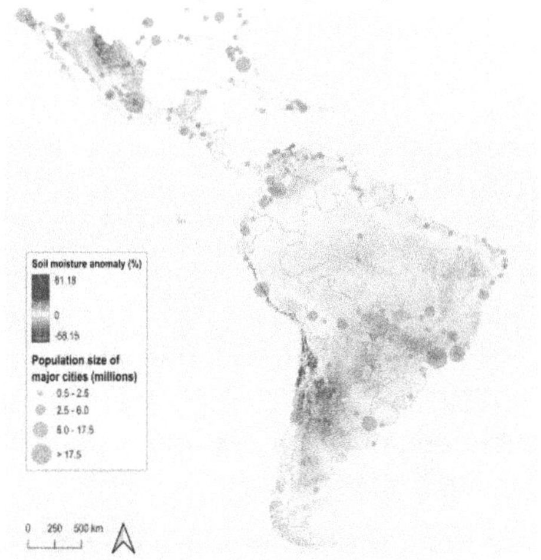

Note: Map C shows soil moisture anomaly (%) 2017-21, compared to 1981-2010.

D. Wide regions across LAC are exposed to wildfire danger

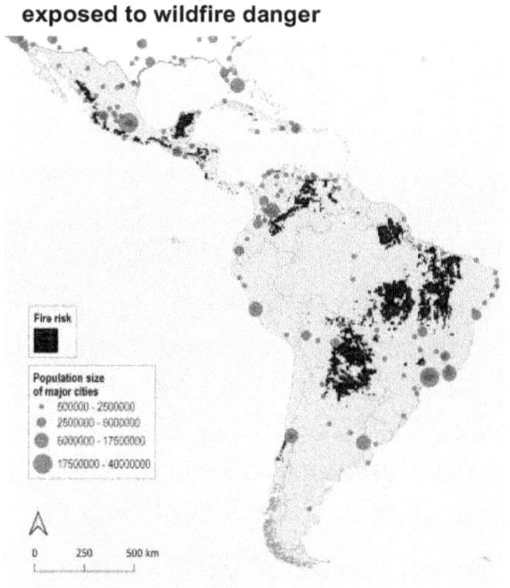

Note: Wildfire danger measures 3 consecutive days of very high or extreme fire danger according to the Canadian Fire Weather Index (FWI), adjusted for biomass availability. Map D shows wildfire danger and population density across the LAC region (2016-20).

Source: (Maes et al., 2022[7]), "Monitoring exposure to climate-related hazards: Indicator methodology and key results", OECD Environment Working Papers, No. 201, OECD Publishing, Paris, https://doi.org/10.1787/da074cb6-en.

Figure 2.3. Climate-related hazards in Latin America and the Caribbean (2/2)

E. Violent storms mostly affect the Southern Cone, while tropical cyclones affect Central America and the Caribbean

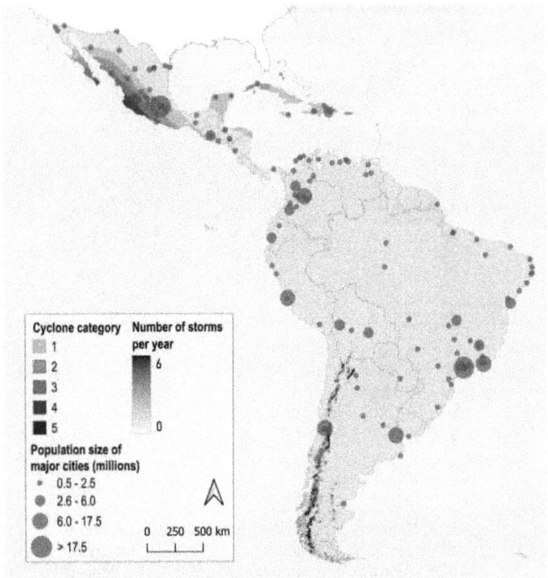

Note: Violent windstorms are measured as yearly number of days with violent windstorms (2016-20 average) where sustained wind gust speed exceeded 28.5 m/s (equivalent to Beaufort class 11). Meanwhile, cyclone categories refer to the Saffir-Simpson Hurricane Wind Scale, which classifies cyclones based on their sustained wind speed as a measure of potential damage. Category 1 cyclones are described as 'very dangerous winds that will produce some damage'. Higher categories cover extensive, devastating and catastrophic damage. The map indicates zones where tropical cyclones are expected to occur at least once every 100 years. Map E shows exposure to violent storms, exposure to tropical cyclones with a 100-year return period and population density across the LAC region.

F. Areas in the LAC region prone to river flooding are often sparsely populated

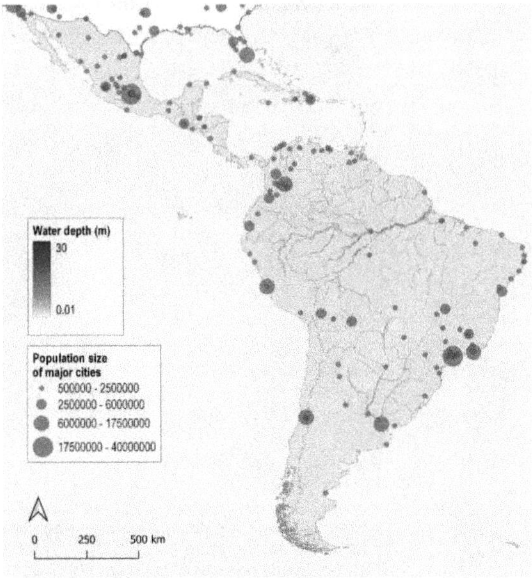

Note: Map F shows exposure to river flooding with a 100-year return period (2020) and population density across the LAC region.

Source: (Maes et al., 2022[7]), "Monitoring exposure to climate-related hazards: Indicator methodology and key results", OECD Environment Working Papers, No. 201, OECD Publishing, Paris, https://doi.org/10.1787/da074cb6-en.

Between 1970 and 2021, South America accounted for 3% of globally reported deaths, with floods being the leading cause of reported deaths. These disasters resulted in USD 115.2 billion in economic losses (WMO, 2021[8]). In total, 17.1% of the 11 933 climate-related extreme weather events registered worldwide between 1970 and 2022 occurred in LAC (OECD et al., 2022[3]). Furthermore, the impacts of climate change are unevenly distributed, with vulnerable communities, including women and children, indigenous peoples, and poor households, often bearing the highest impacts.

The climate change impacts are extensive as they concern vulnerable populations, especially children. In LAC, approximately 169 million children live in areas where at least two climate and environmental shocks overlap and 47 million children, or 1 out of 4, live in areas impacted by at least 4 shocks. Furthermore, about 55 million children are exposed to water scarcity, 60 million are exposed to cyclones, 85 million are exposed to the Zika virus, 115 million children are exposed to Dengue fever, 45 million children are exposed to heatwaves and 105 million are exposed to air pollution (UNICEF, 2021[9]). Hurricanes in the Caribbean, for instance, destroy critical infrastructure for children's well-being and development, such as schools and health facilities. Floods can damage homes, compromise water and sanitation facilities, contaminate drinking water sources, and contribute to the spread of diarrheal diseases, which disproportionately affect young children. Additionally, vulnerable families are forced to migrate due to shocks and scarcity of water and resources. In 2020, weather events internally displaced 2.8 million people in LAC (UNICEF, 2021[9]).

Vulnerabilities to climate change are having direct impacts to national and local economic development and economic sectors in the LAC region. Argentina is already experiencing the climate impacts to agricultural economic activities (Straffelini et al., 2023[10]); (Müller, Lovino and Sgroi, 2021[11]). For Mexico, the present value of crop yield changes, due to high temperatures and precipitation, is estimated at about USD 40 million, twice the national agricultural production of the country in 2012 (Estrada et al., 2022[12]). Peru has estimated the cost of inaction against climate change at between 11%-20% of its gross domestic product (GDP) until 2050, and habitat loss around 9% until 2050 and 22% until 2100 (OECD, 2023[13]).

The LAC region is also highly sensitive to climate system tipping points, i.e. possible catastrophic events that could occur because of current levels of global warming, even if the Paris Agreement targets of 1.5°C and 2°C are achieved. For LAC the tipping elements expected to manifest as changes in the climate system are the collapse of the West Antarctic Ice Sheet; the dieback of the Amazon Forest; as well as the El Niño Southern Oscillation and the Atlantic overturning collapse. Tipping of one of these elements – as well as others occurring in other parts of the globe – could potentially trigger tipping cascades, with global impact (OECD, 2022[14]). Climate tipping points would have further effects on socio-economic systems, as forest loss, rising sea-levels, and damages to infrastructure would impact people's livelihoods and health.

Such challenges require urgent action in adapting to climate change and increasing resilience at the regional, national and local level, as well as integrating adaptation policies and tools to sectoral policies, economic instruments and innovative solutions, including those based on nature or new technologies. Actions to adapt to present and future impacts of climate change would need to be accompanied and aligned with strong mitigation measures, to avoid the worst of global warming (see Chapter 3). This chapter focuses on the challenges discussed during a series of Regional Policy Dialogues in 2023, involving LAC and OECD experts. The analysis is not exhaustive, as it focuses on the points highlighted as a priority for LAC countries during the discussions.

LAC contributions to the international framework for climate change adaptation

Reaching the Global Goal on Adaptation (GGA), as set out in the Paris Agreement (UN, 2015[15]), **is a priority for LAC countries.** Setting the road to reaching the goal is also important and requires countries to assess their strengths and weaknesses to better respond to the impacts of climate change (Climate Analytics, 2021[16]). At the twenty-sixth United Nations Climate Change Conference of the Parties (COP26), countries agreed to create a comprehensive two-year *Glasgow–Sharm el-Sheikh work programme* to address the GGA. The programme emphasises the importance of country-driven, gender-responsive, participatory, and transparent approaches to adaptation action. It considers vulnerable groups, communities, ecosystems, and is guided by the best available science, as well as traditional and local knowledge. It aims to achieve objectives such as the full implementation of the Paris Agreement, enhancing understanding of the GGA, and contributing to the review of overall progress through global stocktakes. It also focuses on improving national planning and implementation of adaptation actions, facilitating communication of priorities, plans, and actions, and establishing robust monitoring and evaluation systems (UNFCCC, n.d.[17]).

In January 2021, the *Adaptation Action Coalition* was formed with the objective of accelerating global action on adaptation to achieve a climate resilient world by 2030. Out of the 33 LAC countries, 8 are now part of the coalition: Argentina, Chile, Costa Rica, Colombia, Jamaica, Paraguay, Peru, and Uruguay (Adaptation Action Coalition, 2022[18]). Finally, the Glasgow Climate Pact included a goal for developed countries to double the funding provided to developing countries for adaptation by 2025, which would represent USD 40 billion for adaptation. It also recognised the critical role of restoring nature and ecosystems in delivering benefits for climate adaptation (UNEP, 2021[19]).

During the twenty-seventh UN Climate Change Conference of the Parties (COP27), countries approved *the Sharm el-Sheikh Implementation Plan*, which included the decision to create a Losses and Damages Fund with over USD 230 million in new pledges. The fund aims to assist developing countries affected by extreme climate change events. It also encourages countries to consider Nature-based Solutions (NbS) for their mitigation and adaptation actions. Additionally, countries approved the institutional arrangements to operationalise the Santiago Network, a portal which links international organisations, experts and bodies with regions, countries and communities that wish to minimise and address losses and damages from climate change. The Santiago Network catalyses technical assistance, and it should be fully operational by the twenty-eighth United Nations Climate Change Conference of the Parties (COP28). The United Nations unveiled a USD 3.1 billion plan to ensure universal coverage of early warning systems within the next five years. However, countries did not define the GGA, instead established a framework for its formulation to be considered and adopted at COP28. Finally, the Sharm El-Sheikh Adaptation Agenda was launched at COP27, aiming to accelerate transformative solutions through system interventions and achieve a set of adaptation outcome targets by 2030 (Adaptation Action Coalition, 2022[18]); (UNFCCC, n.d.[20]); (Carver, 2023[21]).

At a regional level, LAC adopted the *Regional Agreement on Access to Information, Public Participation and Justice in Environmental Matters in Latin America and the Caribbean* known as the *Escazú Agreement*, the first environmental agreement in LAC and the world's first legally binding instrument to include provisions for environmental human rights defenders (UN, 2018[22]). The agreement was adopted in Costa Rica, on 4 March 2018 with the objective to ensure the full and effective implementation of rights related to environmental information access, public participation in decision-making, and access to justice in environmental matters. It also focuses on capacity building, co-operation, and the protection of the right to a healthy environment and sustainable development. Currently, 25 of the 33 LAC countries invited to participate are signatories to the Escazú Agreement. Even though the Agreement has entered into force, implementation requires technological, human-based and NbS, as well as a high level of transboundary collaboration and co-operation on environmental management (López-Cubillos et al., 2021[23]); (UN ECLAC, 2023[24]).

LAC is the second most disaster-prone region in the world. Managing increasing risks from climate change and climate variability is a growing need in the region. The adoption of the *Sendai Framework for Disaster Risk Reduction 2015 – 2030 (Sendai Framework*) and the Paris Agreement has resulted in the need to expand coherence in countries' approaches to climate and disaster risk reduction. Nationally, countries have spread the responsibilities regarding climate change adaptation and disaster risk reduction across different institutions and stakeholders, while internationally they are supported by separate UN agencies and related processes resulting in overlaps and gaps. However, countries have been recognising the benefits of increased coherence. They have been increasingly integrating the two concepts, by developing joint strategies or putting in place processes that facilitate co-ordination across climate change adaptation and disaster risk reduction. There is also a need to ensure that some enabling factors are in place, including strong leadership and engagement of key government bodies, broad stakeholder participation and co-ordination, clear allocation of roles, responsibilities and resources, and monitoring, evaluation and continuous learning. These elements can support the identification of trade-offs and synergies, while minimising redundancies (OECD, 2020[25]).

The LAC region has unevenly reported on indicators of the Sendai's Framework. LAC has notably reduced global disaster mortality and increased the number of national and local disaster risk reduction strategies, as well as expanded international co-operation to support their national actions for the implementation of the Sendai's Framework. Nevertheless, LAC still needs to enhance efforts to substantially reduce the number of affected people to the impacts of climate change and reduce its direct disaster economic losses in relation to GDP. Additional efforts can be made to reduce disaster damage to critical infrastructure and the disruption of basic services, as well as with respect to increasing the availability of and access to multi-hazard early warning systems and disaster risk information and assessments to people (UNDRR, 2022[26]).

Linking climate change to biodiversity loss is well-engraved in the international framework, both through the Convention on Biological Diversity (CBD) and the United Nations Framework Convention on Climate Change (UNFCCC). The CBD fifteenth meeting of the Conference of the Parties (COP15) in 2022 highlighted once more the interconnectedness of climate change and biodiversity loss. The *Kunming-Montreal Global Biodiversity Framework (GBF)*, adopted at CBD COP15, includes four goals to 2050 and 23 targets to be achieved by 2030, including a target for minimising the impact of climate change and ocean acidification on biodiversity, through NbS, ecosystem-based approaches and climate action on biodiversity. Beyond climate change and fundamental to climate resilience, the GBF includes other targets for safeguarding biodiversity and ecosystems, such as to effectively conservate and manage at least 30% of the world's lands, inland waters, coastal areas and ocean; to progressively phase out or reform subsidies that harm biodiversity by at least USD 500 billion per year; to scale up positive incentives for biodiversity, and to cut global food waste in half and significantly reduce over consumption and waste generation (CBD, 2022[27]).

Snapshot of National Adaptation Plans in LAC

NAPs provide a policy tool for countries collecting, developing, adopting and implementing adaptation actions. They serve as a framework, under which countries aim to reduce vulnerability, derived from climate change, strengthen their resilience and increase their adaptive capacity. The development of a NAP has also proven to be a much-accepted process, through which countries align their adaptation actions with other international frameworks and goals, such as the Sendai Framework for Disaster Risk Reduction, and the Sustainable Development Goals (SDGs.

Since 2010 up until 2022, only 36% (12 out of 33) of LAC countries had submitted their NAPs under the UNFCCC process. A few LAC countries have adopted national legislation or policy frameworks on climate adaptation or resilience, while the majority have preferred introducing general legislation or frameworks on climate change. Several LAC countries are also including adaptation considerations in sectoral or other specialised legislation or plans (Annex A). However, overall, there is still a gap between introducing a national plan or framework on climate adaptation, and implementing it. LAC countries are identifying the following major challenges in strengthening their national adaptation pathway: difficulty in aligning the objectives and priorities identified in NAPs with sectoral and sub-national development plans; defining and securing the budget for implementing the NAPs; and ensuring the availability of country-wide, downscaled information on projected climate change impacts.[1] Evidently, only 12% (4 out of 33) of LAC countries have already submitted sectoral NAPs and other outputs, such as a monitoring and evaluation strategy or a communications strategy, supporting implementation (Annex A).

NAPs are not the only tool available for countries wishing to advance with setting and implementing climate adaptation policy measures and actions. Countries are also including climate-resilient or climate adaptation policies in their Nationally Determined Contributions (NDCs) or their Long-Term Strategies (LTS) (Annex A). Despite the fact that all LAC countries have submitted and updated their NDCs, only a few have made progress on their adaptation actions included in their NDCs, and even fewer have submitted or updated their LTS (World Bank, 2022[28]); (NDC Partnership, n.d.[29]). In any case, what is important is to guarantee that policies introduced are aligned with contributions to international targets and national environmental commitments. There is also a need to examine trade-offs and complementarities with sectoral and non-climate policies and to build on synergies with climate mitigation measures. Frequently updating the NAPs and other national plans and strategies related to climate adaptation and based on evidenced-based analysis on global warming, tipping points, and losses and damages, such as provided by the Intergovernmental Panel on Climate Change (IPCC) and the OECD, could help countries to adjust their climate measures and actions to reflect the rapidly changing environment.

Recommendation

- Develop and progressively update National Adaptation Plans submitted to the UNFCCC, and support their implementation through robust legal and regulatory, institutional and financial frameworks.

Aligning adaptation priorities with national commitments and addressing adaptation needs with national policies.

LAC countries are identifying climate change adaptation as a key policy priority for the region. To successfully address the issue, specific climate adaptation actions need to be identified by countries. Several LAC countries have introduced legislation or action plans and roadmaps with specific climate adaptation actions, either under the general climate change policy framework or through sectoral non-environment related policies and strategies, building on the interlinkages between the effects of climate adaptation with vulnerability, economic growth and development (Annex A).

Countries follow differentiated policy approaches, to accommodate national circumstances, vulnerabilities and needs, not allowing direct comparability between the policy options selected. This is especially the case in the LAC region, which is very diverse in terms of economic growth, social development, geography, distribution etc. Irrespective of the particularities in different countries and sub-regions within the LAC region, there are some principal considerations to be taken into account when developing legislation, policies and actions that address climate change adaptation:

- **Align national and local adaptation priorities with countries' commitments**. In many cases, LAC countries have been introducing policy frameworks and legal instruments to reach their pledges towards internationally determined adaptation targets, with clear assignment of responsibilities between national, sub-national and local stakeholders. In the case of Peru, for example, the framework law on climate change establishes not only objectives, but also processes on governing climate change programmes and projects, with special attention paid to cross-cutting actions, which involve different stakeholders throughout the country (OECD, 2023[13]). Paraguay is prioritising specific environmental sectors for action under its NAP and has also set up a plan for its operational implementation (Box 2.1).
- **Align mitigation and adaptation priorities, to safeguard balance between the two aspects of climate change**. Climate mitigation has long received more attention and prioritisation, in both international negotiations and national decision-making, as well as through financing and investments. Measuring the impact of mitigation measures has much advanced, especially since greenhouse gas (GHG) emissions generated from human activities are being calculated, and their decoupling from economic growth is advancing (see Chapter 3). However, measuring vulnerability to climate change and the effects of the often-unprecedented climate phenomena, and quickly updating adaptation policies and aligning them with mitigation measures remains a struggle. Argentina has a legal framework and governance structure overseeing both mitigation and adaptation, also measuring the effectiveness of the measures adopted (Box 2.1).
- **Mainstream adaptation considerations in sectoral policies**. Addressing climate change requires not only climate action, but also alignment of various policy domains, such as finance,

taxation, investment, infrastructure, trade, innovation etc, with climate goals (OECD, 2015[30]). Aligning legal, regulatory and policy frameworks, currently outside the climate policy portfolio, with climate objectives requires a series of commitments and possibly acceptance of short-term trade-offs, which would provide for a more sustainable policy framework in the long term.

Box 2.1. Aligning priorities to address climate change adaptation

Paraguay's prioritisation for climate adaptation

Paraguay has set climate change adaptation as a national priority, with measures introduced in the NDC, NAP and national strategy. In its NAP 2022-2030, Paraguay has identified seven key sectors and has set 25 objectives with the aim to increase resilience at the local and national level in these sectors. The sectors identified are i) resilient urban and rural communities; ii) health; iii) ecosystems and biodiversity; iv) energy; v) agriculture, forestry and food security; vi) water resources; and vii) transport. The objectives set are aligned with the SDGs and the Sendai Framework. The operational implementation of the plan is also introduced, emphasising the roles and links between national and sub-national levels of governance, and setting up a monitoring and evaluation system.

Argentina's plan on climate mitigation and adaptation

In December 2019, Argentina introduced a Law (No. 27520) on climate change, which sought to establish minimum environmental budgets that guarantee actions, instruments and strategies for adaptation and mitigation to climate change, in line with the country's commitments. The law makes provisions for setting up a National Plan for Adaptation and Mitigation to Climate Change, which should cover, among others, i) identifying vulnerabilities and short- medium- and long- term adaptation measures; ii) developing climate scenarios based on vulnerability and socio-economic and environmental trends; and iii) establishing monitoring and evaluations processes of measuring the effectiveness of policy measures and actions adopted. It also sets up a governance structure, headed by a National Cabinet of Climate Change, responsible for monitoring the application of legislative provisions, and supported by an External Advisory Council which consults on a permanent basis on the National Plan. Argentina also recently launched a National Climate Finance Strategy, mainstreaming climate adaptation in financing policies.

Source: (MECON, 2023[31]); (MADES and PNUD, 2022[32]); (Argentina Presidencia, 2019[33]);

Legal certainty and targeted planning over climate adaptation policies can provide a solid ground to accentuate action for climate change adaptation. However, advancing the implementation of adaptation measures requires a more holistic approach, which covers other challenges that several countries, including in the LAC region, are facing:

- Firstly, **implementing the NDCs and NAPs requires a balanced and people-centred approach** for the adaptation measures pursued to benefit local communities, indigenous people and vulnerable groups, and benefit from their knowledge in addressing climate adaptation. For example, in the case of Peru, 84 adaptation measures have been identified to date, with a special focus on early warning systems, actions to address public health issues and strengthening capacity in fishing and agricultural sectors (OECD, 2023[13]). The successful implementation of these measures highly depends on location and the incorporation of local communities needs in the solutions proposed.
- Secondly, **financing must be secured to be able to implement specific policies and advance the adaptation agenda**. Often in LAC countries, the measures proposed are not tied to specific budget lines. In some cases, measures' implementation depends on financing mechanisms, such

as the Global Climate Fund and the Adaptation Fund, and their role in mobilising resources on adaptation. Introducing more creative financing tools – namely micro-insurance on green bonds, green taxonomies, climate risk incorporation in financing processes – could also help transform good adaption proposals into bankable projects, with the involvement of the private sector (OECD, 2023[13]).

- Thirdly, **capacity building is needed**. Building critical skills in public administration to be able to identify adaptation projects which are suitable for financing, and which could be implemented is necessary to advance climate adaptation. In parallel, enhancing national and local capacities to develop climate-related project ideas which consider private sector engagement, local stakeholder acceptance and promote resilience in various sectors, would secure the viability of solutions proposed.

People – Environmental Justice – Communities

Climate change is a global phenomenon, yet it has local impacts. Solutions to climate change adaptation need to be inclusive of local communities and address local vulnerabilities. This applies both in urban and rural areas, which may vary in morphology, vulnerabilities to different climatic and weather events, productive activities that drive the local economy, and therefore local well-being.

Early warning and civil protection systems in LAC

There is a close link between the interventions for climate change adaptation and for disaster risk reduction. These policy areas often share common goals towards increasing resilience, such as protecting communities and infrastructure from the impacts of natural hazards, and minimising losses caused by disasters. They also face overlapping risks, whereby increasing and more intense climate hazards increase the disaster risks and impacts. Increased coherence between the two policy areas, through co-ordinated action between all relevant stakeholders could help improve policy interventions, (OECD, 2020[25]) and support a climate risk-informed local development.

Early warning systems (EWS) are acknowledged as a key element of disaster risk reduction, which aim at supporting people to adapt to climate change and build resilience. Even though EWS have been characterised as a "low-hanging fruit" for adaptation, being an efficient and effective way to protect people, their application requires several prerequisites to reach success. These concern mainly people-centred technology development and transfer, data management and forecasting, enabling innovation, and guaranteeing sustainable funding for constant updates in technology. The UNFCCC launched in 2022 a Rolling workplan of the Technology Executive Committee for 2023-2027, highlighting the need for further collaboration to support accelerated action in innovation and technology development for the wide application of EWS. The Executive Action Plan for the Early Warnings for All presented during COP27 identifies key areas for advancing universal disaster risk knowledge, prioritises the top technical actions to enhance capacity on data and information collection, and sets the ground for aligning and co-ordinating financing instruments to scale-up investments for EWS (WMO, 2022[34]).

EWS are mentioned in over 60% of NDCs submitted by LAC countries, highlighting the need to address climate change phenomena and extreme weather events, as well as reduce water and food security risks. Due to the multiple types of hazards occurring in the region, Multi-Hazard Early Warning Systems (MHEWS) are considered essential tools to address high risks from weather, water, and climate extremes. Yet a recent report from the World Meteorological Organization (WMO) shows that, despite LAC countries facing vulnerabilities ranging from droughts to floods, to landslides, sea-level rise, storms and hurricanes etc, they are also facing early warning capacity gaps. In fact, from the 19 LAC countries that responded to the WMO survey, at least 8 countries have inadequate EWS in place for riverine floods, flash floods and droughts (Figure 2.4). A closer look at the LAC countries shows that the major needs in the region are disaster risk knowledge; detection, monitoring, analysis and forecasting, and disaster preparedness and response. Warning dissemination and communication is also an issue for South America (WMO, 2020[35]).

Figure 2.4. Early Warning System capacity in LAC countries

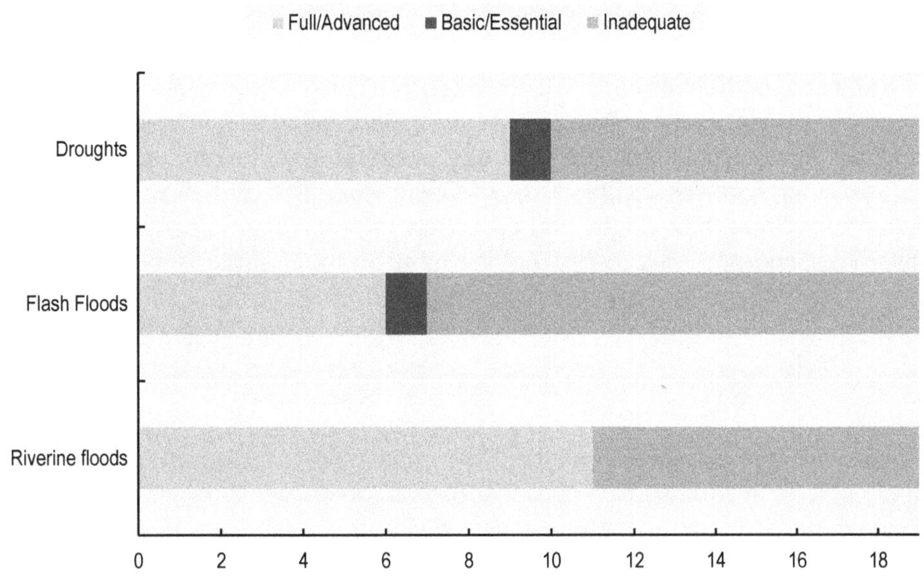

Source: (WMO, 2020[35])

Island States in the Caribbean have been frontrunners in developing their EWS, due to the region's high vulnerability to various natural hazards (hurricanes, floods, droughts, forest fires, volcano eruptions and earthquakes). With the support of the United Nations Development Programme (UNDP), International Federation of Red Cross (IFRC), Caribbean Disaster Emergency Management Agency (CDEMA) and Cuba, islands such as Antigua and Barbuda, Dominica, the Dominican Republic, Saint Lucia and Saint Vincent and the Grenadines applied the Cuban Early Warning Systems Toolbox, which offers tools and activities that countries could undertake to improve their risk knowledge, monitoring and warning systems, dissemination and communication, and response capacities. The programme also included technical trainings, test runs for newly installed meteorological forecast products, a regional measurement tool for monitoring of progress, and information sharing, to spread the lessons learned more broadly in the region (Gazol, 2019[36]).

In addition to EWS, mechanisms to manage the aftermath of extreme weather events or other climate-related hazards are also necessary. The urgent need for primary healthcare, shelter, food, water, sanitation and basic relief items requires appropriate disaster preparedness at the national and local levels, with co-ordination mechanisms set in place and sufficient funding for emergencies. In the medium and long-term, building resilient infrastructure could also help adapt to such events; while investing more on ecosystems' preservation could increase resilience against natural hazards (see below).

Several LAC countries, such as Argentina, Bolivia, Brazil, Colombia, Costa Rica, El Salvador, Guatemala, Mexico, Nicaragua, Panama, Paraguay, Peru, Uruguay and Venezuela, have established civil protection mechanisms to address risk management, preparation and prevention activities, together with co-ordination on emergency and reconstruction systems. Most of these countries have clearly prioritised co-ordination between different government levels for better civil protection, as well as set up funds which cover, among others, natural or climate-related disasters. However, there are still gaps in managing natural disasters, as well as accessing the financial resources available in case of a climate emergency, or even in-kind supplies for the needs of those affected. To overcome such challenges, better co-ordination of actions between different government levels, and dedicated sufficient financial resources to support both risk reduction and emergency response for climate change are needed (Szlafsztein, 2020[37]).

When introducing EWS, or other climate risk reduction mechanisms, considering the particularities of vulnerable groups is key to increasing resilience. Indigenous people, displaced persons, persons with disabilities, rural communities, the elderly, women and children are experiencing differently any social, economic, cultural and environmental change. If not taken into consideration, this could result to increasing inequalities, exacerbating existing ones (Box 2.2). Active collaboration with vulnerable groups can provide additional information on local climate hazards and weather events and assist in prevention and preparedness for local communities. In the case of Costa Rica, active and effective engagement with indigenous communities allows their voices and proposals to be taken into consideration for better early warning. Additional investment in climate-resilient infrastructure and capacity building for responding to such phenomena, would further help improve EWS (OECD, 2023[38]).

Box 2.2. Gender-responsive actions to climate disaster risks in LAC

Climate hazards are not gender-neutral events. Their impacts vary based on gender roles, access to resources, income and other intersecting social identities. Women are usually the ones evacuating last during an extreme weather event, due to their care-giving responsibilities over children and elderly. They are also often less trained on preparedness and response to an extreme weather event. Finally, they may experience less access to information or less capacity to receive and act on early warnings, because of lack of education and illiteracy or lack of technical training. These characteristics apply also to the LAC region.

Transforming climate disaster risk reduction policies and EWS mechanisms to be gender-responsive requires:

- Collecting gender-disaggregated data and setting gender-sensitive indicators. Antigua and Barbuda, Chile, Costa Rica and Ecuador are already providing such disaggregated data form the monitoring of the Sendai Framework.
- Including a gender perspective in climate risk governance. Increasing women's participation in the decision-making processes would help raise their concerns in planning and in reducing vulnerability. Grenada is including women in the discussions at the stages of design, implementation and evaluation of climate mitigation and adaptation strategies.
- Investing in EWS and other mechanisms for climate resilience with a gender perspective. Often investments targeting climate-risk reduction are lacking a gender or inclusiveness perspective, thus missing the opportunity to address inequalities, or even exacerbating them. The Climate Risk Early Warning Systems (CREWS) Caribbean project prioritises investments that support EWS developed with the participation of local communities, including women.
- Providing technical assistance, capacity-building and long-term multi-hazard preparedness. Acknowledging the differentiated impacts of climate disaster to women and men requires incorporating both groups in the preparedness and response interventions. Jamaica includes women in identifying high-risk areas and critical infrastructure that could be affected by a climate disaster. Peru supported financially female-headed households for reconstructing their communities after the 2017 floods.

Source: (Brown et al., 2019[39]); (Value for Women, 2020[40]); (Beltrame and del Pilar Medina, 2022[41]); (CREWS Caribbean, n.d.[42])

Recommendation

- Improve early warning systems to ensure that all people, especially those in communities at greater risk of climate-related extreme weather events in LAC, have access to vital information in real-time, at the individual level, and that local communities participate in the design and implementation of EWS.
- Strengthen or create civil protection systems in LAC, which are equipped and prepared with supplies, trained personnel, infrastructure, and sufficient funds to provide immediate attention, shelter, and comprehensive medical assistance before, during, and after natural disasters.

Reducing vulnerability in urban areas

Urban areas and cities are inevitably gaining more traction in relation to climate change adaptation, as projections show that by 2050 two-thirds of the world population will be living in urban areas. Managing the impacts of this trend would require NAPs revisions, bringing to the forefront the role of urban areas and cities in addressing climate change adaptation.

The LAC region is one of the most urbanised regions worldwide. Despite the disparities between the different types and sizes of cities, it is apparent that many of them are struggling with similar problems such as urban growth, restrictions in urban planning capabilities, and lack of climate risk assessments, which could help identify the type of improvements necessary to combat climate change at the local level.

Almost 21% of the LAC urban population live in slums. Even though this percentage may be less than the world average, which is at 23.9%, it is still not acceptable, considering the residents' living conditions (Figure 2.5). Slums in the LAC region are often affected by natural disasters such as landslides and floods, with the already limited infrastructure (water and sanitation services, electricity, transport and roads etc) being damaged and requiring upgrading (Fay et al., 2017[43]).

Figure 2.5. Percentage of urban population living in slums

2018 data

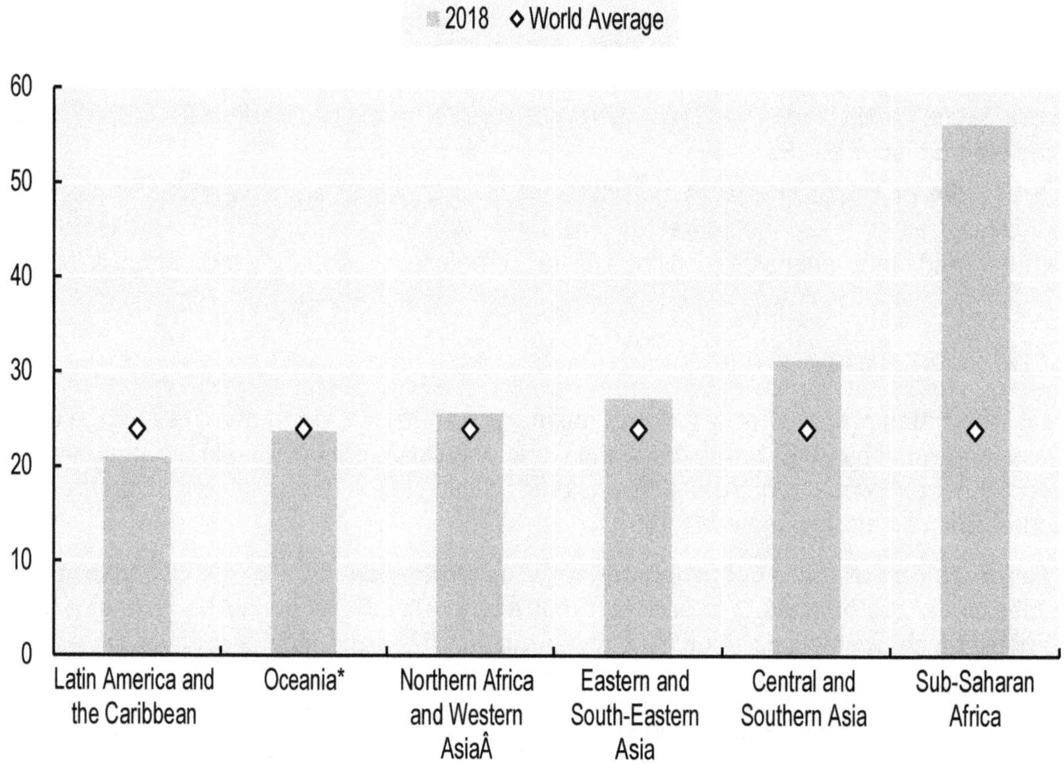

Note: Oceania does not include Australia and New Zealand. World average at 23.9%.
Source: (UNSD, n.d.[44])

From the 12 LAC countries that have submitted a NAP, the majority include targets related to urban planning and land use, though different perspectives are presented. Chile links urban planning with biodiversity and ecosystems' conservation. Costa Rica and Paraguay link it with green corridors in urban areas. Grenada and Saint Lucia present interconnection of urban planning with water resources. Uruguay refers to needed improvements in land use administration and data collection. Overall, there is limited local evidence of connection between urban planning and land use regulatory frameworks with climate risk assessments.

In the case of Caribbean Island states, the issue of urbanisation demands immediate transformative action. Caribbean Small Island Developing States (SIDS) face limitations in formal housing, rising haphazard settlement structures, and inadequate infrastructure for water and sewage treatment, and transport services. These challenges are further aggravated by climate change and extreme weather events in the Caribbean region. Caribbean SIDS are focusing their urban planning measures in NAPs on accessing water resources, expanding green spaces in urban areas, and tackling the effects of increasing migration from rural to urban areas. Mainstreaming climate change mitigation and adaptation into urban planning requires more than simple changes in urban development and land use. It requires improvements in data collection, in climate risk assessments, and in including local communities in the planning, design and development of sustainable infrastructure, as well as securing adequate financing for such works (Mycoo, 2022[45]).

An integrated approach, by which urban planning measures address climate adaptation and help build more climate-resilient cities is needed. Such an approach should include sufficient data collection and monitoring, risk assessment and risk management tools, as well as sufficient budget allocation. Assessing vulnerability at the local level, including local economic activities, would also help local governments improve their management and planning. International development banks and development co-operation agencies are actively supporting climate change adaptation at the local and city level in LAC. Focusing on information collection, monitoring and capacity building, they aim at strengthening resilient urban and local planning (Box 2.3).

Box 2.3. International actors supporting resilient urban and local planning in LAC.

Strategic climate adaptation investment and institutional strengthening plans

The World Bank is supporting medium sized cities in the LAC region in developing *Strategic Climate Adaptation Investment and Institutional Strengthening Plans* for each of them. The exercise also included three assessments: on climate related risks, on institutional adaptive capacities, and on socio-economic capacities to adapt to climate change. In the cases of Castries in Saint Lucia, Cusco in Peru, Esteli in Nicaragua, El Progreso in Honduras and Santos in Brazil, the World Bank activities included mechanisms for data collection and better climate monitoring and risk planning; cross-scale integration of risk management practices; capacity building for local officials working on climate change planning and risk management; better budgetary allocations and private climate financing to build resilience; and a change in risk governance systems from disaster management to long-term risk reduction.

Multi-level governance and planning processes

The German Agency for International Co-operation (GIZ) is also working with LAC countries to improve multi-level governance, to strengthen planning processes and to include land use as a factor affecting several economic activities in the region, such as tourism and agriculture. A necessary part in GIZ projects is developing tools for data collection which allow for vulnerability analysis, as well as identifying strategic frameworks and adaptation models at the local level. For example, on water resources, the exercise not only limits at mapping water basins, but also includes the information in municipality plans for water use. At the same time, capacity building at the municipality level is necessary, to allow for better management and planning.

Source: (World Bank, 2014[46]); (OECD, 2023[13])

Recommendation

- Align regional and urban planning with NAPs and promote an integrated approach to overcome the risk management, capacity and financing gaps.

Sectoral approaches to climate adaptation

Investing in climate-resilient infrastructure

Infrastructure is severely impacted by climate variability and extreme weather events, which may cause damage to buildings, roads and bridges, disruption to transport, water and electricity supply, and possible loss of businesses and people. Climate impacts will have implications on infrastructure investment needs, not only relating to cost but also in guaranteeing that new infrastructure is resilient (OECD, 2018[47]). At the same time, investing in resilient infrastructure has a multiplier effect for the economy, as it reduces the GDP losses (due to reduction of capital destroyed during natural disasters) (Fernández Corugedo, Gonzalez and Guerson, 2023[48]). It is therefore essential to reduce climate risks towards infrastructure, as well as to effectively manage trade-offs between risk minimisation and cost. Prioritising climate-resilient infrastructure is expected to improve both the reliability of service provision and increase asset life. Introducing adaptive approaches to infrastructure, using climate model scenarios, could also reduce uncertainties and risks in the future. Including other socio-economic changes in the analysis would genuinely help achieving climate resilience (OECD, 2018[47]).

Investment needs for infrastructure globally have been estimated at around USD 6.3 trillion annually between 2016 and 2030 (OECD, 2017[49]). Considering countries would have to expedite their actions to achieve their Paris Agreement goals of 1.5°C and 2°C, the infrastructure investment needs are expected to be even greater. However, annual investments do not even reach close to this amount. Only for G20 countries, i.e. the bigger infrastructure investors, estimates of annual investments fall short of the actual needs, emphasising the necessity to close the investment gap (Zelikow and Savas, 2022[50]).

Infrastructure investment needs in the LAC region by 2030 have been estimated at 3.12% of GDP, while from 2008 to 2019 average investment was only 1.8% of GDP (Brichetti et al., 2021[51]). To cover this investment gap and also guarantee that new investment will be resilient to climate change, the mobilisation of additional resources is required. Most of the climate finance mobilised by developed countries in developing countries is tied to climate mitigation projects (67% annual average for the period 2016-2020), while about 24%% covers climate adaptation projects. Despite an increase over the past few years in adaptation finance, the gap between mitigation and adaptation remains significant. Specifically in the LAC region, 74% of climate finance focused on mitigation, with the main targeted sectors being energy (25%), transport (11%) and water supply and sanitation (10.5%) (OECD, 2022[52]).

Increasing climate finance directed to adaptation projects is not only necessary to build resilience against climate change, but also to guarantee more inclusive and sustainable growth. Investing in climate-resilient infrastructure would help not only avoiding losses, but also reducing risks to existing infrastructure and safeguarding social and environmental benefits; the so-called "triple dividend" (Global Center on Adaptation, 2021[53]).

Investing in resilient infrastructure could reduce social inequality. It could provide better water and sanitation services in areas affected by drought, improve forest management with the inclusion of local communities, or improve living conditions in coastal areas. Sustainable infrastructure investment projects which are transparent and take into consideration the local circumstances and the needs of vulnerable communities in the planning, design and implementation phase, would better serve the recipient communities and recognise their expertise and traditional knowledge. Finally, assessing and evaluating the impacts of infrastructure projects with respect to the needs of the most vulnerable, from the investors' perspective (public, private, multilateral, national, subnational), would help revise future prioritisation of investment decisions (Faria, Perutti and Villalba, 2021[54]).

Countries should also consider introducing climate adaptation considerations in investments traditionally financed under the mitigation agenda. Better aligning infrastructure investment planning and financing with long-term, low-emission, resilient and inclusive development pathways will allow for scaling-up energy, transport and industry infrastructure investments. Creating the enabling environment for climate-resilient infrastructure investment also requires alignment between short- and long-term prioritisation of projects, project-level assessment, and capacity building.

Yet, only a few countries around the world are already developing long-term low-emission development strategies, integrating climate considerations in infrastructure planning. In many cases, there is a need for capacity building towards planning, designing and assessing bankable infrastructure projects that are in line with climate goals, both short-term and long-term. Moreover, the approach needs to be holistic and not broken down between the different institutional authorities that may be in charge of infrastructure in different sectors. Whole-of-government planning can help avoid investments with conflicting climate impacts. Creating a 'pipeline' of infrastructure projects, to streamline the process between project conception and financing can also help secure sufficient investment flows for climate-resilient infrastructure (Box 2.4) (OECD, 2018[55]).

Box 2.4. Climate-resilient infrastructure development in Saint Lucia

In the case of Saint Lucia, a Caribbean island which faces many climate-related challenges, long-term planning for infrastructure across different sectors is imperative. Saint Lucia is applying the following tools to benefit the most from climate-resilient infrastructure development:

1. A National Infrastructure Assessment that ensures economic, environmental and social needs are met in future infrastructure planning;
2. Strategic Infrastructure Planning in energy, water supply, wastewater and solid waste sectors; which analyses future changes in demand for these sectors in an integrated manner, taking into consideration the effects of tourist flows;
3. Aligning assessment and planning with the SDGs and the Paris Agreement, guaranteeing that the National Infrastructure Assessment prioritises measures included in the country's NAP;
4. Cross-ministerial co-ordination under the National Integrated Planning and Programme Unit, which is responsible for defining the overarching vision, strategy and roadmap for the island's infrastructure agenda.

Source: (UNEP, 2021[56]); Saint Lucia's National Infrastructure Assessment – Case Study

Recommendation

- Better align infrastructure planning, development, and investments with short- and long-term low emission, climate-resilient and inclusive development strategies at the national level.
- Enhance an enabling environment for the development of climate-resilient infrastructure to limit vulnerability to climate damages.

Achieving climate-resilient water resources management and financing

Global warming, one of the symptoms of climate change, is expected to have uneven impacts on water resources around the globe, with rising frequency of both floods and droughts. Economic activities linked to industry, agriculture and infrastructure development also lead to deforestation and land degradation, phenomena which in their turn affect water sources. Protecting the water cycle and better managing water supplies is essential to address the negative effects on water resources (Rockström et al., 2023[57]).

The LAC region is not homogeneous in the impact of climate change to water resources. The region is both water-rich, being home to over 30% of the world's freshwater resources, but also has arid and semi-arid areas affected by droughts, not to mention the glaciers in the Andes (World Bank, 2013[58]). While in many LAC countries extreme precipitation is an issue, leading to crops' destruction, landslides etc., in others severe droughts and poor water availability and quality are more of a concern. Suriname, Guyana and Trinidad and Tobago suffer most from extreme precipitation events, while Paraguay, Argentina and Brazil are the countries the most affected by droughts (OECD, 2023[1]).

Climate change adaptation has a severe impact on water resources in the LAC region, having a negative effect on biodiversity and ecosystems, as well as on the quality of life for local populations. Destruction of land, forests and ecosystems compounds water risks. In the LAC region, water that evaporates in the Amazon rainforest drives precipitation in most of the continent. Affecting that evaporation-shed, through continuous deforestation, will have consequences on rainfall in several LAC countries, including Argentina, Bolivia and Colombia (Rockström et al., 2023[57]). This interdependence needs to be considered when designing policies on water resources. Further research and data collection on such phenomena would help support policymaking.

Agriculture is overall the major economic activity behind water withdrawal in South and Central America, with 81% and 66% of total water withdrawal respectively. For the Caribbean, about half of total water withdrawal is for municipal use (Figure 2.6). Water, however, is not an infinite source, therefore changes in economic activities, such as agriculture, energy and mining, will affect water allocation. The same applies in cases of increased water demand due to changes in demographics, where a sudden influx of population can create additional stress, especially in areas that suffer from restricted water resources.

Figure 2.6. Agricultural water withdrawal is high in Central and South America

Percentage of water withdrawal by activity

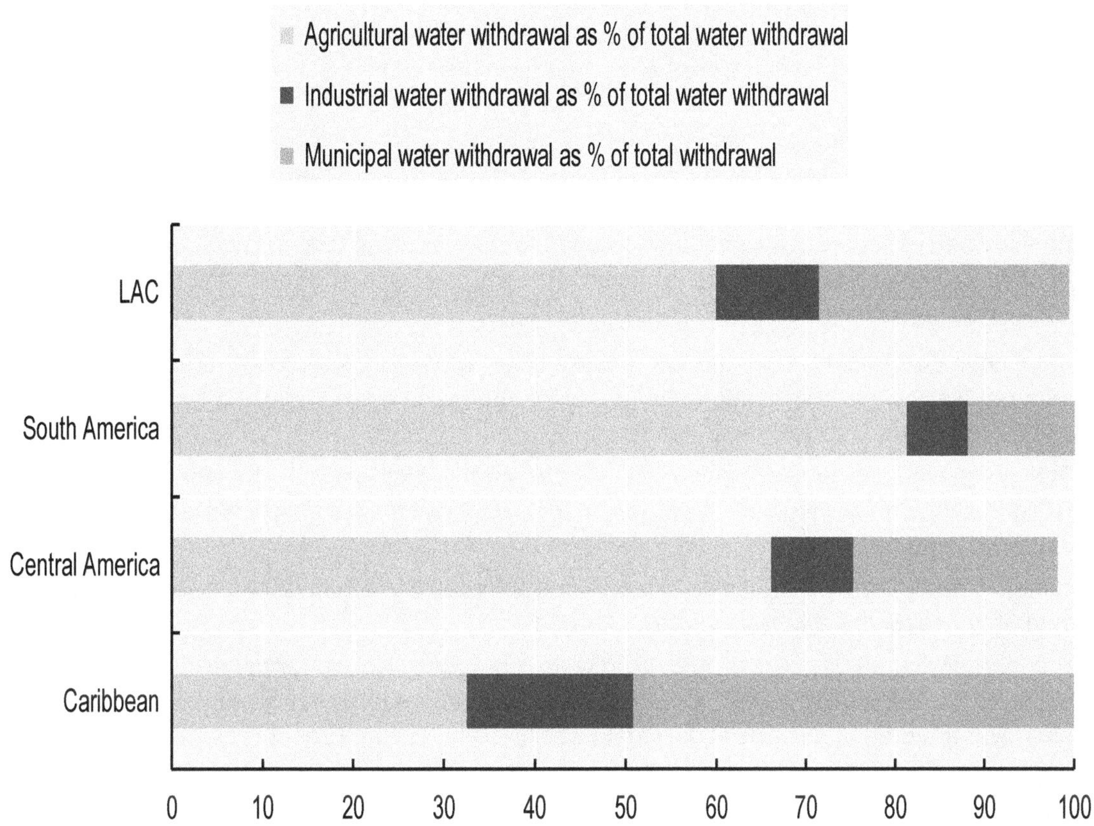

Note: 2020 data. When water withdrawal in a sub-region does not total to 100, this is because of country data available in the AQUASTAT FAO database.
Source : (FAO, n.d.[59]) AQUASTAT dissemination system

Good water demand management is crucial for the region. Countries in Central America showcase the largest gaps in water resources management governance, with the main points missing being river basin management plans, financing instruments for water resources managements, and an integrated information system. In some cases, issues of overlapping responsibilities between different government institutions persist. In South America, institutional, legal, and management tools for water resources management do exist; however, challenges remain, often leading to fragmentation or gaps in water resources management (World Bank, 2022[60]).

Good water management requires a combination of water allocation regimes and economic policy instruments. Water allocation regimes could address issues of water scarcity. They set the process of sharing water resources among different water users, both long-term and short-term, while they may also incorporate seasonal adjustments, depending on cyclical events which impact water supply. LAC countries should reform their water allocation regimes, to better cope with future risks of water resources changes. In the case of Brazil, the OECD has highlighted three sets of measures to address existing weaknesses in water allocation. These could apply, with some flexibility and adaptation, to other LAC countries as well. Suggestions focus on (i) clearly defining available water resources and water use, and encouraging multi-purpose efficient use of water from reservoirs based on water use rights; (ii) introducing or revamping policy instruments such as water use permits with clear issuance criteria, and introducing pricing instruments to facilitate reallocation of water between users; and (iii) clarifying the water governance framework between national and local level, by improving monitoring and enforcement mechanisms for water allocation, strengthening capacity at the local level to better define priorities and plans, and include water users in the decision-making (OECD, 2022[61]).

Economic policy instruments signal the value of water. They can support the sustainable management of water resources, especially when considered together with water allocation regimes. They can also support managing water-related risks, therefore increasing water security, while reflecting externalities in water usage. Abstraction and pollution charges are such type of instruments already applied in some OECD countries. Mexico applies abstraction charges both for ground and surface water, for domestic, industrial, and energy production use. Chile's allocation management regime allows transfer of water entitlements between users, so that water can be used for higher value uses (OECD, 2021[62]). Though the application of such charges may differ depending on target, tax base and structure, when introduced the following should be primarily considered (OECD, 2017[63]):

- Water charges should be analogous to water use and water source. A good inventory of water users per water source can help set a fair water charge system, and could help frame exceptional cases for differentiated pricing, if needed.
- Clear guidance on how to set and implement economic instruments, from the central government to the stakeholders involved in water resources governance and management, could help overcome capacity.
- Economic analysis on resources management, affordability, effect of charges on competitiveness could help design more targeted water charges.
- Transparency in the use of revenues from water charges will allow for better acceptance from local stakeholders. Reusing revenues to further finance improvements in water infrastructure would also help cover the potential financial gap that usually exists in water resources management.

Sustainable urban design could help mitigate flood and scarcity risk in urban environments. On average, about 5% of the population and 4% of the buildings in the LAC region are exposed to risks of river flooding, with Suriname, Guyana and Argentina showing the highest percentages of exposure in the region (OECD, 2023[1]). Reducing the effects of water-related events requires improvements in physical infrastructure, which in turn requires adequate financing and investment. The city of Cartagena in Colombia has set sustainable, resilient economic development as a target. A project aiming at stimulating resilient and sustainable innovations and generating investments for innovative and integrated urban water projects, is being launched. Analysis will cover the complete urban fabric from a physical, social, economic and cultural point of view. Local governmental and non-governmental stakeholders, ranging from investors to indigenous people, are participating in the process, from the analysis and design phase to the development of physical infrastructure (World Water Atlas, n.d.[64]).

Improving the operational performance of water supply and sanitation services can help both with enhancing the operational efficiency of the water management system, and with improving the services offered to the end-consumer. Water management in the LAC region faces low capacity challenges, often leading to technical gaps that hamper the quality of service provided and losses of revenue (World Bank, 2022[60]).Improving the operational performance requires strong, independent economic regulation, that sets performance standards, benchmarks performance of service providers, challenges investment plans, and sets tariffs that drive performance (OECD, 2022[65]); (OECD, 2022[66]).

Investing in a climate-resilient water sector can support efforts to achieve water security. Yet, undervaluing water resources is limiting financial opportunities in such investments. Accelerating finance for water in the context of adaptation requires enabling conditions to be in place. The OECD is developing a score card to assess whether these conditions are in place at national level (OECD, 2023[67]). The score card could be used across countries in the LAC region to review enabling conditions for financing water. In the region, international financing institutions and public development banks have a role to review these enabling conditions and promote alignment with practices than can accelerate finance for water and adaptation and minimise transaction costs.

Recommendation

- Improve water demand management to tackle water scarcity and signal the value of water, through reformed water allocation regimes and better use of economic policy instruments.
- Review the enabling conditions for water financing and sustainable investments in water security.

Biodiversity protection for climate mitigation and adaptation

Biodiversity loss and climate change are interlinked; both constitute threats towards the planet and peoples' well-being, with negative impacts affecting especially the most vulnerable communities and groups. Climate change is one of the five key pressures on biodiversity loss (S. Díaz et al., 2019[68]); (IPBES and IPCCC, 2021[69]), and the loss of biodiversity (e.g. forest loss) is a contributor to climate change.

Biodiversity can also play a key role in limiting climate change. Ecosystems are natural carbon sinks, which can absorb carbon dioxide from the atmosphere. This is especially the case for LAC, one of the richest regions worldwide in biodiversity, with a large forest area, the Amazon, as well as a large ocean basin in the Caribbean Sea. At the same time, adaptation measures, such as restoring mangrove forests, can protect local communities from floods, as well as enhance ecosystems resilience. Due to the interconnectedness, fighting climate change should go hand in hand with minimising biodiversity loss, and vice versa. Acknowledging the interlinkages and mutually addressing the negative impacts would provide for optimal solutions. Maintaining biodiversity requires focused conservation and sustainable use efforts, co-ordinated action, and innovative solutions with strong adaptation characteristics (IPBES and IPCCC, 2021[69]).

Simultaneously addressing climate adaptation and biodiversity challenges, through an integrated approach, would be an opportunity for governments, especially in the LAC region, to address climate-related risks while at the same time building more resilient environments for local communities (OECD, 2021[70]); (UNFCCC et al., 2022[71]). Mainstreaming biodiversity considerations in economic sectors, such as forestry, agriculture and fisheries, can help address underlying causes of biodiversity loss (OECD, 2018[72]). Setting or reviewing existing policy instruments, such as economic incentives (e.g., taxes, fees and charges), and further promoting NbS, could help elevate biodiversity's role in policy making.

Biodiversity conservation through protected areas and biological corridors

Connected and biodiverse ecosystems tend to be more resilient to the effects of climate change. The LAC region is one of the most biodiverse regions globally, with about 40% of the world's species, 16% of the Earth's forests, 40% of freshwater sources, and the second largest coral reef (The Nature Conservancy, 2021[73]).

LAC is the most protected region in the world in terms of coverage (with the exception of the polar region) , and LAC countries have worked to increase the protected surface (land and sea) (Alvarez Malvido et al., 2021[74]). Yet, more efforts are required so that Protected Areas (PAs) are also representative of ecological biodiversity, and that there is sufficient connectivity between them. Such efforts would also help countries reach the CBD Kunming-Montreal global target 3 which calls for the effective conservation and management, though ecologically representative, well-connected and equitably governed systems of protected areas, of at least 30% of terrestrial, inland water, and coastal and marine areas (CBD, 2022[27]).

Currently only nine countries in the region have over 17% of their protected area coverage connected, while on average 33% of PAs are not well connected (Figure 2.7).

Figure 2.7. Protected Areas in the LAC region

2020 data

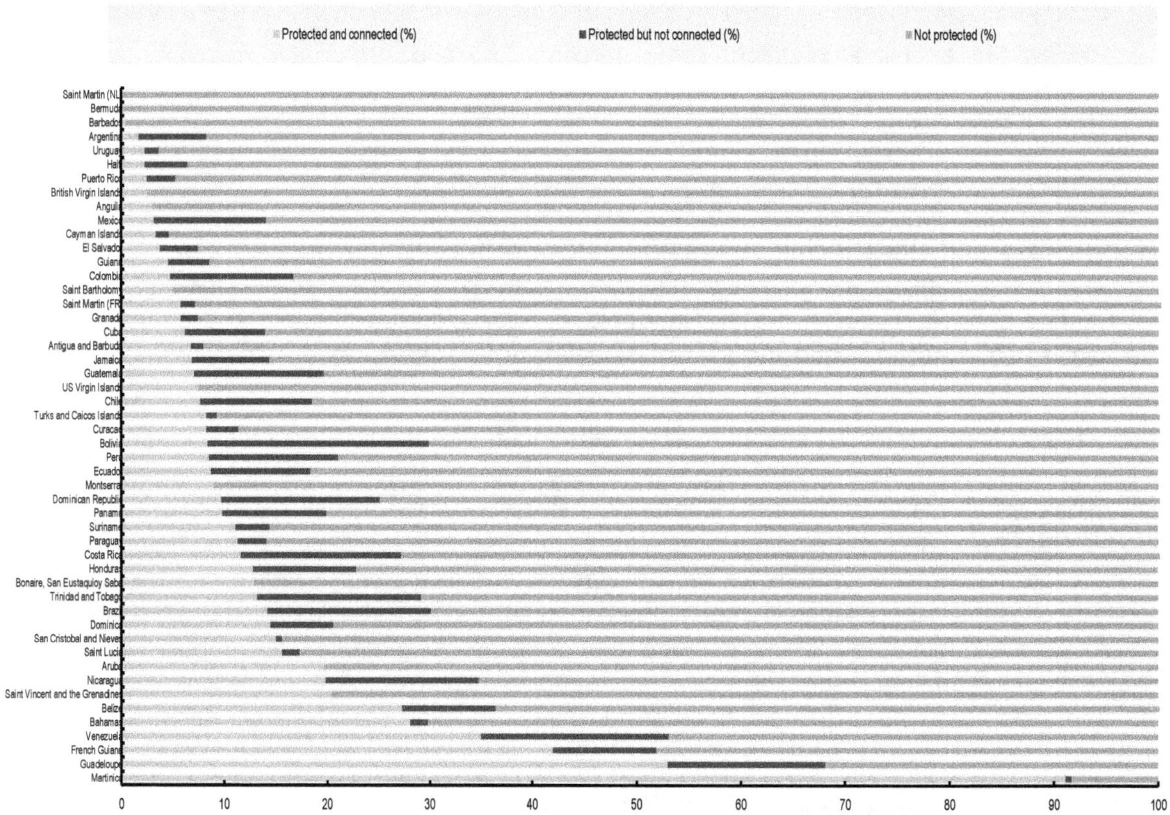

Source : (Alvarez Malvido et al., 2021[74])

Despite efforts to increase PAs, especially by island states in the Caribbean, more needs to be done to guarantee biodiversity conservation in the LAC region. Connecting the various PAs, via biological corridors, and the adoption of Other Effective Area-Based Conservation Measures (OECMs) outside of protected areas, would help build better conservation methods in the future. Such efforts would require enhancing political commitment, engaging local communities who often have knowledge on local ecosystems, and securing necessary technical and financial resources to advance with holistic biodiversity conservation strategies (IPBES and IPCCC, 2021[69]).

Recommendation

- Enhance connectivity of terrestrial and marine Protected Areas (PAs) as it is vital for the conservation of species.
- Effectively protect, expand and maintain the biological corridors of Mesoamerica, the Caribbean, the Amazon, the Andes, and Patagonia, among others, to reverse degradation and restore the integrity of their natural ecosystems.

Mainstreaming biodiversity across economic sectors

Mainstreaming biodiversity across different economic sectors can be achieved through economic instruments, such as taxes, charges, environmentally motivated subsidies, which provide positive incentives to shift to more sustainable behaviour and actions. In the LAC region, seven countries already have biodiversity relevant taxes in place, namely Brazil, Chile, Colombia, Costa Rica, Mexico, Panama, and Paraguay. However, only Chile, Colombia, and Mexico have introduced biodiversity-relevant fees and charges that is a payment by the payer to the general government for a good or service in return (such as a wastewater payment which varies based on the volume of water consumed). The same three countries have also introduced biodiversity-relevant environmentally motivated subsidies (Figure 2.8).

Figure 2.8. Biodiversity-related economic instruments in LAC countries

2021 data

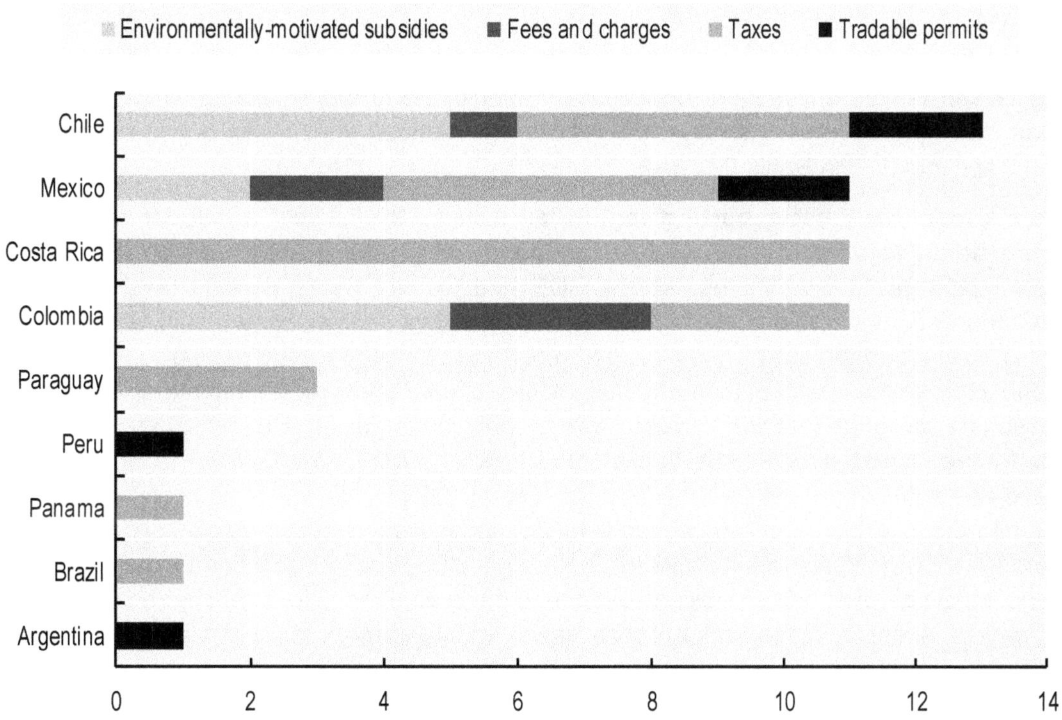

Source: (OECD, 2021[75]), Tracking Economic Instruments and Finance for Biodiversity, https://www.oecd.org/environment/resources/biodiversity/tracking-economic-instruments-and-finance-for-biodiversity-2021.pdf.

Recommendation

- Establish policy instruments that regulate the use and intensity of use of natural resources, respecting the natural cycles and promoting the conservation and sustainable use of biodiversity and ecosystems services. These policies could include objectives of reducing ecosystems vulnerability and GHG emissions, thereby increasing resilience to multiple anthropogenic pressures.

Considering land use, biodiversity and climate change adaptation in agriculture

The LAC region has more than 30% of all forest globally, with high levels of vulnerability due to ecosystems' degradation. At least 20% of the land of these ecosystems is destroyed and another 20% is severely damaged (OECD, 2023[13]). Key factors affecting land degradation in LAC are the expansion of large and small-scale agriculture and livestock, unsustainable infrastructure construction, the expansion of sprawled territories and (illegal) mining (UNCCD, 2019[76]).

LAC countries have incorporated Land Degradation Neutrality (LDN) targets at national level, in line with the Sustainable Development Goals and the LDN initiative driven by UNCCD, while all LAC countries are a party to the UN Convention on to Combat Desertification. Even though degradation goals have been set, and there is also rich traditional knowledge on sustainable land management in the region, it is critical to better protect natural capital and strengthen resilience of ecosystems. Prioritising policy initiatives that serve such purposes will also help address climate change adaptation issues, considering for example the contribution of the Amazonian Forest in controlling global temperatures (UNCCD, 2019[76]).

Land degradation, together with droughts and excess precipitation, also severely affect the agriculture sector. Overall, about 14% of the LAC rural population, that is about 44 000 people, live on degraded agricultural land (OECD, 2023[13]), while in 2021 agriculture covered 15% of total employment in the region (World Bank, n.d.[77]). Climate events, such as landslides, wildfires, temperature increases, storms, droughts and floods, affect most agricultural regions and crops. In cases where such events decrease yields, as in the case of Argentina, the results are reduced agricultural economic activity and increased food insecurity (World Bank, 2022[78]).

LAC is world's largest food net exporting region, as well as the largest producer of ecosystem services, being home to vast forests and savannahs that shape global weather patterns and mitigate climate change. LAC countries, whose GDP and exports highly depend on the agricultural sector, should prioritise land restoration and climate adaptation policies in agriculture and propose measures that will transform the food systems – going beyond planting and harvesting to packaging and consuming - and improve the health of land and soil, by creating certainty on land rights and land access, and using traditional knowledge more effectively. More broadly, countries should investigate the synergies and trade-offs between land use, biodiversity, climate change and food, and move to more coherent and sustainable land use solutions at the national and local level (OECD, 2020[79]). To scale up agriculture, LAC countries can develop long-term processes involving local organisations, share collective learning, and support on developing capabilities of workers in the agriculture and food system. Countries can also strengthen agricultural research and extension systems to generate innovations that increase productivity gains in the region, simplify intellectual property laws and stream product prototype development processes and support research on unattractive productive opportunities like orphan crops or smallholders. Moreover, it is important that LAC countries develop and implement policies aiming to modernise agricultural infrastructure, including information and communications technology, and enact policies with the objective to ensure the establishment of climate-smart agriculture practices (Le Coq, Sabourin and Fouilleux, 2020[80]); (Morris, Sebastian and Perego, 2020[81]).

Recommendation

- Prioritise land restoration and climate adaptation policies in agriculture and introduce measures that will transform the food systems and improve the health of land and soil.

Nature-based Solutions to address climate change

NbS have been introduced by many LAC countries as part of their NDCs. They are measures which protect, sustainably manage and restore nature, while maintaining or enhancing ecosystem services to address socio-economic and environmental challenges (OECD, 2020[82]). Their benefits are undisputable: they provide additional benefits to those gained by ecosystem services, they can be cost-effective, provide multiple co-benefits, and can complement existing non-green infrastructure, while responding to the impacts of climate change with some flexibility. Integrating NbS in long-term climate-resilient infrastructure planning can also contribute in better managing some climate-risks (OECD, 2018[55]).A recent report by the World Resources Institute (WRI), on NbS in the LAC region identified about 150 NbS projects, on water, energy, transport and urban development. In many cases, these projects show multiple benefits in parallel, such as local job creation, improving livelihoods, achieving biodiversity benefits and carbon sequestration (Ozment et al., 2021[83]).

However, **there are still challenges that limit a wider adoption and implementation of NbS** (OECD, 2021[84]); (Ozment et al., 2021[83]). These are also present in the LAC region:

- NbS are yet to be fully integrated in sectoral policies, therefore complementarities and trade-offs between NbS and sectoral policy objectives are not always clear.
- A clear policy framework and investment opportunities, which allow for NbS to be adopted and implemented are often missing, therefore traditional solutions (i.e. for infrastructure) is maintained.
- Multiple government agencies are supporting NbS, yet without the necessary co-ordination. Efficiency and effectiveness may be lost due to unclear responsibilities, duplication of efforts, and scattered funding.
- Technical capacities at the local level may often delay the implementation of a project, which requires first capacity building and training.
- The existing funding and financing framework does not acknowledge NbS' special characteristics, therefore there are limited financing mechanisms to which NbS are eligible for funding.
- There is limited private sector involvement in NbS, which hampers scaling up the efforts. In LAC 94% of the NbS projects have government participation (national or local), with the engagement of civil society, while about 75% depend on grants, with insufficient funding.

Chile, Colombia and Mexico acknowledge the importance of NbS for climate adaptation, through specific references in their NDCs (OECD, 2021[84]). Other LAC countries have also introduced NbS projects, with a high level of participation from civil society and national governments (Figure 2.9). In the case of Colombia's National Development Plan, NbS are to be designed with a community focus, as they could help achieve objectives such as eliminating deforestation, preserving ecosystems and transforming productive sectors through green pathways. Special focus is given in integrating NbS in agriculture, mining and energy, and tourism policies, as means of addressing both climate mitigation and adaptation (OECD, 2023[13]).

Figure 2.9. The vast majority of NbS projects in LAC have some form of government participation

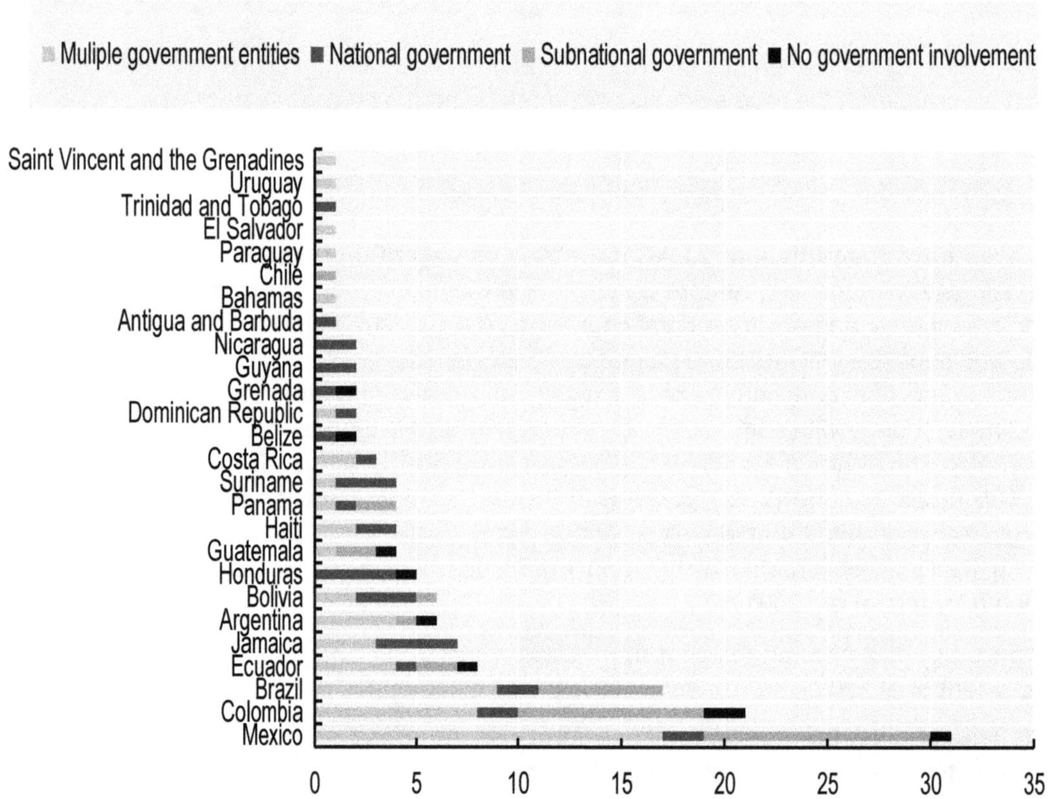

Note: Figure shows stakeholder groups that are leading or participating in the NbS projects. Subnational government include municipalities, cities and states.
Source : (Ozment et al., 2021[83])

Further efforts are required, so that LAC countries can overcome the abovementioned challenges, and successfully upscale NbS to address climate change in a more coherent, co-ordinated manner. Including NbS in policy frameworks is only a first step. Piloting projects is an opportunity to see in practice how to best improve the existing policy instruments, so that they are more inclusive of NbS, especially in economic sectors that require eminent actions to be taken to reduce their GHG emissions and their negative impact to natural resources.

Recommendation

- Integrate and upscale the use of Nature-based Solutions in policy instruments that address climate change mitigation, adaptation and ecosystems' protection.
- Properly value ecosystem services to generate economic compensation for the use of nature, particularly, to channel the revenues to entities and communities that protect nature.

Effective control and zero-tolerance for illegal trade

Illegal trade in environmentally sensitive products can be a major factor leading to the disruption of ecosystems and undermine climate change adaptation and mitigation measures, as well as

challenge national and local economies. Illegal wildlife trade can threaten biodiversity and can have negative implications for ecosystem functions. Reducing the population of a species may lead to changes in the ecosystems, depending on the role these species play and what effects these may have to resilience (Phelps, Board and Mailley, 2022[85]). A major driver of such illegal trade is often the high demand from foreign markets and the large profits for those involved in such exporting activities (OECD, 2012[86]).

Illegal trade in fauna and flora is not adequately monitored, as there is a lack of adequate taxonomic information available, making it difficult to identify species. In addition, there is lack of data and evidence on illegal wildlife trade activities and wildlife crime, limiting the understanding of the vastness of the issue in LAC (UNODC, 2020[87]). In Peru alone, which records illegal wildlife trade activity, around 102 000 live animals of protected species have been confiscated since 2000 (Jabiel, 2002[88]).

Unavailability of scientific information which helps classify species and organisms may impede efforts on safeguarding biological diversity. The Global Taxonomy Initiative, established by CBD COP in 1998, provides training and knowledge exchange between countries, while enriching the database of animal, plant and fungal species (CBD, n.d.[89]). Efforts in the LAC region had intensified to reach the Aichi targets on illegal trade in wildlife, through the enforcement of the Convention on International Trade in Endangered Species of Wild Fauna and Flora (CITES) (UNEP-WCMC, 2016[90]). However, wildlife trafficking persists (Figure 2.10); and together with illegal mining, timber harvesting and illicit crops, cause serious pressure on biodiversity in the region (OECD, 2018[91]). In parallel, the LAC region is showing an increase in numbers of species threatened with extinction, because of overexploitation, habitat fragmentation and loss, and disease (WWF, 2020[92]). Additional measures to combat such activities, in combination with illegal trade, would help minimise biodiversity loss in the region.

Figure 2.10. LAC Wildlife Trafficking 2010-2020

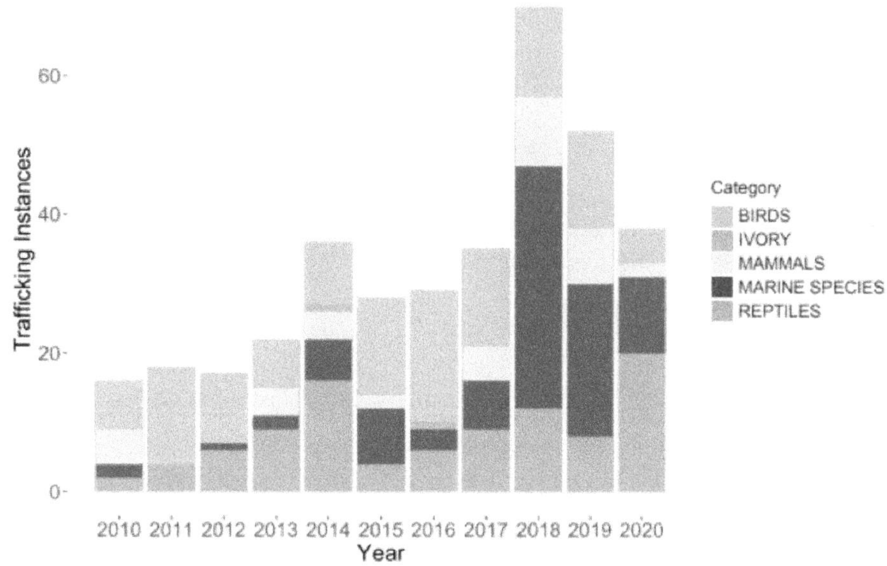

Source: (Connelly and Peyronnin, 2021[93])

While not always the case, **illegal trade of wildlife is often intertwined with other criminal activities and organised crime**, either because criminal groups expand their activities to other illegal trading markets than those they originally covered (for example from trading solely drugs to also trading wildlife) or because they use the same trafficking/smuggling networks (van Uhm, South and Wyatt, 2021[94]).

International co-operation is necessary for combatting illegal wildlife trade. Countries in the Americas have signed the 2019 Lima Declaration on Illegal Wildlife Trade, which calls for strengthened collaboration across source, transit and destination countries; improvements in national regulations for preventing, combatting and eradicating illegal trade; as well as enhancement in the criminal justice system for better response to wildlife trafficking. However, the declaration is not binding, and implementation has been slow (Guynup, 2023[95]).

The LAC region is also home to natural resources such as metals and minerals, including those that are deemed critical for the transition to more sustainable energy resources. Extractive activities in the region often present environmental and social impacts, negatively affecting water, air and soil, biodiversity loss, and affecting local (and indigenous) communities' livelihoods and health. Informal and illegal mining is also linked to organised crime, such as in the case of Colombia, Panama and Peru, where illegal gold mining is used for money laundering and illegal drug trade (OECD, 2022[96]).

Several multilateral and bilateral policy initiatives have been launched in the LAC region or with LAC countries, to increase co-ordination, joint operations and investigations against illegal mining. The International Criminal Police Organisation (INTERPOL) supports LAC countries in developing national, regional and international co-ordinated law enforcement responses, in an attempt to tackle illegal mining. With a focus on Bolivia, Brazil, Ecuador, Panama and Peru, INTERPOL proposes the creation of national multi-agency illegal mining taskforces; and to appoint focal points in enforcement agencies that will be responsible for enforcing and investigating illegal mining crimes (INTERPOL, 2022[97]).

Civil society in LAC has been active in raising awareness both on illegal trade of wildlife and illegal mining, highlighting the damage caused to natural habitats and species, as well as the effect to vulnerable groups and indigenous communities (EIA, n.d.[98]); (IFAW, n.d.[99]); (Villarreal Villamar and Echart Munoz, 2018[100]); (GIATOC, 2016[101]). In the case of the extractive industries, efforts to engage with artisanal and small-scale miners, and to clarify their status and activities through licencing and control, could reduce illegal mining and informality (OECD, 2018[91]).

Recommendation

- Combat illegal extractive activities and trade of threatened wildlife species by making greater multilateral efforts, co-ordinating between international and national authorities, and supporting local authorities, given the association of this activity with criminal groups.

References

Adaptation Action Coalition (2022), *Adaptation Action Coalition: an overview*, https://webarchive.nationalarchives.gov.uk/ukgwa/20230304100218/https://www.gov.uk/government/publications/adaptation-action-coalition-an-overview/adaptation-action-coalition-an-overview (accessed on 26 May 2023). [18]

Almond, R., M. Grooten and T. Petersen (eds.) (2020), *Living Planet Report 2020 - Bending the curve of biodiversity loss*, WWF, https://f.hubspotusercontent20.net/hubfs/4783129/LPR/PDFs/ENGLISH-FULL.pdf. [92]

Alvarez Malvido, M. et al. (eds.) (2021), *Informe Planeta Protegido 2020: Latinoamérica y el Caribe*. [74]

Arga Jafino, B. et al. (2020), *Revised Estimates of the Impact of Climate Change on Extreme Poverty by 2030*, https://openknowledge.worldbank.org/server/api/core/bitstreams/ad7eeab7-d3d8-567d-b804-59d620c3ab37/content (accessed on 12 December 2022). [2]

Argentina Presidencia (2019), *Ley de Presupuestos Mínimos de Adaptación y Mitigación al Cambio Climático Global (27520)*, https://www.boletinoficial.gob.ar/detalleAviso/primera/224006/20191220 (accessed on 13 July 2023). [33]

Beltrame, D. and M. del Pilar Medina (2022), *Towards gender Equality and Women's Leadership for Resilience to Disaster Risks in Latin America and the Caribbean*, https://www.cepal.org/sites/default/files/csw66_-_disaster_risk_reduction_-_en_vf.pdf. [41]

Brichetti, J. et al. (2021), *La brecha de infraestructura en América Latina y el Caribe: estimación de las necesidades de inversión hasta 2030 para progresar hacia el cumplimiento de los Objetivos de Desarrollo Sostenible*, Inter-American Development Bank, https://doi.org/10.18235/0003759. [51]

Brown, S. et al. (2019), *Gender Transformative Early Warning Systems: Experiences from Nepal and Peru*. [39]

Carver, D. (2023), *What was agreed at COP27?*, https://commonslibrary.parliament.uk/what-was-agreed-at-cop27/ (accessed on 26 May 2023). [21]

CBD (2022), *COP15: Final Text of Kunming-Montreal Global Biodiversity Framework*, https://www.cbd.int/article/cop15-final-text-kunming-montreal-gbf-221222 (accessed on 13 July 2023). [27]

CBD (n.d.), *Global Taxonomy Initiative*, https://www.cbd.int/gti/. [89]

Climate Analytics (2021), *What next for the Global Goal on Adaptation?*, https://climateanalytics.org/media/what_next_for_the_global_goal_on_adaptation_2.pdf (accessed on 26 May 2023). [16]

Connelly, B. and H. Peyronnin (2021), *Taking Off - Wildlife Trafficking in the Latin America and Caribbean Region*, https://www.traffic.org/site/assets/files/14510/routes_taking_off_report.pdf. [93]

CREWS Caribbean (n.d.), *CREWS Caribbean: Strengthening Hydro-Meteorological and Early Warning Services in the Caribbean*, https://www.gfdrr.org/en/crews-caribbean (accessed on September 2023). [42]

EIA (n.d.), *Environmental Investigation Agency - What we do*, https://eia-international.org/about-us/what-we-do/ (accessed on 13 July 2023). [98]

Estrada, F. et al. (2022), "Impacts and economic costs of climate change on Mexican agriculture", *Regional Environmental Change*, Vol. 22/4, https://doi.org/10.1007/s10113-022-01986-0. [12]

FAO (n.d.), *AQUASTAT dissemination system*, https://data.apps.fao.org/aquastat/?lang=en (accessed on 10 September 2023). [59]

Faria, F., M. Perutti and D. Villalba (2021), *The Changing Face of Infrastructure in Latin America. Public Sector Perspectives*, https://assets.kpmg.com/content/dam/kpmg/pe/pdf/kpmg_changing_infrastructure_LatinAmerica.pdf (accessed on 13 July 2023). [54]

Fay, M. et al. (2017), *Rethinking Infrastructure in Latin America and the Caribbean - Spending Better to Achieve More*, https://documents1.worldbank.org/curated/pt/676711491563967405/114110-REVISED-Rethinking-Infrastructure-Low-Res.pdf (accessed on 13 July 2023). [43]

Fernández Corugedo, E., A. Gonzalez and A. Guerson (2023), *The Macroeconomic Returns of Investment in Resilience to Natural Disasters under Climate Change: A DSGE Approach*, https://www.imf.org/en/Publications/WP/Issues/2023/06/30/The-Macroeconomic-Returns-of-Investment-in-Resilience-to-Natural-Disasters-under-Climate-534579. [48]

Gazol, C. (2019), *Strengthening Early Warning Systems in the Caribbean South-South Cooperation Strategy*, https://www.undp.org/latin-america/publications/strengthening-early-warning-systems-caribbean-ssc-strategy. [36]

GIATOC (2016), *Organized Crime and Illegal Mined Gold in Latin America*, https://globalinitiative.net/wp-content/uploads/2016/03/Organized-Crime-and-Illegally-Mined-Gold-in-Latin-America.pdf. [101]

Global Center on Adaptation (2021), *A Green and Resilient Recovery for Latin America*, https://gca.org/wp-content/uploads/2021/01/Green-and-Resilient-Recovery-for-LAC-Jan-2021-.pdf?_gl=1*m6llrh*_ga*NzE1MzQ0NjQwLjE2ODc5NTYyMzQ.*_up*MQ... [53]

Guynup, S. (2023), *The Growing Latin America-to-Asia Wildlife Crisis. Can targeted action stop illegal trade in time to prevent widespread losses?*, https://revista.drclas.harvard.edu/the-growing-latin-america-to-asia-wildlife-crisis-can-targeted-action-stop-illegal-trade-in-time-to-prevent-widespread-losses/. [95]

IFAW (n.d.), *A sad truth: Where you find wildlife, you will probably find wildlife crime*, https://www.ifaw.org/international/projects/wildlife-crime-prevention-latin-america-and-caribbean. [99]

INTERPOL (2022), *Illegal Mining and Associated Crimes*, https://www.interpol.int/en/content/download/17495/file/ILM - Illegal mining - Report.pdf. [97]

IPBES and IPCCC (2021), *Co-Sponsored Workshop Report on Biodiversity and Climate Change*, https://www.ipbes.net/sites/default/files/2021-06/20210609_workshop_report_embargo_3pm_CEST_10_june_0.pdf. [69]

IPCC (2022), *Climate Change 2022: Impacts, Adaptation and Vulnerability*, https://www.ipcc.ch/report/ar6/wg2/. [4]

Jabiel, S. (2002), *Illegal wildlife trade hotpot Peru steps up fight against traffickers*, https://dialogochino.net/en/trade-investment/361401-illegal-wildlife-trade-hotspot-peru-fight-trafficking/. [88]

Le Coq, J., E. Sabourin and E. Fouilleux (2020), *Workshop: Stepping Up to the Challenge of Agroecological Transition Through Agricultural Research for Development*, https://hal.science/hal-02776233/document. [80]

López-Cubillos, S. et al. (2021), "The landmark Escazú Agreement: An opportunity to integrate democracy, human rights, and transboundary conservation", *Conservation Letters*, Vol. 15/1, https://doi.org/10.1111/conl.12838. [23]

MADES and PNUD (2022), *Plan Nacional de Adaptación al Cambio Climático 2022-2030*, http://dncc.mades.gov.py/wp-content/uploads/2022/06/Plan-Nacional-de-Adaptaci%C3%B3n-al-Cambio-Clim%C3%A1tico-2022_2030.pdf. [32]

Maes, M. et al. (2022), "Monitoring exposure to climate-related hazards: Indicator methodology and key results", *OECD Environment Working Papers*, No. 201, OECD Publishing, Paris, https://doi.org/10.1787/da074cb6-en. [7]

MECON (2023), *Estrategia Nacional de Financiamiento Climático Internacional para la República Argentina*, https://www.argentina.gob.ar/sites/default/files/estrategia_nacional_de_financiamiento_internacional_para_la_republica_argentina.pdf. [31]

Morris, M., R. Sebastian and V. Perego (2020), *Future Foodscapes: Re-imagining Agriculture in Latin America and the Caribbean*, https://documents1.worldbank.org/curated/en/942381591906970569/pdf/Future-Foodscapes-Re-imagining-Agriculture-in-Latin-America-and-the-Caribbean.pdf. [81]

Müller, G., M. Lovino and L. Sgroi (2021), "Observed and Projected Changes in Temperature and Precipitation in the Core Crop Region of the Humid Pampa, Argentina", *Climate*, Vol. 9/3, p. 40, https://doi.org/10.3390/cli9030040. [11]

Mycoo, M. (2022), *Building Urban Resilience in the Caribbean: Policies, Practices and Prospects*, https://sdg.iisd.org/commentary/guest-articles/building-urban-resilience-in-the-caribbean-policies-practices-and-prospects/ (accessed on 13 July 2023). [45]

NDC Partnership (n.d.), *NDC Content*, https://ndcpartnership.org/node/21071 (accessed on 13 July 2023). [29]

OECD (2023), *3rd LAC Regional Policy Dialogue on Environmental Sustainability: Addressing Climate Change Adaptation in Latin America & the Caribbean*, https://www.oecd.org/greengrowth/3rd-lac-policy-dialogue.htm. [13]

OECD (2023), *Environment at a Glance in Latin America and the Caribbean: Spotlight on Climate Change*, OECD Publishing, Paris, https://doi.org/10.1787/2431bd6c-en. [1]

OECD (2023), *Framework for assessing the enabling conditions to finance water security*, OECD, https://www.oecd.org/water/background-note-enabling-environment-9th-RT-on-financing-water.pdf. [67]

OECD (2023), *OECD Environmental Performance Reviews: Costa Rica 2023*, OECD Environmental Performance Reviews, OECD Publishing, Paris, https://doi.org/10.1787/ec94fd4e-en. [38]

OECD (2022), *Aggregate Trends of Climate Finance Provided and Mobilised by Developed Countries in 2013-2020*, Climate Finance and the USD 100 Billion Goal, OECD Publishing, Paris, https://doi.org/10.1787/d28f963c-en. [52]

OECD (2022), *Climate Tipping Points: Insights for Effective Policy Action*, OECD Publishing, Paris, https://doi.org/10.1787/abc5a69e-en. [14]

OECD (2022), *Fostering Water Resilience in Brazil: Turning Strategy into Action*, OECD Studies on Water, OECD Publishing, Paris, https://doi.org/10.1787/85a99a7c-en. [61]

OECD (2022), *Reform of Water Supply and Wastewater Treatment in Lithuania: Practical Options to Foster Consolidation of Utilities*, OECD Studies on Water, OECD Publishing, Paris, https://doi.org/10.1787/f966a980-en. [66]

OECD (2022), *Responsible Business Conduct in the Extractive and Minerals Sector in Latin America and the Caribbean*, OECD Publishing. [96]

OECD (2022), *Towards Sustainable Water Services in Estonia: Analyses and Action Plan*, OECD Studies on Water, OECD Publishing, Paris, https://doi.org/10.1787/b82d71c6-en. [65]

OECD (2021), *OECD work in support of biodiversity*, https://www.oecd.org/environment/resources/OECD-work-in-support-of-biodiversity-2021.pdf. [70]

OECD (2021), *Scaling up Nature-based Solutions to Tackle Water-related Climate Risks: Insights from Mexico and the United Kingdom*, OECD Publishing, Paris, https://doi.org/10.1787/736638c8-en. [84]

OECD (2021), *Toolkit for Water Policies and Governance: Converging Towards the OECD Council Recommendation on Water*, OECD Publishing, Paris, https://doi.org/10.1787/ed1a7936-en. [62]

OECD (2021), *Tracking Economic Instruments and Finance for Biodiversity*, https://www.oecd.org/environment/resources/biodiversity/tracking-economic-instruments-and-finance-for-biodiversity-2021.pdf. [75]

OECD (2020), *Common Ground Between the Paris Agreement and the Sendai Framework : Climate Change Adaptation and Disaster Risk Reduction*, OECD Publishing, Paris, https://doi.org/10.1787/3edc8d09-en. [25]

OECD (2020), "Nature-based solutions for adapting to water-related climate risks", *OECD Environment Policy Papers*, No. 21, OECD Publishing, Paris, https://doi.org/10.1787/2257873d-en. [82]

OECD (2020), *Towards Sustainable Land Use: Aligning Biodiversity, Climate and Food Policies*, OECD Publishing, Paris, https://doi.org/10.1787/3809b6a1-en. [79]

OECD (2018), *Biodiversity Conservation and Sustainable Use in Latin America: Evidence from Environmental Performance Reviews*, OECD Environmental Performance Reviews, OECD Publishing, Paris, https://doi.org/10.1787/9789264309630-en. [91]

OECD (2018), "Climate-resilient infrastructure", *OECD Environment Policy Papers*, No. 14, OECD Publishing, Paris, https://doi.org/10.1787/4fdf9eaf-en. [47]

OECD (2018), *Mainstreaming Biodiversity for Sustainable Development*, OECD Publishing, Paris, https://doi.org/10.1787/9789264303201-en. [72]

OECD (2018), "Plan infrastructure for a low-emission and resilient future", in *Financing Climate Futures: Rethinking Infrastructure*, OECD Publishing, Paris, https://doi.org/10.1787/9789264308114-5-en. [55]

OECD (2017), *Investing in Climate, Investing in Growth*, OECD Publishing, Paris, https://doi.org/10.1787/9789264273528-en. [49]

OECD (2017), *Water Charges in Brazil: The Ways Forward*, OECD Studies on Water, OECD Publishing, Paris, https://doi.org/10.1787/9789264285712-en. [63]

OECD (2015), *Aligning Policies for a Low-carbon Economy*, OECD Publishing, Paris, https://doi.org/10.1787/9789264233294-en. [30]

OECD (2012), *Illegal Trade in Environmentally Sensitive Goods*, OECD Trade Policy Studies, OECD Publishing, Paris, https://doi.org/10.1787/9789264174238-en. [86]

OECD et al. (2022), *Latin American Economic Outlook 2022: Towards a Green and Just Transition*, OECD Publishing, Paris, https://doi.org/10.1787/3d5554fc-en. [3]

Ozment, S. et al. (2021), *Nature-Based Solutions in Latin America and The Caribbean: Regional Status and Priorities for Growth*. [83]

Phelps, J., S. Board and J. Mailley (2022), *Illegal wildlife trade and climate change - joining the dots*, https://www.unodc.org/documents/data-and-analysis/wildlife/Ilegal_wildlife_trade_and_climate_change_2022.pdf. [85]

Rockström, J. et al. (2023), "Why we need a new economics of water as a common good", *Nature*, Vol. 615/7954, pp. 794-797, https://doi.org/10.1038/d41586-023-00800-z. [57]

S. Díaz et al. (eds.) (2019), *The Global Assessment Report on Biodiversity and Ecosystem Services. Summary for Policymakers of the IPBES Global Assessment Report on Biodiversity and Ecosystem Services*, IPBES Secretariat, Bonn, https://ipbes.net/sites/default/files/inline/files/ipbes_global_assessment_report_summary_for_policymakers.pdf. [68]

Straffelini, E. et al. (2023), "Viticulture in Argentina under extreme weather scenarios: Actual challenges, future perspectives", *Geography and Sustainability*, Vol. 4/2, pp. 161-169, https://doi.org/10.1016/j.geosus.2023.03.003. [10]

Szlafsztein, C. (2020), "Extreme Natural Events Mitigation: An Analysis of the National Disaster Funds in Latin America", *Frontiers in Climate*, Vol. 2, https://doi.org/10.3389/fclim.2020.603176. [37]

The Nature Conservancy (2021), *Together we Find a Way - 2021 Latin America Impact Report*, https://www.nature.org/content/dam/tnc/nature/en/documents/latin-america/2021larannualreport_spreads_low.pdf. [73]

UN (2018), *Regional Agreement on Access to Information, Public Participation and Justice in Environmental Matters in Latin America and the Caribbean*, http://www.cepal.org/es/suscripciones. [22]

UN (2015), *Paris Agreement*, https://unfccc.int/files/essential_background/convention/application/pdf/english_paris_agreement.pdf. [15]

UN ECLAC (2023), *Member Countries of the Escazú Agreement End COP2 in Argentina with a Call for Deepening its Implementation at the National Level*, https://www.cepal.org/en/pressreleases/member-countries-escazu-agreement-end-cop-2-argentina-call-deepening-its (accessed on 26 May 2023). [24]

UNCCD (2019), *The Global Land Outlook, Latin America and the Caribbean Thmatic Report*, https://catalogue.unccd.int/1221_GLO_LAC_E.pdf (accessed on 5 May 2023). [76]

UNDESA (2014), *World Urbanization Prospects*, https://www.un.org/en/development/desa/publications/2014-revision-world-urbanization-prospects.html. [6]

UNDRR (2022), *Midterm Review of the Implementation of the Sendai Framework for Disaster Risk Reduction 2015-2030 for Latin America and the Caribbean*, https://sendaiframework-mtr.undrr.org/media/85823/download?startDownload=true (accessed on 26 May 2023). [26]

UNEP (2021), *Saint Lucia's National Infrastructure Assessment - Case Study*, https://www.unep.org/resources/case-study/saint-lucias-national-infrastructure-assessment-case-study (accessed on 21 September 2023). [56]

UNEP (2021), *What does COP26 mean for adaptation?*, http://www.unep.org/news-and-stories/story/what-does-cop26-mean-adaptation (accessed on 26 May 2023). [19]

UNEP-WCMC (2016), *The State of Biodiversity in Latin America and the Caribbean: A mid-term review of progress towards the Aichi Biodiversity Targets*, https://www.cbd.int/gbo/gbo4/outlook-grulac-en.pdf. [90]

UNFCCC (n.d.), *Decision -/CMA.3 Glasgow-Sharm el-Sheikh work programme on the global goal on adaptation*, https://unfccc.int/sites/default/files/resource/cma3_auv_4ac_Global_Goal.pdf. [17]

UNFCCC (n.d.), *Decision -/CP.27 Sharm el-Sheikh Implementation Plan*, https://unfccc.int/sites/default/files/resource/cop27_auv_2_cover%20decision.pdf (accessed on 26 May 2023). [20]

UNFCCC et al. (2022), *Promoting synergies between climate change adaptation and biodiversity through the National Adaptation Plan (NAP) and National Biodiversity Strategies and Action Plan (NBSPA) processes*, https://unfccc.int/sites/default/files/resource/UNFCCC-NWP_synergies_NAP-NBSAP_technical-brief.pdf. [71]

UNICEF (2021), *9 out of 10 childer in Latin America and the Caribbean are exposed to at least two climate and environmental shocks*, https://www.unicef.org/lac/en/press-releases/children-latin-america-and-caribbean-are-exposed-climate-climate-environmental-shocks (accessed on 6 June 2023). [9]

UNODC (2020), *World Wildlife Crime Report 2020: Trafficking in Protected Species*, https://www.unodc.org/documents/data-and-analysis/wildlife/2020/World_Wildlife_Report_2020_9July.pdf. [87]

UNSD (n.d.), *SDG 11 - Make cities and human setlements inclusive, safe, resilinet and sustainable*, https://unstats.un.org/sdgs/report/2021/goal-11/ (accessed on 13 July 2023). [44]

Value for Women (2020), *Study of the Impacts of Climat Change on the Women and Men of the Caribbean. Pilot Programme for Climate Resilience Countries*, https://www.cif.org/sites/cif_enc/files/knowledge-documents/study-of-the-impacts-of-climate-change-on-the-women-and-men-in-the-caribbean-pilot-programme-for-climate-resilience-countries.pdf. [40]

van Uhm, D., N. South and T. Wyatt (2021), "Connections between trades and trafficking in wildlife and drugs", *Trends in Organized Crime*, Vol. 24/4, pp. 425-446, https://doi.org/10.1007/s12117-021-09416-z. [94]

Villarreal Villamar, M. and E. Echart Munoz (2018), *PACHA: DEFENDING THE LAND Extractivism, conflicts, and alternatives in Latin America and the Caribbean*. [100]

WMO (2023), *State of the Global Climate 2022*, https://library.wmo.int/doc_num.php?explnum_id=11593. [5]

WMO (2022), *Early Warning for All: Exectuive Action Plan 2023-2027 (The UN Global Early Warning Initiative for the Implementation of Climate Adaptation)*, https://library.wmo.int/doc_num.php?explnum_id=11426. [34]

WMO (2021), *WMO Atlas for Mortality and Economic Losses from Weather, Climate and Water Extremes (1970-2019)*, https://public.wmo.int/en/resources/atlas-of-mortality. [8]

WMO (2020), *2020 State of Climate Services - Risk Information and Early Warning Systems*, https://library.wmo.int/doc_num.php?explnum_id=10385. [35]

World Bank (2022), *A Roadmap for Climate Action in Latin America and the Caribbean 2021-2025*, https://openknowledge.worldbank.org/server/api/core/bitstreams/d3e9d5ba-bdea-543b-8e51-e53f39308a73/content. [28]

World Bank (2022), *Argentina Country Climate and Development Report*, http://hdl.handle.net/10986/38252. [78]

World Bank (2022), *Water Matters*, World Bank, https://doi.org/10.1596/37214. [60]

World Bank (2014), *Climate Change Adaptation Planning in Latin American and Caribbean Cities*, https://www.worldbank.org/en/results/2014/01/31/climate-change-adaptation-planning-in-latin-american-and-caribbean-cities (accessed on 13 July 2023). [46]

World Bank (2013), *World Water Day: Latin America leads in water management but inequalities in access remain*, https://www.worldbank.org/en/news/feature/2013/03/22/world-water-day-latin-america-achievements-challenges (accessed on 13 July 2023). [58]

World Bank (n.d.), *Employment in agriculture (% of total employment) Latin America & Caribbean*, https://data.worldbank.org/indicator/SL.AGR.EMPL.ZS?end=2021&locations=ZJ&start=1991&view=chart (accessed on 23 May 2023). [77]

World Water Atlas (n.d.), *Water as Leverage Programme*, https://www.worldwateratlas.org/curated/water-as-leverage/ (accessed on 10 September 2023). [64]

Zelikow, D. and F. Savas (2022), *Mind the gap: Time to rethink infrastructure finance*, https://blogs.worldbank.org/ppps/mind-gap-time-rethink-infrastructure-finance (accessed on 13 July 2023). [50]

Note

[1] These challenges were identified during an OECD Expert Workshop on Priorities on Climate Neutrality and Resilience in LAC, held on the 31st of August 2022.

3 Achieving climate neutrality in the Latin America and the Caribbean region

In the past two decades, the Latin America and the Caribbean (LAC) region has seen a significant rise in emissions, despite contributing to less than 10% of global Green House Gas (GHG) emissions. National pledges, while crucial, fall short of addressing this issue comprehensively. To effectively combat this trend, LAC governments must adopt an integrated approach, prioritising energy efficiency, renewable energy adoption, emissions reduction in transport and agriculture, and forest preservation. The region's diversity results in varying climate impacts and challenges. Based on the discussions in a series of Regional Policy Dialogues and Workshops on these issues among LAC and OECD experts in the context of the OECD LAC Regional Programme (LACRP), this Chapter describes regional challenges, identifies mitigation priorities, and presents policy options for tailored sector-specific climate mitigation strategies.

Introduction

This chapter was developed from discussions held during the 2021 Regional Policy Dialogue on Environmental Sustainability, involving LAC and OECD experts as part of the LACRP. It provides a comprehensive review of the climate change mitigation challenges facing LAC countries and presents a set of policy measures aimed at achieving climate neutrality. Analysis on air pollution and GHG emissions paints a solemn picture, constituting the necessary improvement of regulatory frameworks at the national and local levels. A sectorial approach – with a focus on energy, transport, sustainable mining, cities, agriculture and tourism – highlights the opportunities available towards achieving climate neutrality in the region.

According to the 2022 United Nations Environment Programme (UNEP) Emission Gap Report, based on the Nationally Determined Contributions (NDCs) submitted before and updates since the twenty-sixth United Nations Climate Change Conference of the Parties (COP26), global actions taken to address the climate crisis have been insufficient to stop and reduce GHG emissions. If countries continue with their current policies, global warming is projected to reach 2.8°C by the end of century. However, the implementation of unconditional and conditional NDC scenarios would reduce this to 2.6°C and 2.4°C, respectively, which is still greatly insufficient. Despite calls to "revisit and strengthen" their 2030 targets at COP26, little progress has been made in closing the significant emissions gap for 2030, which represents the disparity between the promised emissions reductions and the reductions required to achieve the temperature goal of the Paris Agreement (UNEP, 2022[1]). The International Energy Agency (IEA) estimates that effective implementation of the pledges announced at the twenty-seventh United Nations Climate Change Conference of the Parties (COP27) could limit global warming to an increase of 1.7°C, thereby providing a pathway towards the more ambitious goal of limiting warming to 1.5°C (IEA, 2022[2]).

It is clear that the time for decisive climate action is now. The urgency of the crisis cannot be overstated since the future of our planet and the well-being of future generations depend on this. Pledges, while important, are insufficient on their own. In such a diverse region, climate change impacts countries differently, and presents a set of challenges as varied as the countries themselves. However, it also presents an opportunity to devise implementation mechanisms that enable the influx of green financial resources into LAC. This approach can catalyse development, foster a green transition, and generate green employment. The success of these depends in their transformation into tangible actions.

Despite LAC contributing to less than 10% of total GHG emissions, its emissions have been significantly increasing in the last 20 years, mainly driven by transport, electricity, and heat production. Moreover, the region plays a crucial role in global mitigation efforts due to its natural carbon capture potential in places such as the Amazon River basin (OECD, 2023[3]). Governments in LAC will need to adopt an integrated approach in order to achieve climate change mitigation goals and international commitments, focused on increasing energy efficiency and renewable energy use, reducing emissions in transport and agriculture, and restoring and protecting forests, mangroves and wetlands. It is important that countries adopt policy mixes that best suit their specific circumstances, ideally articulated as national strategies. At the same time, air pollution represents a real risk to the urban population due to the high level of urbanisation in LAC. Climate change mitigation efforts could also bring important environmental and health co-benefits including reductions in air pollution mortality and morbidity.

COVID-19 and Russia's war of aggression against Ukraine have highlighted and exacerbated the region's vulnerability to external economic shocks, historically rooted in its structural challenges. Global disruptions to the energy and food supplies have increased prices which have forced countries to implement policies aimed at controlling inflationary pressures and protecting the well-being of its citizens, particularly the most vulnerable population. In LAC, during the first five months of 2022, the region witnessed an average price increase of 3.6% higher than the nationally representative household, with estimates suggesting that by the end of 2022, approximately 33.7% of the population would be in poverty and 14.9% in extreme poverty. In this sense, it is crucial for governments to complement monetary measures with fiscal policies that include targeted safety net interventions, as well as to advance towards universal, comprehensive, resilient, and sustainable social protection systems (OECD et al., 2022[4]).

Some countries have established policies, such as regressive energy subsidies to fossil fuels (Cárdenas and Hernández, 2022[5]), **which have negative environmental consequences**, sometimes leading to delays or cancellations in the implementation of NDCs submitted to the UNFCCC. Therefore, countries must plan for a post-pandemic intelligent fiscal consolidation, gradually phasing out measures introduced to support consumption, while considering the inflation caused by higher food and energy prices (Cárdenas and Hernández, 2022[5]); (OECD, 2022[6]).

LAC mitigation contributions in Glasgow and Sharm el-Sheikh

Many LAC countries have made international commitments to reduce their GHG emissions and take action to mitigate the impacts of climate change. At COP26, nearly 200 countries signed the Glasgow Climate Pact, which recognises the urgent need for a rapid, deep, and sustained reduction in GHG emissions, and limit global warming to 1.5°C. The pact calls for increased efforts to collectively reduce GHG emissions through accelerated action and implementation of domestic mitigation measures. Parties are urged to communicate new or updated NDCs and long-term strategies (LTS) and to revisit and strengthen their 2030 targets. Additionally, the Glasgow Climate Pact calls on nations to phase down unabated coal power and inefficient subsidies for fossil fuels (UNFCCC, 2021[7]). Furthermore, countries finalised the *Paris Agreement Rulebook*, which includes agreements on an enhanced transparency framework for reporting emissions, common timeframes for emissions reductions targets, and mechanisms and standards for international carbon markets.

Additional pledges were made at COP26 in key strategic sectors. Some of these include:

- the *Global Methane Pledge*, where countries committed to take voluntary actions to reduce global methane emissions by at least 30% from 2020 levels by 2030, representing 70% of the global economy and nearly half of anthropogenic methane emissions, where 25 out of 105 signatory countries are from LAC[1],
- the *Glasgow Leaders' Declaration on Forests and Land Use*, where, to the date, 145 countries, 24 from LAC[2], committed to halt and reverse forest loss and land degradation by 2030 while delivering sustainable development and promoting an inclusive rural transformation, and
- the *Global Coal to Clean Power Transition Statemen*t with countries committing to scale up the deployment of clean power generation, scale up technologies and policies to achieve a transition away from unabated coal power generation and stop issuance of new permits for new unabated coal-fired power generation projects, new construction of unabated coal-fired power generation projects and to end new direct government support for unabated international coal-fired power generation.

At COP27, countries approved the *Sharm el-Sheikh Implementation Plan*, emphasising the need for immediate, deep, rapid, and sustained reductions in global GHG emissions across all applicable sectors. Countries recognised that limiting global warming to 1.5 °C requires a 43% reduction in global GHG emissions by 2030 compared to 2019 levels. The Plan calls on countries to accelerate the development, deployment, and dissemination of low-emission technologies and the adoption of policies that promote the transition to low-emission energy systems. This includes clean power generation, energy efficiency measures, phasing down unabated coal power, and eliminating inefficient fossil fuel subsidies. The plan also emphasises the importance of providing targeted support to the poorest and most vulnerable, while ensuring a just transition (UNFCCC, 2022[8]).

Global efforts to reduce methane emissions have gained momentum, with the number of countries endorsing the Global Methane Pledge increasing from 105 at COP26 to 150 by the conclusion of COP27. As a result, approximately 95% of countries are either including methane reduction commitments or plan to include them in their next revision of climate goals. Moreover, 50 countries have methane action plans or are working to develop one. More than 70 endorsing countries have already incorporated specific measures to target methane reduction in their NDCs (USA and EU, 2022[9]).

The LAC region has made important developments towards reducing methane emissions. In March 2022, Brazil launched its National Zero Methane Programme, aiming to promote the reduction of methane emissions in alignment with the Sustainable Development Goals (SDGs) (IEA, 2023[10]). The programme also seeks to encourage the use of biomethane and biogas. Chile announced its intention to accelerate methane reduction efforts by 2025, while Colombia indicated its intent to prepare a national methane action plan by COP28 (USA and EU, 2022[9]). Additionally, Mexico is in the planning stages for implementing methane reduction actions under the Global Methane Pledge (USA and EU, 2022[9]).

Furthermore, at COP27 a *Mitigation Work Programme* was launched with the objective of urgently scaling up mitigation ambition and implementation. The programme started immediately after COP27 and will continue until 2026. Governments were requested to revisit and strengthen the 2030 targets in their national climate plans by the end of 2023, as well as to accelerate efforts to phase down unabated coal power and phase out inefficient fossil fuel subsidies.

Snapshot of Nationally Determined Contributions in LAC

Due to the COVID-19 pandemic, many parties submitted new or updated NDCs at COP26 in 2021 instead of in 2020, despite the Paris Agreement requiring parties to submit increasingly ambitious NDCs every five years. While these new and updated NDCs showed some progress, they remained insufficient to bridge the emissions gap for 2030. As a result, the Glasgow Climate Pact, adopted at COP26, called for parties to "revisit and strengthen" their 2030 targets by the end of 2022 (UNFCCC, 2021[7]). In LAC, nine countries sent their updated NDCs by 2022.[3] In the region, some countries have set ambitious emissions reduction targets in their NDCs, while others have focused on adaptation measures or capacity building to support the transition to a low-carbon future (Annex B).

Out of the 33 LAC countries that have submitted GHG emission reduction commitments to the UNFCCC under the Paris Agreement, only 22 have presented clear enough NDCs to infer targets for 2030 and beyond. Moreover, only 16 countries have committed to achieving net zero by 2050 or earlier, and just seven countries cover all GHGs in their pledges (OECD, 2023[3]). The region faces challenges in effectively measuring and monitoring decarbonisation plans, with only the Dominican Republic, Panama, and Peru having proposed or developed national monitoring systems for tracking commitments (OECD et al., 2022[4]). This information gap hampers sound policymaking; for instance, Costa Rica's GHG emission inventories are issued with a significant time lag, with the latest inventory, released in 2021, containing data up to 2017 (Ministry of Environment Costa Rica, 2021[11]) (Annex B).

Challenges for the implementation Nationally Determined Contributions in LAC

There are different ways LAC countries can address climate change and reduce GHG emissions and Short-lived Climate Pollutants (SLCPs), such as carbon dioxide (CO_2), methane, nitrous oxide (N_2O) and fluorinated gases (f-gases), in order to achieve sectoral net-zero targets and climate neutrality goals by 2050. LAC governments should develop and implement mitigation strategies and action plans in a systematic and integrated manner, aligning them with their respective NDCs and the Paris Agreement. These policies and actions will vary depending on the specific challenges in each country and will involve different levels of government and relevant stakeholders, including the private sector and civil society. Some of these include developing climate mitigation policies to reduce air pollution, promoting clean fuels in transport, and enhancing the quality, reliability, and durability of cooking stoves. Moreover, countries in the region can increase the share of renewable energy sources in their energy supply mix, adopt energy-efficient production processes, improve the energy efficiency of consumer goods and services, and conserve and expand carbon sinks like forests and wetlands (OECD, 2023[3]). Committing to deeper emissions reduction targets within their NDCs, transitioning to low-carbon energy systems, and addressing emissions from sectors like transport, agriculture and from land use, land use change and forestry (LULUCF) are essential steps to achieve climate neutrality goals by 2050.

Taking ambitious mitigation actions in diverse sectors across LAC, from renewable energy to sustainable transport and urban development, is vital to combat climate change while aligning with national climate adaptation strategies. Mitigation actions in LAC are needed across different sectors, such as energy (e.g., transitioning from fossil fuels to renewable energy sources and energy efficiency improvements in buildings), transport (e.g., investments in the production and use of low carbon public transport and electric vehicles), urban development/cities, industry/infrastructure development, innovation, agriculture, forestry, land use and tourism. Both NDCs and NAPs are complementary processes (see Chapter 2).

Unlocking the path to a sustainable future in the LAC region demands strategic planning, financial support, and public engagement. Essential factors like economic growth, political will, stability, and strong institutions play a crucial role in providing the necessary investments for net-zero development and emissions reduction, as well as to foster effective mitigation efforts. However, LAC countries often face challenges in funding their NDCs and decarbonisation plans due to the lack of an assigned budget, making them vulnerable to underfunding during crises or external shocks. The LAC governments have recognised they are expecting to shift financial resources away from climate budget due to COVID-19, including co-financing for projects already agreed upon with multilateral climate funds. Considering the growing financial burden of climate change, the LAC countries have consistently asked for support to mobilise climate finance, particularly by involving private sector investors. Expanding technical support for project preparation and improving access to international climate finance is essential to effectively implement its NDCs (NDC Partnership, 2020[12]).

Mitigation strategies should be designed to promote equitable outcomes, addressing existing inequalities within the LAC region while creating green jobs. Additionally, fostering social awareness and developing skills for transitioning to a green economy are vital components to achieve net-zero emissions economies in the region. Empowering citizens with knowledge and understanding of climate change can lead to collective demands for more sustainable practices across sectors. Encouraging behaviours that reduce carbon footprints, such as responsible consumption and waste management, is key to achieving emission reduction targets (OECD, 2023[13]). Furthermore, public engagement in addressing critical environmental issues and advocating for stronger climate policies will provide greater traction and accelerate the implementation of effective mitigation measures.

Air pollution: A major concern in LAC

Air pollution is the primary environmental health risk in LAC, with the most vulnerable populations being children, the elderly and pregnant women (PAHO, 2016[14]). Combustion of fossil fuels are the primary source of particulate air pollution in the region, including $PM_{2.5}$ (Gouveia et al., 2021[15]). Fine particulate matter concentrations are associated with respiratory infections, ischemic heart disease, stroke, cancer, and chronic respiratory diseases. In 2019, chronic respiratory diseases, particularly chronic obstructive pulmonary diseases, were responsible for over 180 000 deaths in LAC, with Brazil accounting for 43% of the cases of the region, followed by Mexico, Colombia, Venezuela, Peru, Cuba, Ecuador, and

Bolivia. The associated average welfare cost in the region was under 3% of GDP, but considering factors like labour productivity losses, medical treatment, and agricultural productivity were considered, this cost would rise further. In the Caribbean, welfare losses due to air pollution reached approximately 7% of GDP in Barbados (OECD, 2023[3]). Additionally, Dominica reached 5%, Grenada 5%, the Dominican Republic 3.8%, Jamaica 3.6%, and Antigua and Barbuda exceeded 3.2% (OECD, 2023[16]).

The percentage of people living in urban areas in LAC has doubled since 1950, with approximately 81% of the region's population living in urban areas in 2021 (World Bank, 2022[17]). The Caribbean has also experienced a significant increase in urbanisation, with the urbanisation rate rising from 36.3% in 1950 to 72.2% in 2020. The Dominican Republic and Haiti have seen the fastest increase of urbanisation rates from 23.7% to 82.5% and from 12.2% to 57.1%, respectively in that same period (OECD et al., 2022[4]).

The high urbanisation rates in LAC have resulted in increased demand for transport, particularly by private vehicles, leading to higher GHG emissions, air pollution, and traffic congestion. Between 2005 and 2015, the region witnessed a 58% growth in car ownership, more than double the global average which was at 27%. Private motorised transport was responsible for 75% of CO_2 emissions and 82% of PM_{10} pollutants (OECD et al., 2022[4]); (SLOCAT, 2021[18]).

Some LAC countries have introduced various policy measures to address air pollution, including green urban planning, more effective use of economic instruments and regulations on emissions from industrial and transport sources, promotion of cleaner fuels and vehicles and the development of sustainable transport programmes. For example, Argentina's *2022 National Plan for Sustainable Transport* aims to establish a roadmap toward 2030 by regulating different modes of transport and promoting the adoption of natural gas and electric mobility (Government of Argentina, 2022[19]). Mexico has implemented the *National Strategy for Air Quality*, which guides and co-ordinates actions between different governmental agencies to control and mitigate pollutant emissions until 2030 (Government of Mexico, 2017[20]).

As of 2020, at least 12 countries in LAC have adopted national emission standards for industries through laws and regulations. These measures include the use of environmental impact assessments (EIAs) to regulate industries, the establishment of industrial emission standards, and policies on efficient resource use for fuel and electricity. Additionally, a total of 17 countries regulate the burning of waste, although only 5 of them do so strictly, as open burning remains a common practice in the region even when regulations exist. Furthermore, at least eight countries in LAC have a national air quality management strategy, framework, or action plan, which is generally implemented through a national environmental action plan. A total of 21 countries in the region had legal instruments that considered ambient air quality standards (UNEP, 2021[21]).

Implementing climate mitigation policies in the LAC region aiming to reduce air pollution can provide multiple co-benefits and synergies, including resource efficiency, economic security, sustainability of ecosystems, biodiversity and increased economic dynamism (UNECE, 2016[22]). Air pollution and climate change are closely related. CO_2 is the major cause of climate change, due to the extraction and burning of fossil fuels, as well as a major source of air pollutants. Many air pollutants contribute to climate change by reflecting or absorbing sunlight, with some pollutants warming and others cooling the earth. These SLCPs include methane and black carbon, which are among the top contributors to global warming after CO_2. The 2018 IPCC special report on the impacts of global warming underlines that deep reductions in non-CO_2 climate forcers, particularly in methane and black carbon, will be vital to reach the Paris Agreement goal of limiting warming to 1.5°C or even 2°C (RIFS Potsdam, 2022[23]).

Sulphur, nitrogen emissions and ground-level ozone impact ecosystems due to air pollution. Emissions of both sulphur dioxide and nitrogen oxides deposit in water, on vegetation and on soils as "acid rain"; with increasing adverse effects on flora and fauna. Acidification affects the ability of ecosystems to provide "ecosystem services", such as nutrient cycling and carbon cycling, but also water provision, on which the planet and human life is dependent (UNECE, 2022[24]).Furthermore, air pollution has negative impacts on both terrestrial and aquatic ecosystems, degrading environments and reducing biodiversity by affecting lower life forms regarding number of species and sensitivity of individual species, such as lichens, bryophytes, fungi, and soft bodied aquatic invertebrates. On land, plants are more affected than animals, but not in freshwater. While most affected species decline as a result of air pollution, it is important to note that there are some species, for instance aphids, which appear to be stimulated by air pollutants, while others are resistant and tend to expand (Air Pollution and Climate Secretariat (AirClim), 1997[25]).

Recognising the connection between GHG emissions and local air pollution, suggests developing integrated strategies that reduce GHG emissions and air pollutants, thus implementing "win-win" solutions for both climate and health policy objectives. Effective pollution prevention and control measures are especially important. They need to be tailored to local circumstances as both the sources of air pollution and severity of exposure vary across and within countries (OECD, 2023[3]).

Air pollution poses an important health risk in LAC

Governments should align environmental and health policies to protect the environment and public health while considering synergies between emission reduction and broader well-being objectives, such as reducing air pollution and improving health. Around 25% of global deaths and diseases can be attributed to avoidable environmental risks, resulting in approximately 13 million deaths annually (WHO, 2019[26]). In LAC, about 13% of premature deaths in high-income countries[4] and 19% in low- and middle-income countries[5] in the Americas are attributable to known avoidable environmental risks, amounting to approximately 1 016 000 deaths each year (Korc and Hauchman, 2021[27]). Air pollution alone leads to 7 million preventable deaths worldwide each year, with over 90% of the population breathing polluted air (WHO, 2019[26]). Furthermore, almost 3 billion people worldwide and 80 million people in LAC still rely on polluting fuels like solid fuels or kerosene for lighting, cooking, and heating. In LAC, ambient and household air pollution was linked to about 250 000 premature deaths in 2016 (WHO, 2019[26]); (Korc and Hauchman, 2021[27]).

Countries in the region should integrate preventive environmental health actions as a core component of universal health coverage through strategies and programmes targeting specific diseases and risks. They should promote the systematic consideration of health in the development of policies and sectors relevant to health, such as energy, transport, housing, labour, industry, food systems and agriculture, water and sanitation, and urban planning. Strengthening governance mechanisms to facilitate cross-sectoral collaboration and comprehensive cost-benefit analysis is important. LAC countries could foster the integration of environmental monitoring (especially in air pollution) and health surveillance to assess health impacts from environmental risks and services, as well as to monitor changes and the implementation of relevant strategies at regional and country levels (WHO, 2019[26]).

Many LAC countries could improve the performance of environmental public health programmes and institutions, to reduce the burden of disease associated with environmental risks. This can be done by placing emphasis on air quality while considering chemical safety, climate change-related impacts, solid waste management, and water and sanitation factors that influence human health and their related behaviours (Korc and Hauchman, 2021[27]). Moreover, it is important that countries consider the health risks on vulnerable populations such as the very young, the elderly and pregnant women (PAHO, 2016[14]).

Black carbon in the transport and the residential sector in LAC

Black carbon (BC) is one of the largest contributors to global warming, following CO_2 (Bond et al., 2013[28]). Despite BC being a SLCP with a lifetime of only days to a few weeks, it significantly accelerates the melting of snow and ice, increasing climate change by reducing the albedo effect.[6] Additionally, BC affects precipitation patterns in the Amazon basin (OECD, 2023[3]), where biomass burning contributes to air pollution and smoke. BC also leads to lower agricultural yields and food security concerns. These impacts directly affect the livelihoods of Andean inhabitants, agriculture, and hydropower generation, the latter accounting for 8% of the total energy supply in LAC, and 54% of electricity production in the region in 2020 (OECD, 2023[3]).

Reducing BC emissions can bring immediate co-benefits to the environment, air quality, and public health. BC and its co-pollutants are significant components of fine particulate matter $(PM)_{2.5}$ air pollution, which is a leading environmental cause of poor health and premature deaths (UNEP and CCAC, 2018[29]). The LAC region contributes less than 10% of the total BC emissions. The transport sector and the combustion of solid fuels in the residential-commercial sector are responsible for about three-quarters of BC emissions in the region, with Brazil and Mexico accounting for more than 60% of it (UNEP and CCAC, 2018[29]). Within the transport sector, high-emitting diesel vehicles are the primary sources of BC emissions (Natural Resources Defense Council, 2014[30]).

Considering the short atmospheric lifetime of BC, targeted policies have proven to be effective in achieving relatively fast climate and health benefits (ICCT, 2009[31]). In the transport sector, it is crucial for LAC to promote clean fuels and adopt common fuel standards that reduce sulphur levels to ultra-low levels, ideally below 15 ppm. Additionally, the region should strengthen its emissions standards for new vehicles by mandating the installation of diesel particulate filters or encouraging the use of comparably effective emerging alternative fuels and advanced vehicle technologies (e.g., natural gas-powered, hybrid-electric, or electric vehicles). Complementary programmes should also be developed to reduce in-use emissions from older diesel vehicles, with a focus on urban fleets, as successful strategies have been implemented in other cases (Natural Resources Defense Council, 2014[30]).

In the residential sector, the use of fuelwood for cooking poses the most significant emissions-related health risks to LAC citizens, particularly affecting lower-income households in rural areas. Approximately 90 million people in LAC relied on solid fuels for cooking in 2017, accounting for around 15% of the region's population. To address this issue, the region could develop and enhance its regulatory frameworks, including measures to improve the quality, reliability, and durability of cooking stoves. Implementing certification and field tests to ensure stoves meet quality standards, alongside policies addressing affordability, accessibility, and awareness of health impacts, will be essential. Supporting sustainable forestry practices and women's economic empowerment can also contribute to addressing the underlying social and environmental issues that necessitate improved cooking stoves (Levy et al., 2020[32]).

Greenhouse gas emissions in LAC

From 1990 to 2019, the LAC region increased its GHG emissions by 61%, despite representing only 6.7% of the global GHG emissions, excluding Forestry, and Other Land Use (LULUCF) (OECD, 2023[3]) and 8.1% including them. This was mainly driven by increased emissions from transport, electricity and heat production, being proportional to its 8.4% share in total world population, and slightly higher than its 6.4% share in global GDP. Total emissions in the Caribbean increased 23.5% from 1990 to 2019, despite it representing only 5% of the region's total emissions throughout that period (OECD et al., 2022[4]). Although the region's contribution to climate change is not significant, LAC, particularly the Amazon River basin, plays a crucial role in global mitigation efforts due to its natural carbon capture potential (OECD, 2023[3]).

There are sectors with high emissions that are rapidly increasing their climate forcer emissions due to the absence of economic incentives for improving, developing, and introducing proper technology and infrastructure (UNEP and CCAC, 2017[33]). In terms of sectoral breakdown, three sectors represented 88.3% of total emissions in LAC in 2019, energy (43.5% including transport), agriculture (25.3%) and LUCF (19.5%). The energy sector remains the most emission-intensive for all three LAC sub-regions, although each one has its particularities. South America's high emitting sectors are agriculture, 28.5%, LUCF, 23.8%, and transport, 13.4%. The Caribbean differs slightly, with electricity and heat accounting for 24.8% followed by agriculture, 15.6% and LUCF, 13.4%, very similar to transport at 11.1%. In Central America, electricity and heat accounts for 23.8% of emissions, while transport accounts for 21.4%, followed by agriculture with 16% (OECD et al., 2022[4]).

Both Brazil and Mexico have shown increased emissions targets compared to previous targets due to a change in the baseline methodology used to calculate the targets in their NDCs. At the same time, Mexico is the only G20 country without a net-zero target by 2050. Per capita emissions vary widely across G20 members, with Mexico not expected to peak its emissions until 2030 under current policies and NDC scenarios, while Argentina and Brazil have already peaked (UNEP, 2022[1]).

LAC's contribution to global net GHG emissions is largely driven by Brazil, Mexico and Argentina, which are the three largest emitters in the region, representing 5.4% of the total global emissions. In 2020, these three countries accounted for 38%, 16%, and 10% of the regional GHG emissions, respectively, making up 63.8% of the region's total GHG emissions. Heavily reliant fossil-fuel exporters like Bolivia, Colombia, Ecuador, Guyana, Suriname, Trinidad and Tobago and Venezuela, represent only 1.7% of global net GHG emissions (Anna Ivanova et al., 2021[34]). Despite significant investments in renewable energy projects over the last decade, the Caribbean remains highly dependent on imported fossil-fuel energy, with most countries being net-energy importers, except for Trinidad and Tobago, Suriname, and Guyana (UN ECLAC, 2021[35]).

Since 2014, emissions in LAC grew at a slower pace than economic growth suggesting a relative decoupling. In order to mitigate and stabilise GHG emissions in the atmosphere, it is crucial to implement both national and international low-carbon strategies and further decouple emissions from economic growth (OECD, 2023[3]). This can be achieved through the adoption of multiple low-carbon strategies, such as increasing the share of renewable energy sources in the energy supply mix, adopting energy-efficient production processes, enhancing the energy efficiency of consumer goods and services, and preserving and expanding carbon sinks, such as forests and wetlands (OECD, 2023[3]). LAC countries could commit to deeper emissions reductions targets on their NDCs and transition to low-carbon energy systems, as well as to reducing emissions from specific sectors such as agriculture and LULUCF, since these sectors account for one third and one fourth of South America's net emissions. In Central America and the Caribbean, energy production and transport are major emitters (OECD, 2023[3]).

Recommendation

- Improve regulatory frameworks for GHG and SLCPs emissions, with particular attention to methane and f-gases, setting sectoral, national and local targets.
- Aim for co-benefits of reducing air pollution with regulating climate mitigation by aligning environmental and health policies and diseases associated with environmental risks.

Methane emissions in LAC are generated by agriculture, coal and gas production and distribution, and waste management.

Methane emissions are an important contributor to global warming, with the largest source of anthropogenic methane emissions being agriculture, responsible for around a quarter of the total emissions, closely followed by the energy sector, which includes emissions from coal, oil, natural gas and biofuels (IEA, 2020[36]). LAC generates approximately 15% of global methane emissions, the main source of emissions are agriculture, at approximately 50%; coal, oil and gas production and distribution, at 40%; and waste management, at 10%. Brazil and Venezuela represent more than half of this figure (UNEP and CCAC, 2018[29]). Reducing SLCPs, such as methane and black carbon, which have a relatively short lifespan in the atmosphere, but potent climate change impacts, can bring immediate co-benefits to the environment, air quality, and public health (UNEP and CCAC, 2018[29]). The IPCC Sixth Assessment Report (AR6) has emphasised that air pollution controls, relying on existing technologies, lead to more rapid improvements in air quality than climate change mitigation, which requires systemic changes. However, reductions in methane and black carbon would significantly improve air quality and reduce adverse effects on human health (Calvin et al., 2023[37]).

Among the most cost-effective and impactful actions that governments can take to achieve climate goals is the reduction of methane emissions from oil and gas operations. Controlling leaks, particularly methane emissions from oil and gas operations, is a crucial aspect of reducing GHG and SLCP emissions. Leaks in the natural gas supply chain can result in significant emissions of methane. It is essential for countries in the region to implement regulations that require regular monitoring of possible leaks in the natural gas distribution system. This could involve conducting regular inspections of pipelines, equipment, and storage facilities, as well as mandatory repairs for any detected leaks. Leak detection and repair (LDAR) programmes, designed to identify and address fugitive leaks, can be implemented. Policies may address equipment standards, inspection frequency, leak thresholds triggering repair requirements, and repair timelines. In 2018, Mexico approved the Guidelines for the prevention and comprehensive control of methane emissions from the hydrocarbons sector. Under the regulation, facilities must develop a Programme for Prevention and Integrated Control of Methane Emissions (PPCIEM) (IEA, 2021[38]), although the country has been regulating this since 2002 (Government of Mexico, 2022[39]). Colombia has implemented regulations that focus on monitoring and repairing leaks in the natural gas system, particularly in hydrocarbon exploration and exploitation (CCAC, 2022[40]). Another approach is to incentivise the use of technologies and practices that can help reduce leaks, such as advanced leak detection systems, remote monitoring technologies, and pipeline integrity management. Satellite, drone, and other aerial measurement methods can aid in locating significant emitting sources (IEA, 2022[41]).

Regulatory instruments should be designed to control and promote the adoption of methane control technologies. Biodigesters are natural systems that utilize organic waste from agricultural activities, mainly animal manure, to produce biogas and organic fertilisers through anaerobic digestion (Dafermos et al., 2014[42]). They can be used to treat waste from landfills, livestock operations, and other sources of organic matter, reducing the amount of methane that is released into the atmosphere. Methane can be used as fuel to generate electricity; capturing and using methane, instead of allowing it to be released into the atmosphere for electricity generation, can help reduce GHG emissions. These solutions are not mutually exclusive and can be used together to address methane emissions. Biodigesters, electricity generation and monitoring technologies can be combined as an integrated solution for controlling methane emissions. For example, methane produced by biodigesters can be used to generate electricity, and monitoring technologies can be used to ensure that the system is operating efficiently.

In LAC, several countries, including Brazil, Chile, Colombia, Cuba, Mexico, and Paraguay, have established regulations regarding biogas. In the case of Cuba, the country still needs to develop policies for biogas production, despite having regulations in place to facilitate the expansion of biogas plants. Argentina, on the other hand, lacks specific national regulations for biogas. Countries should consider the various scales of biodigesters suitable for their territories when developing regulatory frameworks for biodigestion. For example, in Chile, the existing Decree does not mention specific regulations for domestic biodigesters, which operate on a scale of up to 180 kW of nominal power. This imposes excessive requirements on systems designed for household use, impeding family enterprise projects, and demonstration and educational initiatives. Finally, it must be noted that these regulations are often not enforced in the region. In many cases, biogas waste is buried, burned, or sent to landfills, rather than being used to its full potential for energy and materials, such as biofertilisers (IICA & RedBioLAC, 2013[43]).

Fluorinated greenhouse gases(F-gas): three main emitters in LAC

F-gases have a significant impact on climate due to their high global warming potentials, even at small concentrations. They are commonly used as coolants or propellants in air conditioning units, refrigerators, fire protection systems and extinguishers, solvents and aerosols, foams, and insulation materials (International Climate Initiative (IKI), 2020[44]). Argentina, Brazil and Mexico are responsible for nearly 80% of regional total HFCs emissions, with residential applications accounting for 60% of these contributions, followed by 25% from transport and specific industrial uses (UNEP and CCAC, 2018[29]).

Enhanced international co-operation is necessary to phase out F-gases. The *2016 Kigali Amendment to the Montreal Protocol* aims gradually to reduce the production and consumption of HFCs[7] and achieve an 80% reduction in HFCs consumption by 2047. While this amendment is an important step in the right direction, additional actions are still required. Currently, 23 countries in LAC have accepted the Amendment. Mexico has ratified the Kigali Amendment and developed a national strategy to phase out HFCs in sectors such as refrigeration and air conditioning (Ministry of Environment Mexico, 2019[45]). Argentina has also modified its regulations and incorporated the requirement for import and export licenses for HFC substances (Ministry of Environment and Sustainable Development Argentina, 2020[46]).

LAC governments could develop and implement transition policies to accelerate the phase-out of F-gases in key sectors such as tourism, transport, construction, and food supply. These policies may include setting phase-out targets with compliance deadlines, implementing and enforcing regulations that limit the use of F-gases (e.g., building codes prohibiting their use in new constructions) (EIA, 2011[47]), and providing financial incentives for companies and individuals to invest in F-gases alternatives, such as refrigeration systems that use natural coolants like carbon dioxide or ammonia gas, as well as insulation materials with low global warming potential (International Climate Initiative (IKI), 2020[44]). Promoting best practices for food storage and transport, such as insulated or mini containers, can support emissions reduction in the food supply sector. The use of renewable energy can also help reduce the reliance on HFCs in this sector (Syam et al., 2022[48]). The decarbonisation in hard-to-abate sectors will require investments in technologies such as green hydrogen and other low-carbon alternative fuels, including sustainable biofuels (OECD et al., 2022[4]). Countries could also consider phasing down HFCs and products containing them, scaling-up action against their illegal trade, and introducing good practices in refrigerant and end-of-life management (Yamaguchi, 2023[49]); (UNEP and CCAC, 2018[29]).

Sectoral policies

Energy sector: The LAC region is still heavily reliant on fossil fuels.

Fossil fuel dependency in LAC

Fossil fuels still dominate the energy supply at 69% as of 2020 in LAC, despite the significant hydropower and biofuels energy sources and its cleaner primary energy supply compared to the global average. Countries such as Chile, Colombia, the Dominican Republic, and Guatemala still heavily rely on fossil fuels (OECD, 2023[3]). Most Caribbean countries depend on fossil fuel imports, with Trinidad and Tobago, Suriname, and Guyana being the only Caribbean countries with significant domestic energy resources (OECD et al., 2022[4]).

Many LAC countries have made significant progress in developing renewable energy markets and diversifying their energy mix to reduce reliance on fossil fuels and enhance climate resilience, particularly in their hydropower systems. In 2020, renewable energy accounted for 69% of regional electricity generation (OECD, 2023[3]). This is more than double of OECD average of 30%, with 78% coming from hydroelectricity and 22% from solar, wind, biomass, and geothermal sources (OECD, 2023[3]).

In the last two decades, Central America has increased its electricity supply matrix of renewable energy sources from 65% to 77%, followed by the Caribbean with a 3 percentage point increase, due to an increase in the diversification of renewable sources of power; shifting from mainly hydropower to growing shares of thermal, wind, and solar energy. However, there are notable differences across the region, with countries like Paraguay and Brazil generating 100% and 84% of their electricity from hydropower, respectively, while Jamaica relies heavily on fossil fuels, with 87% of its electric power coming from imported oil derivatives (OECD et al., 2022[4]).

There are some positive developments and efforts in LAC to move away from fossil fuel dependency. For instance, Belize banned all petroleum operations in its maritime zone in 2017 through the adoption of the Petroleum Operations (Maritime Zone Moratorium) Act (Government of Belize, 2017[50]). At COP26, the governments of Costa Rica and Denmark led the creation of the *Beyond Oil & Gas Alliance* (BOGA), an international alliance with the objective of achieving the managed phase-out of oil and gas production, although Costa Rica has reduced its leadership role in this area (BOGA, 2021[51]); (Rodriguez, 2022[52]). In 2020, Chile published its *Plan of Phase-out and/or Reconversion of Coal Units*, aiming to eliminate all coal-fired power plants before 2040, with an initial phase established by 2024 (IEA, 2021[53]). In June 2023, during the World Economic Forum, Colombia announced that it would not approve any new oil and gas exploration projects (The Guardian, 2022[54]).

LAC countries could develop and implement energy plans that prioritise the deployment and utilisation of renewable energy sources. Transforming the region's energy mix is crucial to promote well-being and build more resilient societies. To achieve a successful transition to net-zero emissions, a systemic decarbonisation through electrification across all sectors is necessary. These plans should consider various approaches to accelerate the transition to net-zero energy systems. By investing in renewable technologies, some LAC countries can reduce their reliance on imported fossil fuel products, provide lower-cost power, and decrease GHG emissions (OECD et al., 2022[4]).

At the same time, some LAC countries could develop policies aimed at expanding the access to electricity in the region. This objective will improve livelihoods, foster inclusive local economic growth, increase well-being, and contribute to a sustainable, inclusive, and just transition that addresses historical social inequalities. As of 2019, access to electricity reached 95.5%, representing a 15.7% increase over the past two decades (OECD et al., 2022[4]).

Phase-out plans for fossil fuel exploration and production infrastructure could be established. The latest UNEP Production Gap Report highlights that the extraction of coal, oil, and gas is not aligned with agreed climate limits and national net-zero emission targets worldwide. Governments are currently planning to produce more than double the amount of fossil fuels in 2030 than would be consistent with limiting global warming to 1.5°C, and 45% more than consistent with limiting warming to 2°C. Moreover, there are no plans to wind down the production of fossil fuels (UNEP, 2021[55]). Plans aimed at phasing out fossil fuels should include a timeline to cease granting new permits for fossil fuel exploration, production, and infrastructure, as well as a phase-out of all subsidies to fossil fuels (Equitable Climate Action, 2021[56]), and the re-direction of public funding toward the development of low-carbon alternatives alongside improvements in energy security and energy efficiency (OECD, 2022[57]). The energy transition must be fair and inclusive, and it is important to establish effective policies that ensure developing economies, like those in LAC, receive financial assistance and technological know-how for phasing out fossil fuels. Governments should consider implementing support policies for fossil fuel industry workers and communities by promoting training and facilitating new job opportunities (IEA, 2021[58]).

Enhanced international co-operation on managing fossil fuel production is necessary to achieve the Paris Agreement goals. In 2017, the governments from Canada and the UK launched the *Power Past Coal Alliance (PPCA)* to advance the transition from coal power across the world. From LAC, Costa Rica, El Salvador, and Uruguay are part of the PPCA and are coal free, while Peru has committed to phase out coal before 2025 and Chile and Mexico after 2025 (PPCA, 2017[59]). In 2022, the Governments of Vanuatu and Tuvalu launched the proposal for a *Fossil Fuel Non-Proliferation Treaty (FFNPT)*, which is structured around three pillars: i) enable a global just transition; ii) prevent the proliferation of coal, oil and gas by ending all new exploration and production; and iii) phase out existing production of fossil fuels in line with the 1.5°C goal in a fair and equitable manner. The FFNPT has the objective of complementing the demand-side of the Paris Agreement, by addressing the supply- side of fossil fuels and promoting international co-operation in active support (The Fossil Fuel Non-Proliferation Treaty, 2022[60]). Currently, this proposal has been endorsed by LAC cities from Belize, Brazil, Costa Rica, Haiti, and Peru (The Fossil Fuel Non-Proliferation Treaty, 2022[61]).

Recommendation

- Develop and implement energy plans that prioritise the deployment and utilisation of renewable energy sources, while considering expanding affordable and reliable access to electricity.
- Establish and implement phase-out plans for fossil fuel exploration and production infrastructure, including policies aiming to re-direct public funding towards developing low-carbon alternatives.

Renewable energy in LAC

LAC countries need to accelerate their efforts to achieve the 2050 net-zero emissions goals by promoting renewables. In 2020, renewables account for 33% of the total energy supply in the region, compared to the global average of 13%. The primary sources of renewables in LAC include hydroelectric power (9%), biofuels such as firewood and bagasse (18.8%), solar and wind (5.1%), and geothermal (0.9%). Natural gas is the second largest energy source at 31%, slightly surpassing oil at 30%, possibly due to the effects of the COVID-19 pandemic. Coal accounts for 5% and nuclear energy for 1% (OECD et al., 2022[4]).

Ensuring access to energy in LAC is crucial for a green and just transition. In LAC, 17 million people still lack access to electricity, with rural areas facing significant challenges. The COVID-19 pandemic has exacerbated social challenges, leading to increased levels of poverty and inequality, particularly affecting food prices (OECD et al., 2022[4]). Electricity demand in LAC is expected to recover to pre-pandemic levels between 2022 and 2024, with an average annual growth of 3.9% for the rest of the decade (López et al., 2022[62]). The renewable power capacity of Latin America is projected to increase by 45% between 2022 and 2070, with Brazil accounting for over 55% of this growth (IEA, 2022[41]).

To ensure access to electricity in isolated and underdeveloped areas, the use of distributed wind and solar photovoltaic generation is key. Several LAC countries have implemented programmes to promote clean energy access in these areas, such as Peru's National Photovoltaic Household Electrification Programme, Nicaragua's National Programme for Sustainable Electrification and Renewable Energy, Guyana's Hinterland Renewable Energy project, Mexico's Isolated Communities Electrification project, and Brazil's Light for All programme (Grottera, 2022[63]). Additionally, Ecuador's has made significant improvements in off-grid electrification efforts through solar PV in local communities, providing an electromobility solution to improve transport along the Tupungayo River. The project resulted in replacing gasoline outboard engines with electric ones, leading to improved regularity of boat services, reduced emissions, and mitigated noise and water pollution risks. This marked a paradigm shift in providing basic services (energy, water, and mobility) for local communities (OECD et al., 2022[4]).

Several countries in the LAC region have made commitments to increase their use of non-hydro renewable energy, improve energy efficiency, and protect forests or coastal ecosystems through NbS, which can help absorb carbon dioxide from the atmosphere. For example, the Central American

Integration System (SICA), consisting of Belize, Costa Rica, the Dominican Republic, El Salvador, Guatemala, Honduras, Nicaragua, and Panama, established in its 2030 Energy Strategy the goal to diversify the energy matrix by promoting investment in energy infrastructure and clean technologies, as well as the aim to increase the use of other energy sources, particularly geothermal, solar, wind, and modern biomass. The strategy also emphasises the rational and efficient use of energy and aims to accelerate improvements in energy efficiency (UN ECLAC and SICA, 2022[64]). Additionally, SICA has conducted High-Level Dialogues to enhance financial allocations and prioritise NbS to respond to adverse processes and foster resilience in an area with over 60 million inhabitants (El Pais Costa Rica, 2021[65]).

The use of renewable energy in the productive, service, and residential sectors should be promoted in LAC. Green energy plans should prioritise the massive deployment and use of renewable energy in these sectors. It is important to establish achievable targets and projects that aim to transition to renewable energy sources and explore low-cost sustainable technologies for clean energy in electricity production, water heating, cold chains, air conditioning, and heating. The region must boost the demand and supply of renewable energies, especially considering, as mentioned above, that LAC will have an average annual growth of electricity demand of 3.9% throughout the decade. Long-term planning and regional integration must be improved to maximise the use of renewable energy while ensuring energy security (Martínez, 2022[66]). It is important to mention, that renewable energy sources tend to require higher upfront investment than fossil fuelled plans, which is balanced with lower Operation and Maintenance (O&M) costs, leading to a decreased lifetime overall cost (Grottera, 2022[63]).

Digitalisation has transformed the way electricity is produced, transmitted, and consumed due to the shift in consumer behaviour and the transformation of electricity generation through decentralisation. It is crucial that regulators in the region prepare institutions and frameworks for a rapid transformation, with the possibility to re-design network services, and establish tariffs that ensure cost recovery and affordability under changing circumstances. Regulatory frameworks could integrate the benefits of digitalisation in other services, such as electric mobility, and promote access to finance and reduce risk exposure (Grottera, 2022[63]).

Governments should encourage public and private investment in renewable energy projects by implementing mechanisms including subsidies, tax cuts, and policies aimed at phasing out fossil fuel subsidies. Economic instruments to promote renewable energy can be categorised in four groups: i) price regulation, a direct government intervention to set the price of energy; ii) quantity-based instruments, which are market regulations that make a specific outcome mandatory, such as the quantity of renewable energy generated; iii) fiscal instruments, understood as direct budgetary transfers and various forms of taxes like value-added or carbon taxes; and iv) financial instruments that include green bonds and policies that provide financial support to renewable energy projects, directly de-risking investments. Incentives should be extended to productive enterprises, institutions, and households, along with the dissemination of information and training on energy efficiency and renewables (Frédéric Gagnon-Lebrun et al., 2018[67]).

While many countries in LAC have implemented fiscal exemptions for renewable energy products and services, the adoption of carbon taxes remains limited. Most countries in the region have established funds or special credit lines to finance renewable energy, but there is still a need to incorporate policies that address technical aspects like grid access and the integration of renewable energy in other sectors, such as social housing. It is important that countries establish legally binding obligations or enforcement mechanisms, similar to those instituted in Chile, the only country in Latin America to have legally binding targets with clear penalties for non-compliance and a monitoring and enforcement mechanism (Grottera, 2022[63]).

Auction processes have proven to be effective for introducing renewable energy in LAC. By 2017, at least 10 LAC countries had implemented renewable auction policies. These auctions typically involve long-term contracts (15 to 30 years), technology-specific competitions, and a significant focus on solar and wind energy. Net metering policies have also been successful in encouraging small consumers to adopt renewable energy systems. These policies allow consumers to offset their electricity consumption by inputting self-generated surplus electricity into the grid, generating credits that can be utilised later. As of 2018, 17 countries in LAC had implemented net electricity metering policies to promote their adoption, by small consumers such as households and small businesses (Hallack and Tolmasquim, 2020[68]).[8]

Regional and international co-operation needs to be enhanced to accelerate the deployment of renewable energy. In 2019, 16 countries in LAC launched the *Renewables in Latin America and the Caribbean initiative (RELAC)* with the aim of achieving at least a 70% renewable share in the region's electricity matrix by 2030. Moreover, countries seek to develop a specific climate action platform to monitor climate goals for the energy sector (RELAC, 2019[69]). Under RELAC, each member country contributes to the regional target, based on its own NDCs and national conditions. The Inter-American Development Bank (IDB) and the International Renewable Energy Agency (IRENA) provide support to member countries in developing their energy transition strategies, identifying gaps, and prioritising investments to overcome institutional, legal, planning, financial, technical, and regulatory barriers. Moreover, RELAC contributes to the expansion and integration of the regional power sector by establishing the common objective of accelerating the carbon-neutrality of electricity systems in LAC, developing common regulatory and institutional frameworks and enhancing co-ordination between agencies by identifying technical assistance needs, disseminating best practices and channelling climate finance resources (IRENA, 2022[70]); (RELAC, 2019[69]).

Recommendation

- Adopt low-cost sustainable technologies for clean energy used in electricity production, water heating, cold chains, air conditioning and heating.

Expanding Energy efficiency in LAC.

Energy efficiency is the most cost-effective and scalable way to address energy security and climate change targets, including the reduction of GHG emissions. In LAC, economic growth is closely linked to energy consumption, as better access to energy improves the quality of life for many people. However, energy efficiency has not been a priority in the region due to the abundance of renewable resources (such as hydro and geothermal in Central America, as well as wind and solar) and hydrocarbons in some countries (IEA and UN ECLAC, 2015[71]); (Enerdata, 2023[72]). The share of the household budget dedicated to energy ranges between 7% and 9% of income, and for the poorest households, it can exceed 24%, often focused on electricity and gas expenses. While securing energy supplies is important, it is equally important to analyse the role of more efficient and flexible demand in ensuring affordable and reliable energy. Affordable energy is essential to ensure access to basic energy services, including lighting, clean cooking, space cooling, heating, and transport. At the same time, reducing energy bills supports the maintenance of access to these services. Energy efficiency and other demand management measures, such as load shifting and conservation, can provide short and long-term benefits to the energy system and consumers by reducing demand, costs, and emissions, and avoiding the need for more expensive supply-side solutions (IEA, 2023[73]).

Latin America has intensified the implementation of energy efficiency measures and investments. *The Energy Efficiency Information Base*, developed in 2011 by the UN Economic Commission for Latin America and the Caribbean (UN ECLAC) and the French Agency for Ecological Transition (ADEME), monitors energy efficiency trends in Latin American countries and has noted a 70% increase in energy efficiency measures since 2010 and a 30% increase since 2019. Moreover, 30% of the measures are horizontal, meaning they are not sector specific. Among sector-specific measures, households account for 33%, followed by transport at 25%, services at 23%, and industry at 19% (Enerdata, 2023[72]). Energy efficiency translates into budget savings, as most countries in LAC subsidise energy prices. LAC governments should develop energy savings programmes, such as appliance replacement schemes, to lift families out of energy poverty while generating public budgetary savings (IEA, 2023[73]).

One of the main challenges the region will face is adapting to hydropower disruptions driven by climate change. Hydropower accounts for 45% of the electricity supply across the region. Argentina, Chile, Costa Rica, Guatemala, Mexico, and Panama are likely to experience a steady decrease in their hydropower capacity factors due to changing rainfall patterns. Brazil, Paraguay, Uruguay and Venezuela will also experience a mild decrease in their hydropower capacity factors. On the other hand, Colombia, Ecuador, and Peru are expected to have a slight increase in hydropower capacity factors due to increasing precipitation and runoff volume on average (IEA, 2021[74]). To address this issue, countries in the region should enhance the resilience of their hydropower plants and adapt to changing climate conditions. While there is no one-size-fits-all solution, a tailored combination of resilience measures based on a comprehensive assessment of climate risk and impact will help increase their resilience. These measures may include strategic, operational, and physical arrangements categorised as "soft", which consist of strategies, policies, and actions related to the planning, operational management, and recovery of the hydropower system, and "hard", which are associated with the physical enhancement of assets, such as technical and structural improvements to hydropower plants (IEA, 2021[74]).

It is important that LAC countries develop targeted policies, programmes and institutional frameworks to deliver energy savings, overcome barriers to energy efficiency and drive the market for energy efficient products and services. The countries with the biggest historical energy efficiency improvements, such as Mexico, Brazil and Chile, have developed specific institutional frameworks to develop, track and improve energy efficiency policies and programmes. The LAC governments need establish regular data collection and develop indicators as well as awareness campaigns and educational programmes on energy efficiency. Countries in the region may also apply standards and labelling programmes to deliver energy savings in products such as air conditioning and electric motors. Argentina, Colombia, Mexico, Panama, Uruguay and countries in the SICA have all introduced standards and labelling frameworks for appliances and electric motors (IEA, 2023[73]).

Energy efficiency can be as an important source of local jobs. The latest *World Energy Employment report* noted that worldwide energy efficiency accounted for 10.9 million full-time-equivalent jobs in 2019. In Latin America, direct energy efficiency jobs accounted for about 8% of energy sector jobs. In Central and South America, 33% of energy efficiency jobs are in the construction sector, and around 25% in manufacturing (IEA, 2022[75]). At the same time, the ILO has highlighted that decarbonisation has the potential to create 15 million new jobs in LAC by 2030 (Saget, Vogt-Schilb and Luu, 2020[76]).

Recommendation

- Intensify targeted policies, programmes and institutional frameworks to improve energy efficiency. Apply standards and labelling programmes to deliver energy efficient products such as air conditioning and electric motors.

Biofuels is an opportunity in LAC.

Biofuels play a crucial role in decarbonising transport by offering a low-carbon solution for existing technologies, particularly light-duty vehicles in the short term and heavy-duty trucks, ships, and aircraft with limited alternative options in the long term. In 2021, biofuels represented 3.5% of the global transport energy demand, primarily in road transport (IEA, 2022[77]). In 2011, the main producers of bioethanol and biodiesel in LAC were Brazil, Argentina, and Colombia. In 2021, Brazil was the second-largest global producer of biofuels, while Argentina ranked eighth (UN ECLAC, 2011[78]); (Statista, 2022[79]).

According to IEA's renewables analysis and forecast to 2027, global biofuel demand was expected to be 6% higher in 2022 than in 2021, and the demand for ethanol increased in 4% in Brazil during 2021-2022, where rising prices of gasoline and diesel use accelerates demand for biofuels. Moreover, Brazil, along with the USA, Canada, Indonesia, and India make up 80% of global expansion in biofuel use (IEA, 2022[41]).

Biofuels produced from waste and residue resources are expected to meet 45% of total global biofuel demand by 2030. Central and South America produce approximately 28% of global liquid biofuels. Argentina, Brazil, Colombia, and Guatemala produce 24% of biodiesel and 29% of ethanol globally (IEA Bioenergy, 2023[80]). The production of biofuels primarily relies on conventional feedstocks like sugar cane, corn, and soybeans. To mitigate the impact on land use, food prices, and feed prices, it is important to transform biofuel production by advancing feedstocks. New technologies, such as cellulosic ethanol and biomass-based Fischer-Tropsch (bio-FT), can utilise non-food feedstocks to produce low-carbon biofuels for the transport sector. Scaling up technologies that convert woody feedstock into biofuels will be necessary (IEA, 2022[77]).

Biofuels have the potential to significantly reduce global road transport oil consumption. Collectively, biofuels avoided 4% of global road transport oil use (2 million barrels of oil), with nearly 60% of the biofuel demand coming from advanced economies (IEA, 2022[77]). In Brazil, biofuels account for 25% of its transport fuels, with bioethanol being the most important, representing 49% of the combined energy from gasoline and ethanol use. The use of biodiesel is also increasing, aiming to replace diesel in heavy-duty vehicles. As of 2019, biodiesel in Brazil accounted for 9.6% of the energy used in diesel. Brazil has a large fleet of flex-fuel vehicles that can run on either gasohol (a mixture of gasoline and anhydrous ethanol) or hydrous ethanol (IEA Bioenergy, 2021[81]); (OECD/FAO, 2019[82]).

Argentina, Bolivia, Brazil, Colombia, Ecuador, Paraguay, Peru and Uruguay are considered by the IEA as countries that have a robust and fully implemented biofuel programmes, with a blending mandate in place, a regular market of biofuels established and liquid fuel terminals operating normally. Costa Rica, Guatemala, and Mexico have approved legislation and regulation to promote the use of biofuels, some with schedules and programmes to adopt blending mandates. However, debates among consumers, fuel distributors, and biofuel producers persist regarding the convenience, risks, and advantages of biofuels. While Argentina, Brazil, and Colombia have fully implemented biofuel programmes, Guatemala is yet to adopt a national biofuel programme and plans to introduce a 10% ethanol blend in gasoline by 2024 (IEA Bioenergy, 2023[80]).

Sustainability frameworks should be developed and implemented in LAC to ensure that biofuels meet rigorous sustainability requirements verified through third-party certification of biofuel supply chains, including life cycle analysis of GHG emission reductions. Brazil, through its 2017 National Biofuels Policy (RenovaBio) Programme, establishes annual targets for decarbonisation, determined by the federal government, and allocates them among fuel distributors based on their market share. Ethanol, biodiesel, and biogas producers have their CO_2 emission mitigation certified by independent companies using the RenovaCalc model's life cycle analysis (LCA) to assess environmental efficiency. They receive grades that determine the issuance of mitigation credits (CIBIOs) corresponding to their production, which can be traded in the stock market. Fuel distributors need these credits to meet decarbonisation targets, or they may face legal actions. Since the programme's launch in 2020, 75 million CIBIOs have been issued (IEA Bioenergy, 2023[80]).

LAC governments must ensure robust sustainability governance is linked to biofuel policy support, establish mandates, GHG emission intensity reduction targets, and implement carbon pricing and financial incentives aligned with a net-zero trajectory. The expansion of waste and residue-based fuels, lower GHG emissions fuels, and technologies like carbon capture and storage should be prioritised. Additional measures may include loan guarantees and specific biofuel quotas for emerging fuels (IEA, 2022[77]).

International co-operation can facilitate the development of best practices, co-ordinate research, policy implementation, and deployment, as well as promote common sustainability standards to accelerate biofuel adoption. Key initiatives in this regard include *the Biofuture Platform Initiative*, launched in 2020, aiming to promote an advanced low-carbon bioeconomy that is sustainable, innovative, and scalable. This initiative fosters consensus on biomass sustainability, promotes best practices, enables financing, and encourages international co-operation. Argentina, Brazil, Chile, Costa Rica, Mexico, Panama, Paraguay, and Uruguay are part of this initiative (Biofuture Platform, 2020[83]). IEA's *Bioenergy Programme* also plays a significant role in improving co-operation and information exchange between countries with national bioenergy research, development, and deployment programmes. Brazil is currently the only LAC country participating in this initiative (IEA Bioenergy Programme, n.d.[84]). Moreover, the *Global Bioenergy Partnership,* launched in 2006, brings together public, private, and civil society stakeholders in a joint commitment to promote bioenergy for sustainable development. Argentina, Brazil, Colombia, Mexico, and Paraguay are partners of this initiative, while Chile, El Salvador, Panama, Peru, and Uruguay serve as observers (Global Bioenergy Partnership, 2006[85]).

Green and low-carbon hydrogen (GLCH) in LAC

The commercial viability of GLCH needs to be promoted in LAC.[9] While hydrogen is already in use and economically viable for various applications, its current production relies on fossil fuels. The LAC region has significant long-term potential to produce large volumes of competitive low-carbon hydrogen and export it to other global markets, making it a crucial region for a global net-zero emissions future. It is important to note, that despite hydrogen not emitting CO_2 at the end-use stage, current production processes are responsible for large volumes of emissions in the region. Notably, the region's industrial and oil refining sectors contribute about 5% to the worldwide demand for hydrogen, predominantly employed in the production of ammonia, methanol, steel, and refined oil products. The hydrogen production process in the region for 2019 consumed more natural gas than the entire supply in Chile, resulting in the release of more CO_2 into the atmosphere than the cumulative emissions from Colombia's road vehicles. Furthermore, close to 90% of the hydrogen demand in the LAC region in 2019 was concentrated in Argentina, Brazil, Chile, Colombia, Mexico and Trinidad and Tobago which accounted for over 40% of the total hydrogen demand (IEA, 2021[86]).

The region needs to generate a large-scale demand for GLCH, as a feedstock and alternative fuel, creating a virtuous circle between decarbonisation efforts and sustainable industrial development. The LAC region holds immense potential for green hydrogen production, both for domestic consumption and export, thanks to its abundant wind, solar, geothermal, and hydric resources. Additionally, the strategic geographical positioning of LAC provides access to markets in Europe, Asia, and North America. The utilisation of GLCH has the capacity to support countries in decarbonising hard-to-abate sectors such as industry and transport, which contribute to nearly 50% of global GHG emissions. These initiatives offer significant opportunities for an equitable energy transition that places communities at the core, expands energy access, generates new green employment, promotes participation from marginalised groups, advances gender equality, strengthens energy security, and buffers consumers against the volatility of fossil fuel prices (Christiaan Gischle et al., 2023[87]).

Green hydrogen deployment can reduce LAC countries' economic dependence on oil and gas exports, reduce energy price volatility, and provide grid stability by enabling energy storage and adding renewable energy to the grid, particularly in countries suffering intermittency issues associated with renewable energy sources. Countries like Argentina, Bolivia, Brazil, Chile, Colombia, Costa Rica, Mexico, and Peru, have a significant potential for developing a competitive green hydrogen industry. These countries have advantages in the hydrogen market due to their abundance of low-cost renewables and relatively clean electricity mix. Supporting private sector engagement and promoting a regional agenda could foster synergies to increase competitiveness and support industry development in the region (OECD et al., 2022[4]).

Scaling up the production, consumption and export of GLCH can accelerate the energy transition in LAC. Hydrogen has the potential to serve as a feedstock and low-carbon or zero-carbon fuel, facilitating the shift away from fossil fuels, especially in heavy duty vehicles and machinery. Also, as a feedstock, hydrogen can play a role in the production of synthetic fuels, enhancing or improving the combustion processes of biofuels, for example. Hydrogen can also play a crucial role in LAC's energy transition by providing a more sustainable energy solution, enabling food production, and accelerating the decarbonisation of the economy. Moreover, hydrogen and ammonia can act as a substitute for fossil fuels in the power generation sector, as well as in heavy-duty, aviation and maritime transport and fertiliser manufacturing While there were only three hydrogen pilot projects in Latin America in 2019, located in Argentina, Chile, and Costa Rica, the region has now developed a pipeline of over 60 projects as of October 2021, with the aim of exporting hydrogen to Europe and Asia, although most of them are still at an early stage (Oxford Business Group (OGB), 2022[88]); (IEA, 2022[89]). In June 2022, the Argentine province of Tierra del Fuego outlined plans to develop a hydrogen and ammonium industry. The province is trying to use the region's vast wind resources to attract USD 6 billion in investment in technologies to produce the fuel, including investing in wind farms to generate electricity to produce hydrogen. Once established, some of the hydrogen from the project will be used to produce ammonia, which in addition to being used to create fertiliser, can also serve as a carrier fuel to transport hydrogen through branch pipelines to markets (Oxford Business Group (OGB), 2022[88]).

As of 2021, only 33% or 11 countries in LAC had either published or were in the process of developing national hydrogen strategies and roadmaps. These strategic frameworks play a pivotal role in directing hydrogen development towards sectors and applications that align with each country's specific context. They help identify opportunities in the short, medium, and long term while outlining the requisite regulatory, infrastructure, and skill prerequisites. LAC countries could also establish supportive policies that facilitate the initial deployment of critical technologies, offer financial mechanisms for early-stage projects, and implement risk management strategies tailored to different project phases. These efforts should extend beyond emissions reduction, with a strong focus on Research and Development (R&D) (IEA, 2021[86]). Chile launched a *Green Hydrogen Strategy* in 2020 with the goal of establishing 5 GW of electrolyser capacity by 2025 and 25 GW by 2030. It aims to produce the world's cheapest hydrogen by 2030 and become one of the world's top three hydrogen exporters by 2040. Colombia's *National Hydrogen Strategy and Roadmap* aims to facilitate the development of a green hydrogen industry, delivering cost-competitive green hydrogen by 2030. The strategy also considers the production of blue hydrogen using carbon capture, utilisation, and storage (CCUS) to capture emissions. Additionally, Argentina, Bolivia, Brazil, Costa Rica, El Salvador, Panama, Paraguay, Trinidad and Tobago, and Uruguay are in the process of preparing national hydrogen plans (OECD et al., 2022[4]).

LAC countries may integrate hydrogen into policy, institutional, and legal frameworks. It is key that countries understand the value chain and individual potential within each country to develop green hydrogen. Thorough analysis of business cases, economic factors, benefits, and risks is essential, with special attention to cost drivers. This scrutiny enables the creation of robust business models and validation of suitable applications at the country level. Lastly, identifying appropriate policies to bridge viability gaps and cultivate favourable market conditions and financing mechanisms is essential to nurturing green hydrogen development (Cordonnier and Saygin, 2022[90]).

Governments in LAC could develop policies aiming to transform existing industrial and petrochemical hubs where currently grey hydrogen is being consumed to begin the deployment and production of green hydrogen. Petrochemical hubs could use GLCH to produce ammonia, which can be used as feedstock for fertilisers or as fuel for new applications such as shipping. It can also be used to produced methanol, synthetic fuels, or even as a reducing agent to replace coal in iron production (IRENA, 2022[91]). Moreover, refineries use hydrogen to lower the sulphur content of diesel fuel, as well as in the de-sulphurisation of crude oil to make petrol, diesel, and other chemicals (ITM Power, 2020[92]).

The LAC region has the potential to become a green hydrogen industrial hub, considering the growing global demand for hydrogen in line with the expanding global population, industrialisation, and urbanisation. Existing oil and gas infrastructure can be repurposed to accommodate CCU, and storage projects. LAC countries with established natural gas industries may be well-placed to produce and export blue hydrogen, while those with substantial solar and wind resources can make the conversion to green hydrogen. LAC countries that are fossil fuel producers may have an opportunity to offset significant capital expenditures required to develop a hydrogen industry by re-purposing existing oil and gas infrastructure (OECD et al., 2022[4]).

GLCH can be utilised to decarbonise hard-to-abate sectors such as chemicals, steel, road freight, aviation, and shipping, where viable alternatives to fossil fuels are currently lacking. Hydrogen could support the decarbonisation of heavy transport, by replacing diesel mining trucks in countries such as Chile, Colombia, and Peru (OECD et al., 2022[4]). Green hydrogen and its derived products can enable the alignment of these sectors with the net-zero emissions goal. In net-zero scenarios, the use of hydrogen is generally prioritised for hard-to-abate industry sectors with high process heat requirements that cannot be met by other low-carbon alternatives (Cordonnier and Saygin, 2022[90]).

In the maritime sector, the adoption of hydrogen, hydrogen-based fuels such as ammonia, and related technologies offers a tangible pathway for achieving decarbonisation and reducing air pollution from global fleets. To facilitate this transition, robust co-operation is essential among all relevant stakeholders, including shipowners, shipbuilders, fuel producers, and port authorities. Developing a coherent and enduring policy framework, alongside legislation mandating fuel use and infrastructure obligations beyond a certain threshold, will be crucial. The success of maritime decarbonisation hinges significantly on the timely establishment of green hydrogen storage capacities at ports, supported by specific targets for hydrogen and hydrogen-based fuels in the sector's total fuel demand. Furthermore, the integration of the maritime sector into Emission Trading Systems (ETS) could prove instrumental in curbing CO_2 emissions, limiting carbon leakage, and accelerating the shift towards cleaner fuel source (Hydrogen Europe, 2021[93]). Some countries at advanced stages of variable renewable energy (VRE) deployment are also considering its use to enhance electricity system flexibility, since green hydrogen provides a medium for long-term seasonal storage, for instance through the production of synthetic fuels (Cordonnier and Saygin, 2022[90]).

The development of a hydrogen industry in LAC will require government-sponsored demonstration or first- mover projects, as well as collaboration with the industry at the national and regional levels to create market demand, a key factor in raising finance for hydrogen projects. At the same time, it is vital that countries evaluate the potential environmental impacts, risks, impacts, and mitigation measures of activities related to green hydrogen production, storage and transport. Regional co-operation on hydrogen infrastructure development, cross-border regulation, and free trade agreements are essential to support demand creation to increase the commercial viability of regional hydrogen industries (IEA, 2021[86]); (OECD et al., 2022[4]). Regional dialogue, involving a broad spectrum of stakeholders, but especially energy regulators, is key to enable Latin America to exploit synergies in future hydrogen production and demand patterns (Mariano Berkenwald & Jose M Bermudez, 2020[94]).

There are several risks related to the use of hydrogen for both humans and the environment. The production of green hydrogen requires a significant amount of water and could exacerbate existing water shortages, in some areas where water is scarce. While the use of deionised water produced by desalination plants may reduce freshwater demand, it generates a need to discharge a stream of brine into the water sources and soils. The production of ammonia and methanol generates waste and often involves the use of catalysts and other chemicals that can be toxic or harmful to the environment, potentially contaminating water sources and soils during production and transport. Furthermore, the production of renewable energy, needed to power electrolysis, often requires large amounts of land, which could lead to the conversion of natural habitats or agricultural land and pose negative impacts on biodiversity and food security. Land use changes driven by large-scale green hydrogen projects and related large-scale renewable farms may lead to the loss of natural areas, resulting in an increase in vulnerability, community safety and health-related risks and impacts (Signoria and Barlettani, 2023[95]). Finally, hydrogen is a highly flammable gas, and can also present a significant risk to workers' safety during production, transport, and storage.

Recommendation

- Implement policies to create and scale up the necessary demand for green and low-carbon hydrogen as feedstock and alternative fuel, creating a virtuous circle between decarbonisation efforts and sustainable industrial development.

Sustainable mining for a just and green transition

Reaching net-zero emissions by 2050 means quadrupling minerals supply for clean energy specifically by 2040 (IEA, 2022[96]). LAC has the potential to become a significant player supplying key minerals for the energy transition. Minerals pose a growing concern because these are non-renewable, and their deposits are generally geographically clustered, making security of supply a potential risk. The dependence on politically stable emerging markets for mineral sourcing has intensified with the decline of economically competitive deposits in developed nations, and this mounting demand from emerging markets, coupled with the necessity for rare minerals in emerging technologies, coupled with limited substitution options in various applications, and low recycling rates, has accentuated the vulnerability of economies to potential supply disruptions (Coulomb et al., 2015[97]).

In 2017, the region held 61% of global lithium reserves, 39% of global copper reserves, and 32% of global nickel and silver reserves. Argentina, Chile, and Bolivia possess the world's largest reserves of lithium, and there are areas in the region where hydrogen can be produced at very low costs. Chile and Peru also have substantial copper reserves required for the manufacturing of electric vehicles (EVs) (OECD et al., 2022[4]). Historically, mining has accounted for between 13% and 19% of Latin America's incoming foreign direct investment. At present, LAC contributes 35% of the world's lithium supply, with Chile accounting for 26% and Argentina for 6%. The primary reserves of lithium in LAC are concentrated in Argentina (21%) and Chile (11%), while untapped lithium resources in Bolivia remain economically constrained due to infrastructure limitations. The LAC region also holds promise for production in graphite, nickel, manganese, and rare earth elements. Despite Brazil boasting approximately one-fifth of global reserves for each of these resources, its current production levels constitute just a small fraction — 0.2% for rare earth elements and 7% for graphite of the total mineral production (Bernal, Husar and Bracht, 2023[98]).

Mining operations in LAC have been linked to water, air and soil pollution, deforestation, and loss of biodiversity, as well as conflicts over water and land use or lack of community participation (Morales Munoz et al., 2023[99]). Land use change, water use, and waste generation are the three main challenges present throughout the mining value chain. Nonetheless, mining activities also entail other environmental impacts including air and noise pollution due to blasting and transporting activities (IEA, 2022[96]). It is important to strategically integrate environmental considerations at the early stages of project planning to ensure the adoption of sustainable practices and the acceptance of these practices by local communities. Mining projects in the region often face strong opposition from local communities, with approximately 45% of mining conflicts occurring in the LAC, where operations are frequently located in proximity to ecologically sensitive and biodiverse ecosystems that may also host vulnerable communities. The use of heavy machinery required for mining activities can increase the potential for conflicts and challenges. Moreover, taking into account the disparities in wealth within the LAC region, the perceived local benefits or lack thereof from mining projects can contribute to social unrest, leading to protests that halt ongoing mining operations or delay new developments (Bernal, Husar and Bracht, 2023[98]).

To accomplish its full potential, governments in LAC could strengthen the compliance of mining activities to high environmental, social and governance (ESG) standards and promote ways to generate tangible benefits for local communities (Bernal, Husar and Bracht, 2023[98]). The LAC region has the opportunity to expand its production of critical materials like rare earth elements, essential for EV motors and wind turbines, and nickel, a key battery component. The creation of frameworks that attract increased investments in mining and processing activities will be central to success. This requires the development of clear regulations and incentives while ensuring strict adherence to ESG standards. By doing so, the region can effectively prevent and mitigate adverse impacts on both the environment and local communities. Additionally, upgrading national geological surveys to encompass energy-related critical minerals could greatly support future exploration campaigns. For instance, Chile offers comprehensive open-source geological data via its service SERNAGEOMIN, featuring regional and mineral-specific focal points. In Brazil, the geology department (DIPEME) has established a dedicated division focusing on critical minerals, issuing regulations aimed at streamlining administrative processes for strategic mining projects, particularly centered around lithium, rare earth elements, graphite, copper, and cobalt. Colombia, on the other hand, recently developed a strategic roadmap, the Copper Route, designed to amplify the domestic copper industry (Bernal, Husar and Bracht, 2023[98]).

The mining sector needs to undergo a transformation to safeguard the environment while simultaneously boosting mineral recycling rates and the substitutability of minerals. Governments play a crucial role in fostering the adoption of innovative technologies and practices within the mining industry. On a global scale, mining contributes to roughly 11% of total energy consumption. To address this, companies can incorporate renewable energy sources into mineral processing, refining, and transport operations. They can also engage in innovative measures to minimise water usage, improve waste management and reduce their environmental impact. Furthermore, the industry should focus on innovations that curtail mineral demand by promoting recycling and implementing new, less resource-intensive technologies and industrial processes (Marchan, 2019[100]). Governments can promote the improvement of resource efficiency stimulate the transition to a circular economy in material use. Furthermore, they can provide significant support to the metal industry by removing support for primary extraction and processing to stimulate recycled and re-used metals (the secondary metals sector) (McCarthy and Börkey, 2018[101]).

Recommendation

- Ensure that the growing demand for critical minerals, used to develop low-carbon energy technologies, along with the region's strategic position, allows for an integral model of sustainable mining, with low environmental impacts, well-being for local communities, and linkage in regional value chains that enable their transformation and the production of high-value-added final goods.

Transport in LAC: several common challenges

LAC countries face several common challenges concerning the transport sector. Currently, transport accounts for 14.4% of total emissions in South America, 21.4% in Central America, and 11.1% in the Caribbean, representing 26% of the region's final energy consumption (OECD et al., 2022[4]). Furthermore, transport networks in LAC are inadequate and fail to keep pace with urbanisation rates. Public transport usage is declining in LAC, while private motorisation rates are continuously increasing. Overall, low-income households, and women, who rely more on public transport services are the most impacted (Rivas, Suárez-Alemán and Serebrisky, 2019[102]).

Electrifying the public transport sector while implementing policies that promote a transition to renewable power sources are crucial for cost-effective decarbonisation in LAC and for meeting climate change commitments. In 2015, the global average rate of car ownership was 172.8 per 1 000 people, compared to 196 in Latin America and 201 in the Caribbean. The growth of private cars and motorcycles is driven by greater affordability, rising incomes, and the availability and quality of public transport (SLOCAT, 2021[18]). In fact, the motorisation growth rate in this region is among the highest in the world. LAC countries contributed 7% to global new vehicle sales in 2020 (ICCT, 2022[103]). Trucks currently account for about 70% of cargo transport in the region, and this is expected to double between 2015 and 2050. Moreover, electric cars and buses are projected to become the most affordable alternatives by 2025 (Vergana, Fenhann and Santos da Silva, 2020[104]).

To promote clean public transport in LAC, it is crucial to first eliminate diesel subsidies and other pollutant incentives. Subsequently, implementing a tax on fossil fuels and offering financial incentives to public transport operators to transition to cleaner technologies is essential. Governments can promote this transition by establishing carbon-pricing schemes and a kilometre charge that varies depending on the type of vehicle. Research has shown that combining these tax schemes with increased bus electrification efforts could lead to a 45% reduction in CO_2 emissions and a 30-50% decrease in harmful air pollutants, such as CO_2, Volatile Organic Compound (VOC) Gases, Nitrogen Oxides (NO_X), and $PM_{2.5}$, by 2050 (Tikoudis, Udsholt and Oueslati, 2022[105]). The consumption of fossil fuels carries significant environmental costs, with the majority of subsidies being implicit. Environmental costs are often not factored into fossil fuel prices, particularly for coal and diesel. In developing countries, these subsidies to fossil fuels are projected to increase as consumption levels approach those of advanced economies. Eliminating both explicit and implicit fossil fuel subsidies is estimated to prevent 1.6 million premature deaths annually, generate USD 4.4 trillion in additional government revenue, and align emissions with global warming targets. Phasing out these subsidies would also allow for income redistribution, as fuel subsidies disproportionately benefit wealthier households over lower-income ones. To effectively drive these reforms, governments must design, communicate, and implement them as part of a comprehensive policy package highlighting their benefits, and considering a portion of the increased revenues to be earmarked to compensate vulnerable households for potential rises in energy prices (Black, Parry and Vernon, 2023[106]).

Policies should focus on improving public transport infrastructure. Despite the current decline in public transport usage, 68% of all trips in LAC are still made through public transport, making it the region with the highest per capita bus usage in the world. LAC countries should implement policies aimed at expanding dedicated bus lanes, promoting alternative modes of transport, and encouraging the use of low-emission vehicles, technologies, and alternative fuels for public transport. These can include clean diesel (Euro VI equivalent), compressed natural gas (CNG), battery-electric (BEB), hybrid diesel-electric (Hybrid or HBD), biofuels, and hydrogen-powered buses (World Bank, 2019[107]). Additionally, countries could establish reduced fares for passengers using clean public transport to encourage adoption or implement clean vehicle procurement policies, requiring the purchase of public transport vehicles that meet specific standards or use alternative fuels.

Considering the high share of trips made through public transport, LAC region may consider expanding Bus Rapid Transit (BRT). Currently, over 45 cities in Latin America have invested in BRT, collectively representing 63.6% of BRT ridership worldwide (Rodriguez and Vergel Tovar, 2023[108]). With passenger demand expected to surge by 67% in LAC by 2050, it's crucial for countries to prepare for this growth in a sustainable manner. This includes initiatives such as creating and expanding BRT corridors, introducing light rail transit, and electrifying public transport fleets. To achieve this, countries should enhance options for active mobility through the development of better cycling and walking infrastructure and reallocating urban space accordingly. Additionally, integrated land-use planning and transit-oriented development are key to meeting the increased demand while simultaneously improving urban mobility access and sustainability (ITF, 2023[109]). Ensuring service regularity is crucial in encouraging the adoption of these mobility modes. Offering rapid services on trunk routes alone is insufficient, and this presents a unique challenge for trunk and feeder systems and routes that operate in mixed traffic. Reliable service stands as one of the most critical factors in increasing ridership, necessitating innovative and holistic approaches (Institute for Transportation & Development Policy, 2018[110]). Moreover, it is vital for countries to integrate their public transport networks, connecting them with walking and cycling networks and developing dedicated spaces for public transport (Sustainable Mobility for all, 2022[111]).

Achieving transformation and decarbonisation in the transport sector requires a systemic approach that addresses the unsustainable aspects of car dependency and urban sprawl. Policies must be designed to achieve multiple desirable outcomes such as reducing traffic congestion, air pollution, and emissions, while promoting social equity and well-being. Governments can promote the use of active and shared modes of transport by reallocating public space and regulating parking prices. Car-free zones, non-motorised transport infrastructure, and events that restrict car access can encourage walking and cycling. To reduce car dependency and contain urban sprawl, improvements in land-use planning are necessary. Policies supporting shared mobility, telecommuting, and flexible work schedules can further reduce emissions and alleviate peak traffic hours (OECD, 2021[112]); (OECD et al., 2022[4]). Encouraging multimodal on-demand intelligent distribution of freight and passengers in land, river, and maritime transport systems; and expand non-motorised transport infrastructure such as bike lanes or pedestrian paths is vital.

Prioritising the development of zero-emission mobility infrastructure is essential. This includes building net-zero renewable fuel infrastructure in road networks and urban areas, such as biogas and EV stations, as well as improving the efficiency of the biofuel chain. The lack of cost-effective and efficient charging stations presents a barrier to boosting electrification in the transport sector. Therefore, governments should invest in or promote investment in the installation of public charging infrastructure in dense urban areas, highways, and high-performance charging stations for heavy vehicles (Vergana, Fenhann and Santos da Silva, 2020[104]). As vehicle fleets electrify, it is crucial to increase interoperability, ensuring compatibility among key system components such as vehicles, charging stations, charging networks, and the grid, as well as the software systems that support them, enabling seamless and effective operation (Electric Power Research Institute, 2019[113]). Governments can consider requiring the purchase of EVs for government fleets, implementing more rigorous CO_2 standards for heavy-duty vehicles, offering financial incentives such as tax cuts or emissions-based fees, and introducing non-monetary incentives like free parking, priority lanes, and toll exemptions (Vergana, Fenhann and Santos da Silva, 2020[104]). In recent years, there has been significant expansion of charging infrastructure, primarily driven by private stakeholders such as BMW and Enel X (BMW Group, 2020[114]); (Enel X, 2020[115]). Mexico currently has the highest number of public charging stations in the region, while Barbados has the largest coverage of recharge infrastructure based on population density and number of registered EVs (Vergana, Fenhann and Santos da Silva, 2020[104]).

To achieve full adoption of EVs in LAC, it is essential to strengthen the application of policy instruments to acquire the industrial capacity needed to promote net zero emissions modes of transport for 2050, including solutions such as biofuels and EVs. The goal should be to develop the necessary industrial capacity to replace all internal combustion vehicles with zero-emission alternatives in 2050. The adoption of electric passenger cars in the region is still at a very early stage, with only 0.6% of sales in Costa Rica and Colombia, and 0.5% in Chile (ICCT, 2022[103]). In 2018, Costa Rica implemented a law on fiscal incentives for the promotion of EVs (Government of Costa Rica, 2018[116]). Additionally, in 2019, Ecuador's Organic Law on Energy Efficiency mandated that all vehicles incorporated into the public transport system from 2025 must be electric. The law also introduced differentiated or preferential fees for public and private vehicles and mandated local governments to incentivise the use and circulation of EVs (Government of Ecuador, 2019[117]).

Introducing stringent emissions standards and targets for public transport vehicles can reduce GHG emissions and air pollution in the LAC region. So far only Colombia and Costa Rica have established targets for phasing out GHG-emitting public transport in official policy documents. Costa Rica pledged that 30% of their public transport would be zero emissions by 2035 and aims to achieve 85% zero-emission fleet by 2050 (Government of Costa Rica, 2018[118]). Colombia, on the other hand, has committed to having fully electrified public transport by 2035 (Government of Colombia, 2019[119]); (ICCT, 2020[120]). In 2020, the LAC region had the second highest number of implemented Sustainable Urban Mobility Plans worldwide, and National Urban Mobility Plans are increasingly being used (SLOCAT, 2021[18]). It is important to mention that improving engine efficiency is a transition measure, considering the time needed to develop electric infrastructure, as well as complete shift towards EVs in LAC.

There is need to speed up the implementation of comprehensive net-zero solutions in LAC to reduce GHG emissions in aviation, maritime, and rail transport. To achieve this goal, it is essential to encourage the increased use of sustainable fuels and low-carbon synthetic fuels. LAC governments may also impose challenging deadlines to eliminate non-zero emission aircraft, ships, and trains from circulation, starting with those coming from the most profitable sectors, such as cruise ships in maritime transport.

Aviation contributes approximately 2% to 3% of global CO_2 emissions and accounts for 12% of emissions within the transport sector. Sustainable Aviation Fuels (SAFs), derived from biological or non-fossil feedstocks (commonly referred to as biojet), offer a promising solution to replace or complement conventional aviation fuels, significantly reducing GHG emissions throughout the product's lifecycle. Several countries have already taken steps to encourage the adoption of SAFs and low-carbon aviation fuels. Brazil, for instance, has implemented a National Biokerosene Programme, mandating federal agencies and institutions to support SAF-related projects through measures like tax incentives. In 2021, Colombia passed Law 2169, calling upon the Ministries of Energy and Transport to promote the development and utilisation of SAFs. The Ministry of Energy is also actively working on establishing a national standard for SAF promotion and use. While the LAC region has initiated various efforts related to alternative aviation biofuels, it currently lacks specific public policies or strategic frameworks on this subject. Counties in LAC should enhance institutional collaboration by establishing treaties, interinstitutional and intersectoral agreements, and by encouraging both public and private research. These efforts will help structure a productive aerial biofuels chain involving diverse stakeholders (Torroba et al., 2023[121]).

Emissions from international shipping account for 2-3% of global emissions annually. This is projected to grow overall and increase relative to other parts of the economy, which will be able to electrify and curtail emissions faster. In order to meet the Paris Agreement goals, a full-scale transition to scalable zero-emission technologies over the coming decades is needed. LAC finds itself facing several untapped opportunities connected to the global maritime ecosystem's transition to scalable zero-emission fuels. For international shipping to fully decarbonise it will be necessary to accelerate the shift to scalable zero-emission fuels, in particular green hydrogen in the form of fuels including green ammonia and green methanol. As previously mentioned, the region can highly contribute to green hydrogen production, potentially creating opportunities to generate and transport hydrogen to demand centres with low production capacity like Europe and parts of North East Asia. To accelerate the transition countries could support green fuel production, green port development, or R&D projects focusing on domestic fleets (Global Maritime Forum, 2023[122]).

Box 3.1. Carbon Offsetting and Reduction Scheme for International Aviation (CORSIA)

In 2016, the International Civil Aviation Organization (ICAO) approved the Carbon Offsetting and Reduction Scheme for International Aviation (CORSIA), with the aim of reducing the net-climate impact of aviation, and imposed CO_2 offset requirements in its various phases. These requirements primarily involve airlines acquiring emission rights, with the option of using biofuels. CORSIA's implementation stands as a significant milestone for the international community, as it represents the world's first global mechanism directly addressing CO_2 emissions in a specific sector, achieved through consensus among governments, industry stakeholders, and international organisations. While CORSIA serves as a mechanism to encourage long-term production, it may prove insufficient to fully credit the complete life cycle benefits of SAFs. Therefore, it becomes crucial to consider specific SAF policies that not only promote production but also consumption. The correct formulation of public policies allows the development of the industry by promoting the constant, growing and widespread use of SAFs.

Source: (Torroba et al., 2023[121])

Recommendation

- Strengthen the application of policy instruments to acquire the industrial capacity needed to promote net-zero emissions modes of transport for 2050, including the local production and use of biofuels and low-carbon synthetic fuels and EVs.
- Implement policies aiming to decarbonise freight and passenger transport. Expand non-motorised transport infrastructure such as bike lanes and pedestrian paths.
- Introduce stringent emissions standards and targets for public transport vehicles. Promote clean fuels and common fuel standards that reduce sulphur levels to ultra-low levels. Establish complementary programmes to reduce emissions from older diesel vehicles, focusing on urban fleets.

Cities and Urban development in LAC

The urban population share in LAC is projected to be 89% by 2050 and the urbanisation rate in the Caribbean has increased from 36.3% in 1950 to 72.2% in 2020. To address climate change and work towards achieving carbon neutrality by 2050, it is crucial to develop and implement ambitious policies and measures in urban areas to transition towards sustainable and net-zero emission (OECD et al., 2022[4]); (UN ECLAC, 2018[123]). Cities account for approximately 75% of global energy consumption and 70% of global CO_2 emissions. At the same time, they also present a vital opportunity to drive progress towards climate goals, as they contribute to 80% of the global GDP. Taking sustainable actions in cities could potentially reduce urban emissions from buildings, transport, materials, and waste by around 90% by 2050 (IEA, 2021[124]).

The decarbonisation of buildings and infrastructure is crucial for achieving net-zero emissions, efficiency, and resilience in the buildings and construction sector. Globally, the buildings and construction sector accounted for 36% of final energy use and 37% of energy and process-related CO_2 emissions (UNEP, 2021[125]). In Latin America, the buildings sector accounted for 24% of final energy use and 21% of process-related CO_2 emissions, excluding emissions from manufacturing building materials such as steel, cement, and glass. The Global Buildings Climate Tracker, which monitors progress towards the Paris Agreement goals, indicates that the buildings and construction sector is on track to achieve complete decarbonisation by 2050. However, the changes in building use during the pandemic are expected to have a negative impact on progress unless efforts to decarbonise the sector increase significantly (UNEP, 2021[125]); (IEA, 2020[126]).

There has been some progress towards sustainable urban mobility and public transport in LAC. As mentioned above, LAC has the second-highest number of Sustainable Urban Mobility Plans, and the use of National Urban Mobility Plans is increasing in the region. Brazil has played a leading role by making it mandatory for cities with over 200 000 residents to develop and implement these plans. Similar efforts are underway in countries such as Argentina, Bolivia, Chile, Colombia, Costa Rica, Cuba, the Dominican Republic, Ecuador, Guatemala, Mexico, Paraguay, Peru, and Uruguay (MobiliseYourCity, 2022[127]). Furthermore, other LAC countries have taken specific actions to promote sustainable public transport. For instance, Chile has acquired electric low-emission buses for its public transport system (UNEP, 2019[128]). Paraguay aims to power 33.4% of its public transport with green hydrogen by 2030 (Government of Paraguay, 2021[129]). Peru has implemented projects to enhance electric transport (LATAM Mobility, 2021[130]), and Uruguay has introduced legal incentives to switch to electric buses and promote investments in electro-mobility (Transport Decarbonisation Alliance, 2023[131]).

Green public procurement can be an essential tool to promote circular construction developments, encourage the use of circular business models, incorporate secondary materials, and encourage repair and reuse actions through public purchases (OECD et al., 2022[4]). Countries can also establish credible standards and policies that promote green buildings and sustainable construction practices. These practices should include the reuse and recycling of construction materials, reducing energy consumption, and minimising GHG emissions associated with the construction, use, and maintenance of buildings. Meeting the goals of the Paris Agreement requires a 30% reduction in energy consumption in buildings by 2030 in comparison with 2018 (GlobalABC, IEA and UNEP, 2020[132]). In LAC, the municipality of Mendoza (Argentina) uses its public procurement system to enable a triple-impact economy (economic, social and environmental) by allowing procuring agencies to prioritise goods and services from companies certified as B Corporations (i.e. complying with environmental, social and governance criteria) (OECD et al., 2022[4]).

In LAC, the implementation of urban public transport policies should be prioritised, aimed at reducing city commute times and transitioning towards more sustainable urban transport. Population in LAC often face longer waiting times and commutes compared to developed nations, even for shorter distances. On average, people in LAC spend 77 minutes on public transport weekly, surpassing the 64-minute average in advanced economies. Additionally, the waiting time at stops or stations in the region is higher at 21 minutes, compared to 14 minutes in advanced economies (Rivas, Suárez-Alemán and Serebrisky, 2019[102]). The reduction of commuting emissions significantly contributed to the decrease in GHG emissions in 2020, highlighting the importance of minimising commuter emissions for achieving a sustainable future and meeting international abatement targets. To this end, countries could consider promoting remote working to foster innovation and induce behavioural changes in the population, emphasising the benefits of work-life balance through remote work, raising awareness about the environmental impact of commuting, and encouraging the adoption of zero-carbon transport (Sutton-Parker, 2021[133]).

Cities can implement stricter energy efficiency standards in public buildings. Cities in LAC can leverage public buildings and procurement to promote energy efficiency and sustainability and attract private investments. Implementing stricter energy efficiency standards for public buildings and using public projects as catalysts for wider investment in energy efficiency can be effective strategies. Additionally, cities can drive innovation by launching pilot projects and using green finance to incentivise investments in building energy efficiency. Governments could encourage the development of innovative business models that make energy efficiency measures more accessible and affordable, further promoting energy efficiency in the region (OECD, 2022[134]).

Many countries in LAC should strengthen the enforcement of regulatory frameworks for decarbonising buildings. The region should strengthen the enforcement of mandatory energy codes for buildings, provide a roadmap for stricter regulations and strategies, test functional regulations for existing buildings, and establish regulatory frameworks that facilitate integrated action. Many new constructions lack strong codes and mandatory minimum energy performance. Existing codes need to be strengthened to prioritise passive and affordable construction strategies, implement mandatory building energy codes, adopt passive designs, and reduce cooling needs. Regarding existing buildings, LAC countries must accelerate action on building retrofits and quality by developing and implementing affordable low energy decarbonisation strategies, increasing renovation rates for existing high-density development and low-income housing (GlobalABC, IEA and UNEP, 2020[132]).

Implementing efficient waste management policies, such as waste separation, proper collection and treatment infrastructure and recycling practices can substantially reduce methane emissions while improving the quality of life in cities. Improving regulatory frameworks for GHG and SLCP emissions in waste management is essential, with particular attention to methane emissions. Open dumps remain the most common form of final solid waste disposal in many LAC cities, generating substantial amounts of methane emissions. According to the Pan American Health Organization (PAHO), the region produces over 436 000 tonnes of solid waste per year, and 50% of this waste is disposed of in open dumps (PAHO, 2011[135]). Adopting a circular economy approach will contribute to the decarbonisation of built environment through minimised material use and maximised reuse (OECD, 2022[134]).

Digitalisation presents a significant opportunity for achieving zero emissions in LAC cities. By 2024, an estimated 83 billion connected devices and sensors worldwide will generate vast amounts of data on air quality, energy consumption, geospatial data, and traffic patterns, which can provide valuable insights for effective and sustainable urban planning and policies. To accelerate the transition to net-zero emissions and maximise the potential of cities, governments need to design inclusive policies and programmes that integrate equity and inclusion into urban digital and energy transitions. This requires investment in human resources, training programmes, partnerships, research and development, and innovation to enhance digitalisation and energy capabilities. Access to timely, robust, and transparent data, including energy use and transport patterns, is critical for digitalisation-based solutions and business models. Governments should also facilitate financing and promote financial innovation to overcome barriers, create new opportunities, and establish conditions for innovative financing schemes. The adoption of international standards and benchmarks is necessary to ensure interoperability and monitor progress towards net-zero emissions. Lastly, knowledge-sharing networks and the integration of urban environments into large-scale energy transition programmes will foster a successful transition (IEA, 2021[124]).

Sustainable Construction

Brazil and Mexico rank among the top 20 producers of cement globally regarding the construction sector, and the regional demand is expected to increase due to the need for infrastructure development and reconstruction in the face of climate change impacts. LAC has approximately 272 operational cement plants and experiences high consumption of bagged cement due to self-building and informal housing construction. It is crucial for policy approaches in this industry to consider the region's inequalities, as LAC faces a significant housing deficit, and any increase in construction prices could adversely impact poor households relying on self-construction schemes (Villagrán-Zaccardi et al., 2022[136]).

LAC countries should adopt comprehensive policy frameworks that focus on reducing industry emissions, including specific carbon prices and low-emission standards. It is essential for countries to increase investment and financing in R&D of low-carbon technologies, such as carbon capture and storage (CCS) and alternative raw materials for clinker production (IEA, n.d.[137]). In order to achieve durability and resilience of infrastructure, the region should target long lifespan of construction which can provide a significant long-term reduction of emissions. Moreover, reducing the clinker factor by increasing emerging supplementary cementitious materials is one of the most straightforward strategies for reduction emissions. To achieve climate targets by 2050, technology will be needed, some of examples are the implementation of CCS, oxy-fuel, green hydrogen, intelligent plants to process reduce uncertainties related to the product performance, and Carbon Capture Utilisation (CCU) to convert CO_2 into materials with added value, for example, through mineral carbonation of industrial waste or natural minerals (Villagrán-Zaccardi et al., 2022[136]).

It is important to promote green building certifications. These certifications can go beyond mandatory regulations and assess factors such as energy efficiency, sustainable materials, water management, indoor air quality, and waste management, among other environmental and social aspects (OECD, 2022[134]). Several internationally recognised green certifications exist, including Leadership in Energy and Environmental Design (LEED), the Building Research Establishment Environmental Assessment Method (BREEAM), the WELL Building Standard, the Green Star, and the Living Building Challenge. However, there is a lack of regionally developed green certifications in LAC. Currently, multinational corporations that dominate the construction industry in the region typically rely on international certifications, and existing regulations are not stringent enough to encourage widespread adoption of green certifications. Therefore, the number of certified projects in the region remains low compared to other countries. In 2022, for instance, over 520 new projects were registered for LEED certification, with 317 projects successfully obtaining certification, bringing the regional total to more than 2 778 certified projects covering over 48.3 million square meters of space. The main countries for LEED certification in the region are Brazil, Mexico, Chile, and Colombia, representing 78% of the annual certified projects. Although the number of certified projects has been increasing in recent years, it still lags significantly behind the USA, which had 69 066 buildings accredited with the LEED certification by 2019 (GBCI, 2022[138]).

Recommendation

- Establish credible frameworks, standards and policies that promote sustainable buildings and construction practices in cities, thereby recycling materials and reducing greenhouse gas emissions associated with construction.

Industry and trade of industrial goods

Carbon footprint of products will become a factor for global markets in the future. The carbon footprint of products is becoming increasingly significant in global markets and is expected to continue shaping the future due to the rising demand for sustainable products, growing regulations and policies aimed at emissions reduction, supply chain management practices, and investor pressure on the private sector to be environmentally accountable. LAC, being the largest net-exporting region in the world, holds a vulnerable position in terms of transition risks and potential decreases in competitiveness, despite not fully realising its agricultural production potential (Zeigler and Ginya, 2014[139])). Certain countries in the region play a vital role as exporters of agricultural products. For example, Brazil, Argentina, and Paraguay are among the top five global exporters of soybeans, while Brazil and Colombia fall into the same category for coffee (Observatory of Economic Complexity, 2021[140]). Brazil and Argentina also hold significant global export shares for beef (Cook, 2023[141]).

LAC countries need to develop and implement policies that safeguard the exports of key national products. Mutual recognition of equivalent standards and agreements on trade in organic products can be beneficial for the region. Chile, for instance, has been recognised as an equivalent third country for organic products since 2018, and Argentina and Costa Rica have initiated negotiations in this regard (OECD et al., 2022[4]).

To address the carbon footprint of key national products, LAC countries should consider implementing policies such as establishing carbon pricing schemes and emission standards for high carbon footprint products. Trade policies that take into account the footprint of products from countries and trading blocs, such as the European Union (EU), can significantly impact LAC exports. LAC is a crucial supplier of agribusiness products and raw materials to the EU. In 2021, the EU27 received 8.9% of total exports from LAC, with Brazil accounting for 34.4% of LAC exports, followed by Mexico (15.5%), Argentina (9.3%), Chile (7.3%), and Peru (6.3%). International green regulations like the Green Deal will impose demands for food chain traceability, transparency, compliance, and due diligence, as well as low-carbon, organic, and sustainable production, and reinforcement of the circular economy. These regulations also introduce additional controls on the use of antibiotics, hormones, biologically active substances, feed additives, and chemical residues. Consequently, EU policies such as the proposal for a regulation on deforestation-free products, the Fit for 55 Package, the New Circular Economy Action Plan, the Farm to Fork Strategy, and the Biodiversity Strategy for 2030 may have implications for LAC (OECD et al., 2022[4]). Governments will be compelled to adopt costly actions to align with new standards and requirements while adopting sustainable production practices, which may require investment in capacity building, infrastructure, or technology.

Agriculture, Forestry, and land-based sectors

There is a need to establish sustainable agriculture practices due to the increase in agricultural emissions and the growing challenges of hunger and food insecurity. Between 1990 and 2019, emissions from agriculture in LAC increased by approximately 32%, while agriculture, fisheries, and mining accounted for 6% of the final energy consumption (OECD et al., 2022[4]). In recent years, LAC has witnessed a rise in hunger and food insecurity levels, reaching their highest point in 15 years due to the COVID-19 pandemic. This resulted in 59.7 million people experiencing undernourishment and 237 million people facing moderate or severe food in security in 2020. Haiti, Venezuela, Nicaragua, Guatemala, Honduras, Bolivia, and Ecuador were among the countries with the highest prevalence of undernourishment. The region also grapples with adult obesity and childhood overweight, which have increased over the past two decades, leading to significant economic, social, and health impacts. These issues contribute to decreased productivity, increased disability, premature mortality, and higher treatment costs (FAO, 2021[142]).

LAC is the region with the largest producer of ecosystems services and has highest net food exports in the world, accounting for 16% of total global good and agricultural exports. The Food and Agriculture Organization (FAO) estimates that by 2024, net food exports from LAC countries will reach USD 60 billion, three times their value in 2000. The LAC region's share of world exports of commodities like bananas, sugar, and soybeans exceeds 50%, followed by lesser shares for coffee, beef, poultry, and corn, accounting for more than 25% of world exports of each commodity. Moreover, at the regional level, agriculture and livestock are responsible for 70% of habitat conversion, and deforestation rates are three times higher than the global average (FAO, 2016[143]). Beyond the loss of forests and habitats, agriculture accounts for over 70% of freshwater resource extractions in the region (FAO, 2016[143]); (Dávila, 2011[144]) and is among the leading causes of land and soil degradation and biodiversity loss (FAO, 2020[145]). LAC also hosts 57% of the world's remaining primary forests and a third of all plant species. Nearly half of the region's surface is covered by forests that store a large amount of carbon estimated at 104 gigatonnes (WMO, 2021[146]).

Forest loss is a prevailing trend in the LAC region, primarily due to the emergence of new uses of land for agriculture, forestry, and stockbreeding, as well as urban expansion and highway

construction to a lesser extent. Over the past two decades, Brazil has experienced the highest total forest area loss, reaching 544 690 km^2, with an annual deforestation rate of approximately 10%, and 11 088 km^2 of deforestation in 2020. Nicaragua and Paraguay have also faced significant forest loss rates, although on a smaller scale in the same period. In contrast, Chile and Costa Rica stand out as the only LAC countries that have managed to increase their forest cover by 15% and 6%, respectively from 2000 to 2020, thanks to robust governmental enforcement of laws, secure land tenure protecting property rights, and efforts to combat illegal deforestation and unsustainable agricultural and livestock practices (OECD et al., 2022[4]).

Brazil, for instance, has implemented different types of innovations to promote more sustainable agricultural and livestock sectors. The 2010 Sector Plan for Adaptation to Climate Change and Low Carbon Emissions in Agriculture, known as the ABC plan, sought to fortify innovation within tropical soils. From 2010 to 2020, the plan concentrated on the development of sustainable agricultural production technologies,[10] resulting in the mitigation of 170 million tonnes of CO_2e over two decades. Building on its success, the plan was updated for 2020-2030 (ABC +) to include encompassing new technologies such as bio inputs, sustainable irrigation systems, and intensified livestock farming. These innovations aim to expand across an additional 72 million hectares, potentially curbing more than 1 billion tonnes of CO_2e. Notably, the ABC+ strategy incorporates an Integrated Landscape Approach that holistically considers various components of rural landscapes, harmonising natural elements like carbon, water, soil, and biodiversity with agricultural production in a sustainable manner (OECD et al., 2022[4]).

Food and energy plans should be further integrated. The increasing demand for food, feed, fuel, and fibre offers substantial opportunities for the agriculture sector, yet effective government policies must address challenges such as boosting productivity growth, enhancing environmental sustainability, including the reduction of GHG emissions, and improving adaptation and resilience against climate change and unforeseen shocks. It is important that countries promote initiatives focused on avoiding and/or reducing deforestation and the degradation of vegetation resources, contributing to mitigation and adaptation to climate change (OECD, 2022[147]).

The interconnections among water, food, and energy lie at the core of sustainable development. Policy measures should emphasise the expansion of renewable energy sources and the establishment of integrated land, soil, and water systems that promote efficiency throughout the entire agrifood chain, aiming to conserve water, energy, and ecosystems (United Nations, 2021[148]). Biomass by-products from agri-food activities can be used to produce energy for processing, storage and cooking. Residues generated from crop production and livestock can be an important source of bioenergy while considering the competing end uses (e.g., as animal feed) (IRENA and FAO, 2021[149]).

LAC should prioritise the development of national bioeconomy strategies that recognise territorial specificities and establish or adapt educational programmes. The region needs policies that promote sustainable production models, ensuring the sustainability of natural resources that agriculture depends on, increasing the provision of ecosystem services, and enhancing climate resilience. Improved environmental management can bring significant national benefits beyond ecosystem protection, including the long-term sustainability of LAC's prominent position in global food markets. To achieve the best environmental outcome and political acceptability, measures should be implemented as close as possible to the point of emission, considering their impact. Often, a combination of policies such as "polluter pays" and "beneficiary pays," along with environmental regulations, will be necessary (OECD, 2018[150]).

Replacing traditional food production systems with better and scalable methods is essential. Agricultural strategies that prioritise ecosystem services can significantly enhance critical functions. The implementation of diversified farming systems, such as agroforestry and silvopasture, offers substantial benefits including increased biodiversity, improved soil quality, enhanced carbon sequestration, greater water-holding capacity in surface soils, heightened energy-use efficiency, and enhanced resistance and resilience to climate change (Kremen and Miles, 2012[151]). These techniques also contribute to biodiversity preservation and habitat connectivity, effectively complementing protected areas and enhancing overall resilience to climate change (Kremen and Miles, 2012[151]).

Agri-food systems must become more efficient, resilient, inclusive, and sustainable to ensure access to sufficient, safe, and nutritious food. Strengthening the resilience of vulnerable and non-vulnerable populations in LAC is crucial, particularly in the face of extreme weather events. The ability to resume productive and economic activities is essential for recovery. LAC countries should have a clear understanding of the most exposed communities and geographical areas. Establishing climate risk repositories and maps that are shared with all relevant stakeholders is vital for informing climate change adaptation measures and prioritisation (OECD et al., 2022[4]).

The promotion of protected and precision agriculture is essential for efficient and sustainable food production. Smart villages, based on digital technologies and innovations, can enhance rural areas and communities, supporting quality of life, public services, and new opportunities for rural value chains (European Commission, 2018[152]). Sustainable biofactories are necessary for promoting the circular economy and sustainable water use in agriculture, treating wastewater and generating renewable energy while avoiding waste and environmental impact (UNFCCC, 2018[153]).

Recommendation

- Develop and implement integrated plans for sustainable energy, food security, and bioeconomy, considering the use of renewable energy sources and sustainable practices in agriculture, food waste minimisation, and the promotion of technological innovations with a resilience perspective.

Sustainable Tourism in LAC

As for other sectors, immediate action is necessary to address the existential crisis of climate change, reduce carbon emissions, pollution, and enhance energy and resource efficiency while preventing the depletion of biodiversity and ecosystems resulting from tourism activities. Tourism is both impacted by and highly dependent on the quality of the environment. This dependency requires adaptation to climate and other changes to be addressed alongside actions to mitigate and reduce the environmental impacts from tourism, while supporting the well-being of communities. It is vital that countries accelerate the transition to a greener tourism economy, translating commitments into tangible actions and outcomes, and integrating environmental objectives into tourism policies. This requires the implementation of active tourism policies and recovery measures aimed at driving the shift towards greener tourism business models and value chains. Such efforts can improve environmental outcomes for destinations while delivering benefits to local economies and communities, with a focus on considerations such as decarbonisation, climate change adaptation, ecosystem restoration, and inclusiveness (OECD, 2022[154]).

Tourism serves as a vital driver in LAC economies, contributing to foreign exchange, income, and employment. In 2019, the tourism industry accounted for 42% in the Caribbean and 10% in Latin America of total exports (goods and services). Additionally, it made up 26% of total GDP in the Caribbean and 10% in Latin America. Due to its labour-intensive nature, the tourism sector also provided 35% of employment in the Caribbean and 10% in Latin America (UN ECLAC, 2020[155]). Reliably estimating tourism's carbon footprint is challenging, but recent estimates range from 8% to 11% of global emissions. (OECD, 2022[154]). Potential negative environmental impacts associated with unplanned tourism growth include rapid urban growth, unorganised land use, resource depletion, destruction of fragile ecosystems, contamination of water bodies, and aesthetic deterioration of landscapes and urban environments (Altés, 2006[156]).

However, by implementing sustainable practices, the industry can reduce tourism's negative environmental impacts (OECD, 2018[157]) and attract environmentally conscious tourists. Moreover, tourism can also raise awareness of cultural and environmental values and help finance the protection and management of protected areas, and the preservation of biological diversity (OECD, 2021[158]).

Valuing landscapes and biodiversity should be fundamental principles of sustainable tourism in LAC to ensure long-term sustainability and enhance economic, environmental, and social benefits for local communities and visitors. The Latin America Development Bank (CAF) presented its new work proposal at FITUR 2023 to promote a model of living and regenerative tourism that contributes to mitigating the effects of climate change, preserving biodiversity, enhancing cultural heritage, and reactivating economies. The proposal aims to improve the well-being of rural communities, indigenous peoples, and Afro-descendants; protect and restore biodiversity and value ecosystem services; reduce vulnerability to natural disasters resulting from climate change through resilient infrastructure and monitoring systems; improve government planning processes; promote circular economy practices; and create new spaces to enhance creative and cultural economies, such as museums, galleries, theatres, or creative districts (CAF, 2023[159]).

Digitalisation of the tourism sector is an urgent priority to allow destinations to modernise, innovate, and generate more responsible travellers, who engage positively with host communities Countries need to take proactive measures to ensure that their tourism sectors can fully benefit from opportunities offered by the digital transition, addressing gaps in skills and infrastructure that many tourism businesses and destinations still face. There is an opportunity to develop policies that accelerate the dual transition towards greener and digital tourism, and this is true also for the LAC region. This includes exploiting the opportunities digitalisation opens up for marketing, product and destination development, as well as investing in human capital and skills to embrace digital solutions to promote greener tourism (OECD, 2022[154]). Governments should also actively promote collaboration among stakeholders within the tourism ecosystem. This collaborative approach can enhance the ability to respond to events, share valuable information and experiences, and gain a deeper understanding of both risks and opportunities. Lastly, countries should work on developing long-term integrated strategies with a sustainable tourism vision, clear goals, and targets, along with action plans and mechanisms for resource leverage and government co-ordination (OECD, 2022[154]).

Promoting sustainable tourism development and management presents an ongoing challenge, given the considerable variations in issues and impacts across different destinations (OECD, 2021[158]). To address this, there is a growing emphasis on the potential of certification schemes and similar tools to advance sustainable tourism practices. Countries can establish certification programmes for sustainable tourism activities, designed to minimise their environmental footprint and ensure equitable compensation for the ecosystem services they rely on, ultimately fostering a regenerative economy. Certification schemes represent just one approach to promote sustainable tourism, an area that has acquired increased attention for various reasons, both positive and negative. Concerns include the proliferation of schemes, their effectiveness in driving sustainable behaviours, and associated costs. In the tourism industry, third-party certification schemes have become common, while some countries are considering developing their own schemes tailored to specific objectives. These often concentrate on influencing the practices of businesses and destinations rather than the behaviours of travellers (OECD, 2021[158]).

The use or promotion of certification schemes could, under circumstances, promote ecotourism or certified tourism in protected natural areas that respect the ecosystem and have a minimal environmental footprint. These eco- or sustainability certifications serve as labels that assess the incorporation of sustainable practices and performance based on environmental, social, and economic criteria. These certifications validate an organisation's sustainability strategy by verifying claims and providing external validation on aspects such as responsible supply chain management, legal compliance, and environmental and social risk management practices. Moreover, certifications also exist for key performance areas like energy management, emissions control, sustainable food practices, and accessible tourism. In many cases, these individual labels and programmes are locally managed and approved to address the region's specific and most significant impacts (GDSM, 2022[160]). At the same time, when introducing certification schemes, one should also consider the proliferation, veracity and success in promoting a shift to more sustainable behaviours, as well as the costs involved. Translating ambitions into relevant and meaningful actions to promote sustainable tourism development and management is an area of ongoing work, not least because the issues and impacts vary considerably between destinations. In this context, there is a growing focus on the potential for certification schemes and other tools to promote sustainable tourism activities.

Tourism can be a driver of positive change in global poverty reduction efforts. *The 2030 Agenda for Sustainable Development* highlights tourism as a driver of positive change in global poverty reduction efforts for both advanced and emerging economies. While tourism has the potential to contribute to all 17 SDGs, specific targets for inclusive and sustainable economic growth, sustainable consumption and production, and the sustainable use of oceans and marine resources are included in SDG 8, 12, and 14 respectively. Achieving these goals will require significant public intervention to create the necessary conditions for private sector growth, as well as co-ordination and dissemination of policy approaches and education and capacity building at the national and sub-national levels (OECD, 2018[157]).

Recommendation

- Develop comprehensive long-term strategies for sustainable tourism, supported by action plans. Promote the green tourism transition by leading through governmental example and ensure that all publicly funded or procured tourism infrastructure adheres to the highest environmental standards, contributing to climate-resilient development.
- Promote the certification of sustainable tourism businesses based on internationally agreed standards, as a tool to mainstream sustainable practices, reduce the negative impact on the environment, meet national sustainable development goals, and encourage more sustainable consumer choices and behaviour.

References

Air Pollution and Climate Secretariat (AirClim) (1997), *https://www.airclim.org/* -, https://www.airclim.org/sites/default/files/documents/Factsheet_7_0.pdf (accessed on August 2023). [25]

Altés, C. (2006), *El turismo en América Latina y el Caribe y la experiencia del BID*, https://publications.iadb.org/es/publicacion/13709/el-turismo-en-america-latina-y-el-caribe-y-la-experiencia-del-bid (accessed on August 2023). [156]

Anna Ivanova et al., A. (2021), *Climate Change Challenges in Latin America and the Caribbean*, IMF, https://www.imf.org/-/media/Files/Publications/REO/WHD/2021/English/CH3.ashx. [34]

Arias, P. et al. (eds.) (2023), *IPCC, 2023: Climate Change 2023: Synthesis Report. Contribution of Working Groups I, II and III to the Sixth Assessment Report of the Intergovernmental Panel on Climate Change [Core Writing Team, H. Lee and J. Romero (eds.)]. IPCC, Geneva, Switzerland.*, Intergovernmental Panel on Climate Change (IPCC), https://doi.org/10.59327/ipcc/ar6-9789291691647. [37]

Bernal, A., J. Husar and J. Bracht (2023), *Latin America's opportunity in critical minerals for the clean energy transition*, https://www.iea.org/commentaries/latin-america-s-opportunity-in-critical-minerals-for-the-clean-energy-transition (accessed on 2 August 2023). [98]

Biofuture Platform (2020), *https://biofutureplatform.org/*, https://biofutureplatform.org/ (accessed on 20 May 2023). [83]

Black, S., I. Parry and N. Vernon (2023), "Fossil Fuel Subsidies Surged to Record $7 Trillion", *IMF Blog*, https://www.imf.org/en/Blogs/Articles/2023/08/24/fossil-fuel-subsidies-surged-to-record-7-trillion. [106]

BMW Group (2020), "BMW Group amplía su corredor eléctrico abierto en México, con una nueva estación de carga rápida en Puebla, y se convierte en el más grande de Latinoamérica.", *BMW Group amplía su corredor eléctrico abierto en México, con una nueva estación de carga rápida en Puebla, y se convierte en el más grande de Latinoamérica.*, https://www.press.bmwgroup.com/mexico/article/detail/T0305245ES/bmw-group-ampl%C3%ADa-su-corredor-el%C3%A9ctrico-abierto-en-m%C3%A9xico-con-una-nueva-estaci%C3%B3n-de-carga-r%C3%A1pida-en-puebla-y-se-convierte-en-el-m%C3%A1s-grande-de-latinoam%C3%A9rica?l (accessed on 17 March 2023). [114]

BOGA, B. (2021), *https://beyondoilandgasalliance.org/*, https://beyondoilandgasalliance.org/who-we-are/ (accessed on 14 March 2023). [51]

Bond, T. et al. (2013), "Bounding the role of black carbon in the climate system: A scientific assessment", *Journal of Geophysical Research: Atmospheres*, Vol. 118/11, pp. 5380-5552, https://doi.org/10.1002/jgrd.50171. [28]

CAF (2023), *https://www.caf.com/*, https://www.caf.com/es/conocimiento/visiones/2023/01/la-nueva-voz-de-america-latina-en-el-turismo-global/ (accessed on 19 March 2023). [159]

Cárdenas, M. and A. Hernández (2022), *The Economic Impact of the War in Ukraine on Latin America and the Caribbean*, https://www.undp.org/sites/g/files/zskgke326/files/2022-08/PDS-Number29%20Ucrania%20EN.pdf. [5]

CCAC (2022), *ccacoalition.org - The Climate and Clean Air Coalition and its partners helped spur a multi-year effort to build Colombia's capacity to rein in methane emissions, culminating in groundbreaking policy*, https://www.ccacoalition.org/news/colombia-mandates-methane-emissions-reductions-fossil-fuel-sector-first-region (accessed on July 2023). [40]

Christiaan Gischle et al., C. (2023), *Unlocking Green and Just Hydrogen in Latin America and the Caribbean*, IDB, https://publications.iadb.org/publications/english/viewer/Unlocking-Green-and-Just-Hydrogen-in-Latin-America-and-the-Caribbean.pdf (accessed on May 2023). [87]

Cook, R. (2023), *https://beef2live.com/*, https://beef2live.com/story-ranking-countries-export-beef-usda-0-106903 (accessed on 2023). [141]

Cordonnier, J. and D. Saygin (2022), "Green hydrogen opportunities for emerging and developing economies: Identifying success factors for market development and building enabling conditions", *OECD Environment Working Papers*, No. 205, OECD Publishing, Paris, https://doi.org/10.1787/53ad9f22-en. [90]

Coulomb, R. et al. (2015), "Critical Minerals Today and in 2030: An Analysis for OECD Countries", *OECD Environment Working Papers*, No. 91, OECD Publishing, Paris, https://doi.org/10.1787/5jrtknwm5hr5-en. [97]

Dafermos, G. et al. (2014), *peerproduction.net - Transforming the energy matrix: transition policies for the development of the distributed energy model*, http://peerproduction.net/issues/issue-7-policies-for-the-commons/peer-reviewed-papers/transforming-the-energy-matrix/. [42]

Dávila, C. (2011), *https://www.un.org/ - Water and the green economy in Latin America and the Caribbean: regional*, https://www.un.org/waterforlifedecade/green_economy_2011/pdf/session_7_lac.pdf (accessed on 2023). [144]

EIA (2011), *End in sight: Phasing out fluorinated Green House Gases in Europe. EIA position paper on HFCs in the Review of the EU F-Gas Regulation*, https://eia-international.org/wp-content/uploads/EIA-End-in-Sight1.pdf (accessed on July 2023). [47]

El Pais Costa Rica (2021), *Países del SICA tras financiamiento ambiental y climático*, https://www.elpais.cr/2021/05/15/paises-del-sica-tras-financiamiento-ambiental-y-climatico/. [65]

Electric Power Research Institute (2019), *Interoperability of Public Electric Vehicle Charging Infrastructure*, https://www.eei.org/-/media/Project/EEI/Documents/Issues-and-Policy/Electric-Transportation/Final-Joint-Interoperability-Paper.pdf (accessed on September 2023). [113]

Enel X (2020), "Primer corredor panamericano 100% eléctrico", *Primer corredor panamericano 100% eléctrico*, https://www.enelx.com/ar/es/noticias/estrenamos-primer-corredor-100-electrico (accessed on 2023). [115]

Enerdata (2023), *https://www.enerdata.net/*, https://www.enerdata.net/publications/executive-briefing/empowering-sustainable-development-through-energy-efficiency-latin-america.pdf (accessed on 5 July 2023). [72]

Equitable Climate Action (2021), *https://equitableclimateaction.org/*, https://equitableclimateaction.org/phasing-out-fossil-fuels/ (accessed on 15 June 2023). [56]

European Commission (2018), , https://ec.europa.eu/enrd/sites/default/files/enrd_publications/smart-villages_orientations_digital-strategies.pdf (accessed on 2023). [152]

FAO (2021), *Latin America and the Caribbean – Regional Overview of Food Security and Nutrition 2021*, FAO, https://doi.org/10.4060/cb7497en. [142]

FAO (2020), *Land use in agriculture by the numbers*, https://www.fao.org/sustainability/success-stories/detail/en/c/1295695/ (accessed on 2023). [145]

FAO (2016), *2016 State of the World's Forests*, https://www.fao.org/3/i5588e/i5588e.pdf (accessed on April 2023). [143]

Frédéric Gagnon-Lebrun et al., F. (2018), *Economic Instruments to Leverage Clean Energy Investment*, IISD, https://www.iisd.org/system/files/publications/economic-instruments-clean-energy.pdf (accessed on 2023). [67]

GBCI (2022), *https://www.gbci.org/*, https://www.gbci.org/year-review-gbci-latin-america-2022 (accessed on August 2023). [138]

GDSM (2022), *https://www.gds.earth/*, https://www.gds.earth/wp-content/uploads/Certifications-Guide.pdf (accessed on August 2023). [160]

Global Bioenergy Partnership (2006), *https://www.globalbioenergy.org/*, https://www.globalbioenergy.org/ (accessed on 24 May 2023). [85]

Global Maritime Forum (2023), *https://www.globalmaritimeforum.org/ - Global maritime decarbonisation: New opportunities for Latin America*, https://www.globalmaritimeforum.org/content/2023/05/Insight-brief_Global-maritime-decarbonisation-new-opportunities-for-Latin-America.pdf (accessed on 6 September 2023). [122]

GlobalABC, IEA and UNEP (2020), *GlobalABC Roadmap for Buildings and Construction: Towards a zero-emission, efficient, and resilient buildings and construction sector*, IEA, https://globalabc.org/sites/default/files/inline-files/GlobalABC_Roadmap_for_Buildings_and_Construction_2020-2050_3.pdf (accessed on 2023). [132]

Gouveia, N. et al. (2021), "Ambient fine particulate matter in Latin American cities: Levels, population exposure, and associated urban factors", *Science of The Total Environment*, Vol. 772, p. 145035, https://doi.org/10.1016/j.scitotenv.2021.145035. [15]

Government of Argentina, G. (2022), *Argentina.gob.ar*, https://www.argentina.gob.ar/normativa/nacional/resoluci%C3%B3n-668-2022-372773/texto (accessed on August 2023). [19]

Government of Belize, G. (2017), *faolex.fao.org - Petroleum Operations (Maritime Zone Moratorium) Act*, https://faolex.fao.org/docs/pdf/blz175462.pdf (accessed on 27 May 2023). [50]

Government of Colombia, G. (2019), *minamibiente.gov.co - Ley por medio de la cual se promueve el uso de vehiculos eléctricos en Colombia y se dictan otras disposiciones*, https://www.minambiente.gov.co/wp-content/uploads/2021/06/ley-1964-2019.pdf (accessed on August 2022). [119]

Government of Costa Rica, G. (2018), *cambioclimatico.org - Plan Nacional de Descarbonización - Gobierno de Costa Rica 2018-2050*, https://cambioclimatico.go.cr/wp-content/uploads/2019/02/PLAN.pdf (accessed on August 2023). [118]

Government of Costa Rica, G. (2018), *https://www.pgrweb.go.cr/ - Sistema Costarricense de Información Jurídica*, https://www.pgrweb.go.cr/scij/Busqueda/Normativa/Normas/nrm_texto_completo.aspx?nValor1=1&nValor2=85810 (accessed on February 2023). [116]

Government of Ecuador (2019), *https://www.recursosyenergia.gob.ec/*, https://www.recursosyenergia.gob.ec/wp-content/uploads/2022/12/20190319-S_R_O_449_19_MARZO_LEY-ORGANICA-DE-EFICIENCIA-ENERGETICA.pdf (accessed on March 2023). [117]

Government of Mexico, G. (2022), *Diario Oficial de la Federación - NORMA Oficial Mexicana NOM-009-SECRE-2002, Monitoreo, detección y clasificación de fugas de gas natural y gas L.P., en ductos.*, https://www.dof.gob.mx/nota_detalle_popup.php?codigo=736171. [39]

Government of Mexico, G. (2017), *www.gob.mx - Estrategia Nacional de Calidad del Aire, Visión 2017-2030*, https://www.gob.mx/cms/uploads/attachment/file/195809/Estrategia_Nacional_Calidad_del_Aire.pdf (accessed on August 2022). [20]

Government of Paraguay (2021), *Actualización de la NDC de la República del Paraguay*, https://unfccc.int/sites/default/files/NDC/2022-06/Actualizaci%C3%B3n-NDC%20VF%20PAG.%20WEB_MADES%20Mayo%202022.pdf (accessed on 2023). [129]

Grottera, C. (2022), *Reducing emissions from the energy sector for a more resilient and low-carbon post-pandemic recovery in Latin America and the Caribbean*, https://repositorio.cepal.org/server/api/core/bitstreams/55f4e544-5070-4933-9301-ac32b8ef1675/content (accessed on May 2023). [63]

Hallack, M. and M. Tolmasquim (2020), *https://blogs.iadb.org/*, https://blogs.iadb.org/energia/en/renewable-energy-policies-in-latin-america-and-caribbean-auction-and-net-metering/ (accessed on August 2023). [68]

Hydrogen Europe (2021), *How hydrogen can help decarbonise the maritime sector*, https://hydrogeneurope.eu/wp-content/uploads/2021/11/How-hydrogen-can-help-decarbonise-the-maritime-sector_final.pdf (accessed on 2023). [93]

ICCT (2022), *Zero-emission vehicle deployment: Latin America*, https://theicct.org/wp-content/uploads/2022/04/EMDE-Latin-America-briefing-A4-v2.pdf (accessed on 2023). [103]

ICCT (2020), *Growing Momentum: Global Overview of Government Targets for Phasing Out Sales of New Internal Combustion Engine Vehicles*, https://theicct.org/growing-momentum-global-overview-of-government-targets-for-phasing-out-sales-of-new-internal-combustion-engine-vehicles/ (accessed on August 2023). [120]

ICCT (2009), *A policy-relevant summary of black carbon climate science and appropriate emission control strategies*, https://theicct.org/sites/default/files/BC_policy-relevant_summary_Final.pdf (accessed on 2023). [31]

IEA (2023), *Boosting Efficiency. Delivering affordability, security and jobs in Latin America*, https://iea.blob.core.windows.net/assets/c8972f43-55af-4368-83a6-865f2d17b461/Boostingefficiency_Deliveringaffordability%2CsecurityandjobsinLatinAmerica.pdf (accessed on 4 July 2023). [73]

IEA (2022), *Biofuels*, https://www.iea.org/energy-system/low-emission-fuels/biofuels (accessed on 6 June 2023). [77]

IEA (2022), "Hydrogen Projects Database", *Hydrogen Projects Database*, https://www.iea.org/data-and-statistics/data-product/hydrogen-projects-database/ (accessed on 16 August 2023). [89]

IEA (2022), *Renewables 2022: Analysis and forecast to 2027*, https://iea.blob.core.windows.net/assets/ada7af90-e280-46c4-a577-df2e4fb44254/Renewables2022.pdf (accessed on July 2023). [41]

IEA (2022), *The Role of Critical Minerals in Clean Energy Transitions*, IEA, https://iea.blob.core.windows.net/assets/ffd2a83b-8c30-4e9d-980a-52b6d9a86fdc/TheRoleofCriticalMineralsinCleanEnergyTransitions.pdf (accessed on 2023). [96]

IEA (2022), *World Energy Employment*, https://iea.blob.core.windows.net/assets/a0432c97-14af-4fc7-b3bf-c409fb7e4ab8/WorldEnergyEmployment.pdf (accessed on May 2023). [75]

IEA (2022), *World Energy Outlook*, https://www.iea.org/reports/world-energy-outlook-2022. [2]

IEA (2021), *Climate Impacts on Latin American Hydropower*, IEA, https://iea.blob.core.windows.net/assets/8fa86b9d-470c-41a6-982e-70acd3fbdda4/ClimateImpactsonLatinAmericanHydropower_WEB.pdf (accessed on May 2023). [74]

IEA (2021), *Coal Phase-out and/or Reconversion of Coal Units*, https://www.iea.org/policies/13500-coal-phase-out-andor-reconversion-of-coal-units (accessed on 9 March 2023). [53]

IEA (2021), *Driving Down Methane Leaks from the Oil and Gas Industry: A Regulatory Roadmap and Toolkit*, https://www.iea.org/reports/driving-down-methane-leaks-from-the-oil-and-gas-industry (accessed on August 2023). [38]

IEA (2021), *Empowering Cities for a Net Zero Future*, https://www.iea.org/reports/empowering-cities-for-a-net-zero-future (accessed on 2023). [124]

IEA (2021), *Hydrogen in Latin America: From near-term opportunities to large-scale deployment*, OECD Publishing, Paris, https://doi.org/10.1787/68467068-en. [86]

IEA (2021), *Net Zero by 2050: A Roadmap for the Global Energy Sector*, https://www.iea.org/reports/net-zero-by-2050 (accessed on 2023). [58]

IEA (2020), *GlobalABC Regional Roadmap for Buildings and Construction in Latin America 2020-2050*, https://www.iea.org/reports/globalabc-regional-roadmap-for-buildings-and-construction-in-latin-america-2020-2050 (accessed on April 2023). [126]

IEA (2020), *IEA Methane Tracker 2020*, https://www.iea.org/reports/methane-tracker-2020 (accessed on August 2023). [36]

IEA (n.d.), *Cement*, https://www.iea.org/energy-system/industry/cement (accessed on 24 June 2023). [137]

IEA Bioenergy (2023), *https://task39.ieabioenergy.com/ - Biofuels in Emerging Markets*, https://task39.ieabioenergy.com/wp-content/uploads/sites/37/2023/03/Biofuels-in-Emerging-Markets.pdf (accessed on 19 May 2023). [80]

IEA Bioenergy (2021), *https://www.ieabioenergy.com/ - Implementation of bioenergy in Brazil – 2021 update*, https://www.ieabioenergy.com/wp-content/uploads/2021/11/CountryReport2021_Brazil_final.pdf (accessed on 19 May 2023). [81]

IEA Bioenergy Programme (n.d.), *https://www.ieabioenergy.com/*, https://www.ieabioenergy.com/ (accessed on 2023). [84]

IEA, I. (2023), *National Programme for the Reduction of Methane Emissions - Zero Methane*, https://www.iea.org/policies/17045-national-programme-for-the-reduction-of-methane-emissions-zero-methane. [10]

IEA and UN ECLAC (2015), *Regional Energy Efficiency Policy Recommendations - Latin America and the Caribbean*, https://iea.blob.core.windows.net/assets/761ae750-0ef2-48cc-b5a8-241e605af41b/EEPolicyRecom_LatinAmerica_Caribbean.pdf (accessed on 2023). [71]

IICA & RedBioLAC (2013), *Estado actual de la biodigestión en América Latina y el Caribe*, https://repositorio.iica.int/bitstream/handle/11324/21579/BVE23069184e.pdf?sequence=1&isAllowed=y. [43]

Institute for Transportation & Development Policy (2018), "Improving BRT Systems in Latin America", *Improving BRT Systems in Latin America*, https://www.itdp.org/2018/12/04/improving-brt-latin-america/ (accessed on 8 September 2023). [110]

International Climate Initiative (IKI) (2020), *https://www.international-climate-initiative.com - Alternatives to harmful F gases*, https://www.international-climate-initiative.com/en/topics/homeissuesmitigationf-gases-alternatives-to-harmful-f-gases/ (accessed on July 2023). [44]

IRENA (2022), "Hydrogen", *Hydrogen*, https://www.irena.org/Energy-Transition/Technology/Hydrogen#:~:text=It%20can%20be%20used%20to,replace%20coal%20in%20iron%20production (accessed on 15 June 2023). [91]

IRENA (2022), *Renewable Energy in Latin America and the Caribbean Towards a Regional Energy Transition*, https://www.irena.org/events/2022/Jun/Renewable-Energy-in-Latin-America-and-the-Caribbean-Towards-a-Regional-Energy-Transition (accessed on 12 March 2023). [70]

IRENA and FAO (2021), *Renewable Energy and Agri-food Systems: Advancing Energy and Food Security towards Sustainable Development Goals*, IRENA and FAO, https://doi.org/10.4060/cb7433en. [149]

ITF (2023), *ITF Transport Outlook 2023*, OECD Publishing, Paris, https://doi.org/10.1787/b6cc9ad5-en. [109]

ITM Power (2020), *https://itm-power.com/*, https://itm-power.com/markets/refinery-hydrogen (accessed on June 2023). [92]

Korc and Hauchman, K. (2021), *Advancing environmental public health in Latin America and the Caribbean*, https://doi.org/10.26633/RPSP.2021.118 (accessed on July 2023). [27]

Kremen, C. and A. Miles (2012), "Ecosystem Services in Biologically Diversified versus Conventional Farming Systems: Benefits, Externalities, and Trade-Offs", *Ecology and Society*, Vol. 17/4, https://doi.org/10.5751/es-05035-170440. [151]

LATAM Mobility (2021), *Peru: Government to Introduce Bill to Promote Electromobility*, https://latamobility.com/en/peru-government-to-introduce-bill-to-promote-electromobility/ (accessed on 2023). [130]

Levy, A. et al. (2020), *Clearing Up the Smoke: Untapping the Potential of Tailored Clean Cooking Programs in Latin America*, Inter-American Development Bank, https://doi.org/10.18235/0002786. [32]

López, D. et al. (2022), *La ruta energética de América Latina y el Caribe*, Banco Interamericano de Desarrollo, https://doi.org/10.18235/0004433. [62]

Marchan, E. (2019), "Latin America and the Caribbean's mining sector is key to fighting climate change", *Latin America and the Caribbean's mining sector is key to fighting climate change*, https://blogs.iadb.org/energia/en/latin-america-and-the-caribbean-mining-sector-key-to-fighting-climate-change/ (accessed on 2 August 2023). [100]

Mariano Berkenwald & Jose M Bermudez, M. (2020), *https://www.iea.org/ - Latin America's hydrogen opportunity: from national strategies to regional cooperation*, https://www.iea.org/commentaries/latin-america-s-hydrogen-opportunity-from-national-strategies-to-regional-cooperation (accessed on 1 June 2023). [94]

Martínez, R. (2022), *Energy transition powering transformative sustainable development in Latin America and the Caribbean*, https://www.cepal.org/sites/default/files/news/files/ppt_challenges_eclac.pdf (accessed on 21 June 2023). [66]

McCarthy, A. and P. Börkey (2018), "Mapping support for primary and secondary metal production", *OECD Environment Working Papers*, No. 135, OECD Publishing, Paris, https://doi.org/10.1787/4eaa61d4-en. [101]

Ministry of Environment and Sustainable Development Argentina (2020), *https://www.argentina.gob.ar/ - Argentina regula los gases de efecto invernadero que contribuyen al cambio climático*, https://www.argentina.gob.ar/noticias/argentina-regula-los-gases-de-efecto-invernadero-que-contribuyen-al-cambio-climatico (accessed on 2023). [46]

Ministry of Environment Costa Rica, M. (2021), *Inventario Nacional de Emisions por fuentes y absorción por sumideros de Gases de Efecto Invernadero*, https://cambioclimatico.go.cr/wp-content/uploads/2022/06/InventarioGEI2017.pdf. [11]

Ministry of Environment Mexico (2019), *https://dsiappsdev.semarnat.gob.mx/ - Hoja de Ruta para implementar la Enmienda de Kigali en México*, https://dsiappsdev.semarnat.gob.mx/datos/portal/Hoja_de_ruta_EK.pdf (accessed on 2023). [45]

MobiliseYourCity (2022), *https://www.mobiliseyourcity.net - MobiliseYourCity's projects in Latin America*, https://www.mobiliseyourcity.net/mobiliseyourcitys-projects-latin-america (accessed on 16 February 2023). [127]

Morales Munoz, H. et al. (2023), *Climate security and critical minerals mining in Latin America: How can business help?*, https://climate-diplomacy.org/magazine/environment/climate-security-and-critical-minerals-mining-latin-america-how-can-business#:~:text=However%2C%20mining%20operations%20in%20the,or%20lack%20of%20community%20participation (accessed on 3 August 2023). [99]

Natural Resources Defense Council (2014), *nrdc.org - Cleaning Up Latin America's Air: Reducing Black Carbon Emissions Can Benefit the Climate and Public Health Quickly*, https://www.nrdc.org/sites/default/files/latin-america-diesel-pollution-IB.pdf (accessed on July 2023). [30]

NDC Partnership, N. (2020), *NDC Partnership*, https://ndcpartnership.org/sites/default/files/Insight_Brief-Finance_in_LAC_NDCs_October-2020.pdf. [12]

Observatory of Economic Complexity (2021), *Soybeans*, https://oec.world/en/profile/hs/soybeans (accessed on 2023). [140]

OECD (2023), "Air quality and health: Mortality and welfare cost from exposure to air pollution", *OECD Environment Statistics* (database), https://doi.org/10.1787/c14fb169-en (accessed on 11 September 2023). [16]

OECD (2023), "Climate change", in *Environment at a Glance in Latin America and the Caribbean: Spotlight on climate change*, OECD Publishing, Paris, https://doi.org/10.1787/5584ad47-en. [3]

OECD (2023), *Job Creation and Local Economic Development 2023: Bridging the Great Green Divide*, OECD Publishing, Paris, https://doi.org/10.1787/21db61c1-en. [13]

OECD (2022), *Agricultural Policy Monitoring and Evaluation 2022: Reforming Agricultural Policies for Climate Change Mitigation*, OECD Publishing, Paris, https://doi.org/10.1787/7f4542bf-en. [147]

OECD (2022), *Decarbonising Buildings in Cities and Regions*, OECD Urban Studies, OECD Publishing, Paris, https://doi.org/10.1787/a48ce566-en. [134]

OECD (2022), *OECD Economic Outlook, Interim Report March 2022: Economic and Social Impacts and Policy Implications of the War in Ukraine*, OECD Publishing, Paris, https://doi.org/10.1787/4181d61b-en. [6]

OECD (2022), *OECD Tourism Trends and Policies 2022*, OECD Publishing, Paris, https://doi.org/10.1787/a8dd3019-en. [154]

OECD (2022), *Support for fossil fuels almost doubled in 2021, slowing progress toward international climate goals, according to new analysis from OECD and IEA*, https://www.oecd.org/newsroom/support-for-fossil-fuels-almost-doubled-in-2021-slowing-progress-toward-international-climate-goals-according-to-new-analysis-from-oecd-and-iea.htm#:~:text=The%20OECD%20and%20IEA%20have,energy%20security%20and%20energy%20effi (accessed on 16 May 2023). [57]

OECD (2021), "Managing tourism development for sustainable and inclusive recovery", *OECD Tourism Papers*, No. 2021/01, OECD Publishing, Paris, https://doi.org/10.1787/b062f603-en. [158]

OECD (2021), *Transport Strategies for Net-Zero Systems by Design*, OECD Publishing, Paris, https://doi.org/10.1787/0a20f779-en. [112]

OECD (2018), *Human Acceleration of the Nitrogen Cycle: Managing Risks and Uncertainty*, OECD Publishing, Paris, https://doi.org/10.1787/9789264307438-en. [150]

OECD (2018), *OECD Tourism Trends and Policies 2018*, OECD Publishing, Paris, https://doi.org/10.1787/tour-2018-en. [157]

OECD & RE-CIRCLE (2018), *https://www.oecd.org/ - Government Support for Primary and Secondary Metal Production*, https://www.oecd.org/environment/waste/Policy-Highlights-Government-Support-for-Metal-Production.pdf (accessed on August 2023). [161]

OECD et al. (2022), *Latin American Economic Outlook 2022: Towards a Green and Just Transition*, OECD Publishing, Paris, https://doi.org/10.1787/3d5554fc-en. [4]

OECD/FAO (2019), *OECD-FAO Agricultural Outlook 2019-2028*, OECD Publishing, Paris/Food and Agriculture Organization of the United Nations, Rome, https://doi.org/10.1787/agr_outlook-2019-en. [82]

Oxford Business Group (OGB) (2022), *https://oxfordbusinessgroup.com/ - Green hydrogen and Latin America's energy transition*, https://oxfordbusinessgroup.com/articles-interviews/green-hydrogen-and-latin-americas-energy-transition (accessed on 28 May 2023). [88]

PAHO (2016), *Air Quality*, https://www.paho.org/en/topics/air-quality (accessed on 16 July 2023). [14]

PAHO (2011), *Pan American Health Organization - Residuos sólidos*, https://www.paho.org/ (accessed on 2023). [135]

PPCA, P. (2017), *https://poweringpastcoal.org/*, https://poweringpastcoal.org/ (accessed on August 2023). [59]

RELAC (2019), *https://hubenergia.org/es/relac*, https://hubenergia.org/es/relac (accessed on August 2023). [69]

RIFS Potsdam, R. (2022), *https://www.rifs-potsdam.de - Links between Greenhouse Gases, Climate change and Air Quality: Air Pollution and Climate Change*, https://www.rifs-potsdam.de/en/output/dossiers/air-pollution-and-climate-change (accessed on 8 August 2023). [23]

Rivas, M., A. Suárez-Alemán and T. Serebrisky (2019), *Stylized Urban Transportation Facts in Latin America and the Caribbean*, Inter American Development Bank, https://doi.org/10.18235/0001606. [102]

Rodriguez, D. and E. Vergel Tovar (2023), *Bus Rapid Transit and Urban Development in Latin America*, https://www.lincolninst.edu/sites/default/files/pubfiles/2188_1514_Bus_Rapid_Transit_in_Latin_America_0113LL.pdf (accessed on 20 July 2023). [108]

Rodriguez, S. (2022), *Costa Rica backs away from leading oil and gas phaseout coalition*, Climate Home News, https://www.climatechangenews.com/2022/11/03/costa-rica-cop27-oil-gas-phase-out-coalition/. [52]

Saget, C., A. Vogt-Schilb and T. Luu (2020), *El empleo en un futuro de cero emisiones netas en América Latina y el Caribe*, Banco interamericano de Desarrollo, https://doi.org/10.18235/0002509. [76]

Signoria, C. and M. Barlettani (2023), *Environmental, Health, Safety, and Social Management of Green Hydrogen in Latin America and the Caribbean*, Inter-American Development Bank, https://doi.org/10.18235/0004888. [95]

SLOCAT, P. (2021), *Latin America and the Caribbean Regional Overview*, https://tcc-gsr.com/wp-content/uploads/2021/06/1.5-Latin-America-and-the-Caribbean-.pdf. [18]

Statista (2022), *https://www.statista.com/ - Leading countries based on biofuel production worldwide in 2022*, https://www.statista.com/statistics/274168/biofuel-production-in-leading-countries-in-oil-equivalent/ (accessed on 18 May 2023). [79]

Sustainable Mobility for all (2022), "How to unlock public transport for climate and sustainable development: six areas for action", *How to unlock public transport for climate and sustainable development: six areas for action*, https://www.sum4all.org/data/files/how_to_unlock_public_transport_for_climate_and_sustainable_development-six_areas_for_action.pdf (accessed on 8 September 2023). [111]

Sutton-Parker, J. (2021), "Determining commuting greenhouse gas emissions abatement achieved by information technology enabled remote working", *Procedia Computer Science*, Vol. 191, pp. 296-303, https://doi.org/10.1016/j.procs.2021.07.037. [133]

Syam, M. et al. (2022), "Mini Containers to Improve the Cold Chain Energy Efficiency and Carbon Footprint", *Climate*, Vol. 10/5, p. 76, https://doi.org/10.3390/cli10050076. [48]

The Fossil Fuel Non-Proliferation Treaty (2022), *https://fossilfueltreaty.org/*, https://static1.squarespace.com/static/5dd3cc5b7fd99372fbb04561/t/6358a9ce7c826e6c3f0c225a/1666755041757/Fossil+Fuel+Treaty+Briefing+for+Government+Officials.pdf (accessed on 18 June 2023). [60]

The Fossil Fuel Non-Proliferation Treaty (2022), *https://fossilfueltreaty.org/*, https://fossilfueltreaty.org/endorsements (accessed on 2023). [61]

The Guardian (2022), *Colombia announces halt on fossil fuel exploration for a greener economy*, The Guardian, https://www.theguardian.com/world/2023/jan/20/colombia-stop-new-oil-gas-exploration-davos. [54]

Tikoudis, I., T. Udsholt and W. Oueslati (2022), "Tackling air pollution in dense urban areas: The case of Santiago, Chile", *OECD Environment Working Papers*, No. 195, OECD Publishing, Paris, https://doi.org/10.1787/4c8a4f94-en. [105]

Torroba, A. et al. (2023), *Descarbonizando los cielos: biocombustibles sostenibles de aviación*, Inter-American Institute for Cooperation on Agriculture, https://repositorio.iica.int/handle/11324/21441?locale-attribute=en. [121]

Transport Decarbonisation Alliance (2023), *Uruguay incentivises electric vehicle acquisition*, https://tda-mobility.org/uruguay-incentivises-electric-vehicle-acquisition/#:~:text=Uruguay's%20Ministry%20of%20Industry,from%20all%20over%20the%20country. (accessed on 2023). [131]

UN ECLAC (2021), *cepal.org - Conceptualizing a circular economy in the Caribbean: perspectives and possibilities*, https://repositorio.cepal.org/server/api/core/bitstreams/e469c033-81c9-4638-878e-2c3437695299/content. [35]

UN ECLAC (2020), *Medidas de recuperación del sector turístico en América Latina y el Caribe: una oportunidad para promover la sostenibilidad y la resiliencia*, https://repositorio.cepal.org/server/api/core/bitstreams/86ac5966-d3c1-4297-a90f-650ca471ad4f/content (accessed on August 2023). [155]

UN ECLAC (2018), *Urban and Cities Platform of Latin America and the Caribbean*, https://plataformaurbana.cepal.org/en#:~:text=Highlighted%20indicators&text=Currently%2C%2081.2%25%20of%20the%20population,Caribbean%20live%20in%20urban%20areas.&text=By%202050%2089%25%20of%20the,will%20live%20in%20urban%20areas (accessed on 2023). [123]

UN ECLAC (2011), *Brazil, Argentina and Colombia Lead Biofuel Production in the Region*, https://www.cepal.org/en/pressreleases/brazil-argentina-and-colombia-lead-biofuel-production-region (accessed on 18 May 2023). [78]

UN ECLAC and SICA (2022), *Estrategia Energética Sustentable 2030 de los países del SICA*, ECLAC and Sistema de la Integración Centroamericana (SICA), https://repositorio.cepal.org/server/api/core/bitstreams/43105667-395f-48f4-a46c-5134d2e42fea/content (accessed on 20 June 2023). [64]

UNECE, U. (2022), *unece.org - Air pollution, ecosystems and biodiversity*, https://unece.org/air-pollution-ecosystems-and-biodiversity (accessed on 17 August 2023). [24]

UNECE, U. (2016), *unece.org - The co-benefits of climate*, https://unece.org/DAM/Sustainable_Development_No._2__Final__Draft_OK_2.pdf (accessed on August 2023). [22]

UNEP (2022), *Emissions Gap Report 2022*, https://www.unep.org/resources/emissions-gap-report-2022. [1]

UNEP (2021), *2021 Global Status Report for Buildings and Construction*, https://globalabc.org/sites/default/files/2021-10/GABC_Buildings-GSR-2021_BOOK.pdf (accessed on 19 April 2023). [125]

UNEP (2021), *Actions on Air Quality in Latin America and the Caribbean – Executive Summary*, https://wedocs.unep.org/handle/20.500.11822/36699 (accessed on August 2023). [21]

UNEP (2021), *The Production Gap: 2021 Report*, UNEP, https://productiongap.org/wp-content/uploads/2021/11/PGR2021_web_rev.pdf (accessed on 6 April 2023). [55]

UNEP (2019), *Electric buses put Chile on the path to a healthier tomorrow*, https://www.unep.org/news-and-stories/story/electric-buses-put-chile-path-healthier-tomorrow (accessed on 2023). [128]

UNEP and CCAC (2018), *Integrated Assessment of Short-lived Climate Pollutants in Latin America and the Caribbean*, https://www.ccacoalition.org/sites/default/files/resources//CCAC_SLCP%20LAC%20Assessment%20FULL_Web%202_0.pdf. [29]

UNEP and CCAC (2017), *Progress and Opportunities for Reducing Short-lived Climate Pollutants across Latin America and the Caribbean*, https://www.mce2.org/images/docs/UNEP%20159%20Technical_Report_SLCPs%20in%20LAC_2018_3.pdf (accessed on July 2023). [33]

UNFCCC (2018), *https://unfccc.int/ - Santiago Biofactory | Chile*, https://unfccc.int/climate-action/un-global-climate-action-awards/planetary-health/santiago-biofactory-chile (accessed on 24 August 2023). [153]

UNFCCC, U. (2022), *Sharm el-Sheikh Implementation Plan*, https://unfccc.int/sites/default/files/resource/cop27_auv_2_cover%20decision.pdf. [8]

UNFCCC, U. (2021), *Report of the Conference of the Parties serving as the meeting of the Parties to the Paris Agreement on its third session, held in Glasgow from 31 October to 13 November 2021*, https://unfccc.int/sites/default/files/resource/cma2021_10_add1_adv.pdf. [7]

United Nations (2021), *Water, Food and Energy*, https://www.unwater.org/water-facts/water-food-and-energy. [148]

USA and EU (2022), *Global Methane Pledge: From Moment to Momentum*, https://www.state.gov/global-methane-pledge-from-moment-to-momentum/. [9]

Vergana, W., J. Fenhann and S. Santos da Silva (2020), *Zero carbon in Latin America and the Caribbean: The opportunity, cost and benefits of decoupled decarbonization of the powert and transport sectors in Latin America and the Caribbean*, UNEP, https://www.unep.org/resources/report/zero-carbon-latin-america-and-caribbean (accessed on March 2023). [104]

Villagrán-Zaccardi, Y. et al. (2022), "Overview of cement and concrete production in Latin America and the Caribbean with a focus on the goals of reaching carbon neutrality", *RILEM Technical Letters*, Vol. 7, pp. 30-46, https://doi.org/10.21809/rilemtechlett.2022.155. [136]

WHO (2019), *Health, environment and climate change - Draft WHO global strategy on health, environment and climate*, https://apps.who.int/gb/ebwha/pdf_files/WHA72/A72_15-en.pdf?ua=1 (accessed on July 2023). [26]

WMO (2021), *https://public.wmo.int/ - New report shows impacts of climate change and extreme weather in Latin America and Caribbean*, https://public.wmo.int/en/media/press-release/new-report-shows-impacts-of-climate-change-and-extreme-weather-latin-america-and (accessed on July 2023). [146]

World Bank (2022), *Urban population (% of total population) - Latin America & Caribbean*, https://data.worldbank.org/indicator/SP.URB.TOTL.IN.ZS?locations=ZJ (accessed on September 2023). [17]

World Bank (2019), *Green your bus ride: Clean buses in Latin America - Summary Report*, https://documents1.worldbank.org/curated/en/410331548180859451/pdf/133929-WP-PUBLIC-P164403-Summary-Report-Green-Your-Bus-Ride.pdf (accessed on 2023). [107]

Yamaguchi, S. (2023), "The nexus between illegal trade and environmental crime", *OECD Trade and Environment Working Papers*, No. 2023/02, OECD Publishing, Paris, https://doi.org/10.1787/8dae4616-en. [49]

Zeigler, M. and T. Ginya (2014), *The Next Global Breadbasket: How Latin America Can Feed the World: A Call to Action for Addressing Challenges & Developing Solutions*, https://publications.iadb.org/publications/english/viewer/The-Next-Global-Breadbasket-How-Latin-America-Can-Feed-the-World-A-Call-to-Action-for-Addressing-Challenges--Developing-Solutions.pdf (accessed on 22 April 2023). [139]

Notes

[1] Countries that have not signed are Bahamas, Bolivia, Haiti, Nicaragua, Paraguay, St. Vincent & Grenadines, Suriname, Venezuela.

[2] Argentina, Belize, Brazil, Chile, Colombia, Costa Rica, Cuba, Dominican Republic, Ecuador, El Salvador, Guatemala, Guyana, Haiti, Honduras, Jamaica, Mexico, Nicaragua, Panama, Paraguay, Peru, Saint Lucia, Saint Vincent and the Grenadines, Suriname, and Uruguay.

[3] Bahamas, Bolivia, Brazil, Dominica, El Salvador, Guatemala, Haiti, Mexico, Uruguay.

[4] High-income countries: Antigua and Barbuda, Bahamas, Barbados, Canada, Chile, Saint Kitts and Nevis, Trinidad and Tobago, United States of America, Uruguay.

[5] Low- and middle-income countries: Argentina, Belize, Bolivia (PlurinationalState of), Brazil, Colombia, Costa Rica, Cuba, Dominica, Dominican Republic, Ecuador, El Salvador, Grenada, Guatemala, Guyana, Haiti, Honduras, Jamaica, Mexico, Nicaragua, Panama, Paraguay, Peru, Saint Lucia, Saint Vincent and the Grenadines, Suriname, Venezuela.

[6] The effect produced by the light and heat of the sun being reflected back from surfaces on Earth into the atmosphere.

[7] Hydrofluorocarbons (HFCs) are a group of synthetic gases primarily used for cooling and refrigeration. Many HFCs are very powerful, short-lived climate pollutants with an average atmospheric lifetime of 15 years.

[8] Panama (2008); Mexico, Uruguay, Barbados, Costa Rica (2010); Brazil, Chile, El Salvador (2012), Colombia, Honduras, Guatemala (2014); The Bahamas, Jamaica (2015); Suriname (2016); Nicaragua (2017); Argentina (2018).

[9] Low-carbon hydrogen includes green hydrogen (hydrogen from renewable electricity), blue hydrogen (hydrogen from fossil fuels with CO_2 emissions reduced by the use of Carbon Capture Use and Storage) and aqua hydrogen (hydrogen from fossil fuels via the new technology).

[10] Pastures recovery, crop livestock forestry and agroforestry systems, no tillage system, biological nitrogen fixation, planted forests and animal waste treatment.

4 Cross-cutting policy areas for climate resilience and neutrality in the Latin America and the Caribbean region

Addressing climate change requires comprehensive, cross-cutting policies to ensure that government efforts are not isolated within a single sector. Climate change is a complex issue that affects multiple aspects of society, including the economy, education, health, and social equity. Governments in Latin America and the Caribbean (LAC) need to develop integrated strategies and a comprehensive and horizontal approach to address and enable synergies on issues such as climate governance, finance, and environmental information. Based on the discussions in a series of Regional Policy Dialogues and Workshops on these issues, this Chapter discusses critical policy priorities that can impact multiple sectors, providing a foundation for addressing immediate and long-term challenges ensuring that climate neutrality and resilience are incorporated in the region's development agenda.

Introduction

Current climate change mitigation and adaptation policies alone do not suffice to achieve net-zero emissions and climate resilience, neither globally, nor regionally, nor at the national and local levels. Climate change has an impact not only on environmental, but also economic and social issues. Therefore, introducing cross-cutting and horizontal policies with interlinkages to climate change, such as governance, financing, innovation, education, and gender equality, will help provide a more comprehensive policy framework to achieve net-zero emissions and climate resilience in the region; as well as support the green transition.

The Latin America and the Caribbean (LAC) region faces high vulnerability to the impacts of climate change and requires an increasing need to prioritise adaptation action. Decarbonisation plans and actions targeting the energy and transport sectors have been proposed by the governments and offer opportunities to cut the emissions. However, the challenge lies in translating these ambitions into measurable outcomes. Achieving full integration of climate policy, budgets aligned with the goals of the Paris Agreement, and developing project pipelines demands co-ordination across multiple ministries and the adoption of an effective whole-of-government approach. Additionally, it requires ensuring that national planning and budgetary allocations are aligned with each country's Nationally Determined Contributions (NDCs). Mainstreaming climate change implies that climate policy should no longer be confined to environmental concerns alone. Instead, sustainable policy responses must be systematically integrated into public and private planning and decision-making processes (OECD, 2015[1]). Given the budget constraints in LAC countries, public spending must be optimised to focus on building resilient infrastructure and housing, as well as developing renewable energy sources. Furthermore, climate policies must take into account the unique context of high poverty and inequality levels in LAC. While there are no one-size-fits-all policy recommendations, it is possible to provide general guidelines to emphasise key priorities and next steps for future policymaking (Cárdenas, Bonilla and Brusa, 2021[2]).

Incorporating cross-cutting policies ensures that climate change efforts are not isolated within a single sector. Climate change is a complex issue that affects multiple aspects of society, including the economy, education, health, and social equity. By integrating policies across different sectors, a holistic approach can be adopted to tackle the multifaceted challenges posed by climate change. For instance, addressing finance and investment policies can help mobilise resources for climate-friendly projects, while education policies can raise awareness and promote sustainable practices among the population.

Countries worldwide are actively implementing policies aimed at reducing their emissions, encompassing strategies like carbon pricing mechanisms and energy efficiency measures, alongside support for low-carbon technology research, development, and deployment. However, these measures must be expanded and deepened to effectively redirect investments away from fossil fuels towards a low-carbon energy mix. Unfortunately, global and regional policies often fail to align with climate objectives and sometimes even conflict with them. Fiscal systems inadvertently promote higher fossil energy consumption and production (OECD, 2015[1]). Moreover, the investment climate does not consistently support long-term climate-focused infrastructure. Thus, countries must re-evaluate their policy frameworks to ease the transition to low-carbon economies, understanding that policy misalignments can undermine climate efforts while also recognising that resolving these misalignments can lead to other critical policy objectives such as increased infrastructure investment, more inclusive economic growth, enhanced energy security, and a healthier environment. Currently, existing policies and economic interests primarily favour fossil fuels and carbon-intensive activities, but aligning these policies with a low-carbon economy can drive a broader reform agenda for more sustainable, resilient, and inclusive growth. This includes adopting more progressive tax codes, promoting pro-growth long-term infrastructure investments, and developing energy and transport systems that prioritise cleaner air, better public health, and a diversified energy supply (OECD, 2015[1]).

A comprehensive policy framework that incorporates cross-cutting policies can enhance the long-term sustainability and resilience of LAC. Climate change is an on-going and evolving issue, and policies need to be adaptable and responsive to changing circumstances. By examining the interlinkages of climate change with other policy areas, can provide the ground to design and address both immediate and long-term challenges, ensuring that climate action is embedded in the region's development agenda.

Securing environmental information and data is critical to help monitor the progress in implementing all policy measures, whether they cover mitigation, adaptation or a cross-cutting policy in the region. Environmental information can maximise the impact of future climate actions and help enhance long-term sustainability.

Cross-cutting policies enable synergies and maximise the impact of climate change actions. By integrating policies on gender equality, for example, the unique vulnerabilities and capacities of women can be considered in climate action plans. This can lead to more inclusive and effective strategies that empower women to contribute to climate solutions and enhance their resilience to climate impacts.

For climate policies to be more effective, all relevant stakeholders should identify and address significant misalignments with the low-carbon transition in their respective portfolios. Additionally, beyond the national level, better alignment of policies across countries can enhance effectiveness and mitigate concerns related to potential distortions of competition. It is important that countries in LAC prioritise the scaling up of sustainable, low-carbon investment and finance. This includes developing taxation measures that go beyond the energy sector alone, fostering widespread low-carbon innovation, promoting climate-friendly international trade practices, and revisiting electricity markets to provide the necessary long-term price signals for investment in high capital cost, low-carbon technologies. Furthermore, a focus on sustainable urban mobility, especially in urban areas, should be a key consideration. Strengthening incentives for sustainable land use to reduce deforestation, restore degraded lands, adopt low-carbon agricultural practices, and enhance carbon sequestration in soils and forests is also important (OECD, 2015[1]).

This chapter covers the above points, which were highlighted through a series of Regional Policy Dialogues and Workshops, with the participation of LAC and OECD experts. It focuses on cross-cutting policy areas, which are imperative for addressing climate change in a comprehensive manner.

Climate governance and policymaking

Climate change governance is complex, as it involves multiple actors and stakeholders, at the international, national and local levels. Action to address climate change requires co-operation among many governmental and non-governmental actors. Moreover, it requires multilevel governance due to the multilevel causes and impacts, as well as the participation of all social actors to provide an effective response.

Effective policy implementation is essential to achieve climate change mitigation and adaptation policy goals. One of its prerequisites is effective climate change governance, which encompasses interventions that target changes in environmental incentives, knowledge, institutions, decision-making processes and behaviours. It involves regulatory processes, mechanisms, and organisations, through which political actors influence environmental actions and outcomes (Lemos and Agrawal, 2006[3]).

Understanding the nature of multilevel governance provides a base to strengthen and promote innovation, enhance problem-solving capacity, facilitate learning, and improve decision-making efficiency, while also enabling the creation of adaptable mechanisms tailored to specific contexts, topics, and sectors. Multilevel climate governance ensures coherence between local, national, and international plans and policies, fostering collaboration, innovation, and learning among actors and authorities at various levels. This approach allows to establish shared objectives, mechanisms, policies and solutions, creating structures for information exchange, decision-making, follow-up, monitoring, and reporting, and ultimately enhancing collaboration between actors at different levels by defining clear roles, relationships, and responsibilities (Cognuck González and Numer, 2020[4]).

Committing to international partnerships

International partnerships and co-operation play a crucial role in addressing global challenges, particularly in the context of climate change. The LAC region, with its diverse ecosystems and vulnerable populations, is particularly susceptible to the impacts of climate change. Committing to international partnerships and fostering co-operation is of utmost importance for the region to effectively tackle climate policies and ensure a sustainable future.

International partnerships can enhance capacity in the region. By joining forces, countries can pool their resources, expertise, and knowledge to address climate change challenges more effectively. They can share experiences, best practices, and research, enabling each country to learn from others' successes and failures. Knowledge sharing can also foster innovation and promote the adoption of sustainable practices across the region.

The Amazon Cooperation Treaty Organisation (ACTO) provides a platform where countries share commitments to promote and co-ordinate the sustainable development and conservation of the Amazon Rainforest. This intergovernmental organisation was established in 1978 by Bolivia, Brazil, Colombia, Ecuador, Guyana, Peru, Suriname, and Venezuela, which collectively signed the Amazon Cooperation Treaty (ACT), with the primary aim of providing a legal framework that acknowledges the significance and cross-border nature of the Amazon ecosystem. During the most recent Amazon Summit, held in August 2023 in Belém do Pará, attending countries endorsed the Belem Declaration, which, among other key points, acknowledges the invaluable contributions of indigenous peoples, local communities, women, and youth in tropical forest conservation efforts. The declaration reaffirms a shared commitment to forest preservation, the mitigation of deforestation drivers, biodiversity conservation, and the pursuit of an equitable ecological transition. It emphasises the importance of international co-operation as the most potent means to uphold commitments aimed at reducing deforestation and forest degradation and highlights the need for developed countries to fulfil their commitments over climate financing (Government of Brazil, 2023[5]). The Leticia Pact for the protection of the Amazon Forest, also adopted through the ACTO, and the Escazú Agreement for the fair integration of local communities and indigenous peoples are additional examples of multilateral co-operation whose implementation will allow the comprehensive consolidation of achievements at the national level in the long term.

International partnerships also strengthen countries collective bargaining power. By forming partnerships, countries can present a united block in international climate negotiations, prioritise their joint challenges and advocate their specific needs. International partnerships address current implementation shortcomings of multilateral agreements and instruments, align national and regional priorities with multilateral sustainability goals, and facilitate technology transfer and capacity building. This is achieved through policy dialogues and the exchange of experiences through peer learning. Furthermore, international partnerships can play a crucial role in assisting LAC countries in addressing trade challenges when adapting to new international green norms and regulations (OECD et al., 2022[6]).

Developing climate change policies at the national level [top-down and bottom-up approaches]

Considerations and benefits of a top-down approach

In some respects, a top-down approach is necessary as it emphasises the need for governments to formulate policies with well-defined targets, establish robust laws, regulations and standards, and develop guidelines for national and sub-national governments. Sectorial institutional arrangements can support relevant stakeholders to reduce greenhouse gas (GHG) emissions, particularly in hard-to-abate-sectors such as cement, steel, and petrochemicals, as well as areas like construction and power generation, while also reducing dependence on fossil fuels. A top-down approach also facilitates engagement from a range of stakeholders and enables seamless integration across policy realms, spanning energy, transport, agriculture, urban planning, and economic development, with due consideration for social and economic consequences, especially among vulnerable communities. High-level inter-ministerial committees and working groups are mechanisms that can foster co-ordination, integrate climate change mitigation and adaptation efforts across different sectors and levels of government, and involve external stakeholders to enhance the inclusiveness of the policy-making process (UNFCCC, 2019[7]); (OECD, 2021[8]). Simultaneously, these mechanisms offer a comprehensive means to holistically address environmental concerns, set priority actions, allocate vital financial resources, and implement monitoring, reporting, and evaluation (MRV) systems for assessing policy effectiveness, to enhance accountability and help identify areas for improvement.

Political will and leadership play a crucial role in achieving effective legal and institutional co-ordination in LAC, as well as in progressing towards climate-resilient, low-carbon economies, and heightened climate ambitions. The political leadership within each country must show its dedication to both the development and execution of climate change policies. Bridging the gap between global expectations and political commitments is crucial, along with elevating ambitions in mitigation, adaptation, and climate finance.

Such a top-down approach to climate change mitigation policies could address a number of challenges in LAC. It could: i) set specific emission reduction targets, as well as financial regional commitments; ii) facilitate the development of internal market mechanisms, as well as MRV systems, along with compliance regimes that ensure the achievement of goals and targets; iii) help prevent carbon leakage; and iv) provide countries with the necessary information to develop effective, efficient, and evidence-based policies (Marr, Marett and Wohlgemuth, 2018[9]); (IEA, 2020[10]). It is important to note that while both top-down and bottom-up approaches are necessary in addressing the complexity of climate change, a top-down approach is particularly crucial for climate change mitigation policies due to these particularities.

At the same time, countries must acknowledge the importance of balancing top-down initiatives with a bottom-up approach involving local communities (explained in the bottom-up approach section of this chapter). Combining both approaches can lead to more effective and efficient climate policy progress (Hermansen and Sundqvist, 2022[11]). Limiting consideration to only top-down or bottom-up approaches could result in sub-optimal solutions for the communities most affected by, but least resourced to adapt to climate change (Qamar and Archfield, 2022[12]). Top-down actions establish overall goals and targets, while bottom-up actions provide specific and concrete solutions to achieve those targets. This combination can result in more effective climate change mitigation policies by providing a legal framework, financial resources, and global or national co-ordination, while empowering local communities to take action and address local needs and priorities.

Box 4.1. Examples of top-down policy approaches and inter-ministerial groups in LAC

Costa Rica's *2019 National Decarbonisation Plan*, which aims to make the country carbon neutral by 2050. The plan includes measures to reduce GHG emissions, such as promoting renewable energy sources, implementing energy efficiency measures, and expanding carbon sequestration efforts.

In 2020, Peru established a High-Level Commission on Climate Change, with the responsibility for proposing climate change mitigation and adaptation actions, aiming to achieve net-zero GHG emissions by 2050 and progressively increasing Peru's NDCs. Additionally, it prepares technical reports and proposes updates to align the country's NDC with global climate objectives. It is led by the President of the Council of Ministers; and it includes ministers from various sectors and government institutions.

The Dominican Republic set the National Council for Climate Change and Clean Development Mechanism in 2008. This government institution co-ordinates and promotes the implementation of mitigation and adaptation policies and actions in the country. It formulates and approves the investment strategy for Clean Development Mechanism projects. The Council is chaired by the President of the Republic; other members are the Ministers of Environment and Natural Resources, Economy, Planning and Development, Agriculture, Foreign Relations, Finance, Industry and Commerce, Public Health and Social Assistance and Tourism. Other stakeholders also attend the meetings, namely the heads of the Central Bank of the Dominican Republic, the National Energy Commission, the Office for the Reorganisation of Transport, the Superintendence of Electricity, the Dominican Corporation of State Electric Companies, the Association of Banks of the Dominican Republic, the Association of Industries of the Dominican Republic, private generators of the national energy sector, the National Council of Private Enterprise and representatives of civil society organisations.

Source : (Government of Costa Rica, 2018[13]); (Ministry of Environment Peru, n.d.[14]); (Presidéncia de la República Dominicana, n.d.[15])

Enhancing inclusiveness by taking into consideration local communities and vulnerable groups - bottom-up approach

The bottom-up approach is people-centred, allowing the generation of knowledge based on their understanding of present conditions, risks, and responses. This approach emphasises the importance of individual elements or components that contribute to a holistic system or solution. It focuses on recent and present vulnerability thresholds, studying local responses empirically to define local priorities and concerns. It includes finer geographical scales and examines physical, ecological, and social processes, as well as current sensitivity to weather and climate. Additionally, it evaluates plausible policy options within technological, ecological, or perceived social limits while considering various normative measures of risk to vulnerable populations (Conway et al., 2019[16]).

Climate change impacts disproportionately affect the poorest and most vulnerable, implying a need for adaptation strategies and disaster risk management strategies to manage existing climate impacts and risks. Sub-national governments play a vital role in transitioning to a climate-neutral economy and fulfilling international environmental commitments. They are also key actors in mitigation and adaptation efforts due to their jurisdiction over crucial policy domains for the climate-neutral transition (OECD, 2022[17]). A bottom-up approach is important as it enables the development of community-based action, aiming to achieve equity and efficacy in policy implementation within communities (Qamar and Archfield, 2022[12]). Bottom-up assessments provide a better understanding of specific contexts, the transmission of impacts through socio-economic organisation, local and risks (Conway et al., 2019[16]).

Developing and implementing a bottom-up approach presents significant challenges, as they tend to be resource-intensive due to their contextual nature. Acquiring sufficient detailed information about complex systems for decision-making is challenging, and generalising findings or lessons to other contexts is problematic. Additionally, there is a lack of awareness and means to acquire innovative solutions, and uncertainty persists regarding physical changes, socio-economic developments, and the costs and benefits associated with different approaches or time scales. To address these challenges, bottom-up processes should aim to increase comparability between different cases and be developed on past successful cases (Box 4.2) (Conway et al., 2019[16]); (Boteler et al., 2015[18])).

Box 4.2. Examples of bottom-up approaches in LAC

From 2018 to 2019, Peru initiated a consultation process with indigenous communities to develop regulations for the country's Climate Change Law. This process marked a significant milestone in shaping public policies for climate action in Peru, as it represented the first-ever consultation of its kind in South America for the approval of national regulations. The primary goal was to establish a strong foundation for the development of public policies that incorporate the perspectives of all stakeholders, following an open-door policy and a participatory, inclusive, and decentralised approach. The outcome of this process resulted in 152 agreements, of which 147 have been successfully implemented.

Since 1984, stakeholders in Belize have collaborated to protect the natural environment through an informal arrangement known as co-management. More recently, the government of Belize formalised these efforts with the introduction of a new Protected Areas Co-management Framework. These agreements, which are specific to individual sites, encompass a wide range of responsibilities, including financial accountability, transparency, and data reporting. Additionally, they foster stronger collaboration between the government of Belize and conservation partners. By 2016, Belize had established 48 protected areas under co-management, representing nearly 50% of all protected areas in the country. These initiatives have delivered significant socio-economic benefits to local communities, fostered robust collaborative governance structures at multiple levels, and sustained self-organisation to promote co-management over time. Furthermore, in 2014, the Global Support Initiative for territories and areas conserved by Indigenous Peoples and local communities (ICCA-GSI) was established. This initiative aims to enhance the recognition and effectiveness of biodiversity conservation, sustainable livelihoods, and resilience to climate change in such territories and areas. Phase 1 of ICCA-GSI is currently underway in 26 countries, including Argentina, Belize, Brazil, Colombia, Ecuador, Guatemala, Paraguay, Peru, and Suriname in LAC.

Source: (MINAM, 2022[19]); (Williams and Tai, 2016[20]); (SGP, n.d.[21]); (Government of Belize, 2022[22])

It is crucial for LAC countries to develop policies that enhance bottom-up approaches for climate change mitigation and adaptation. LAC countries could promote the development of participatory methods and approaches to identify key barriers and opportunities for implementing local strategies and plans. They should establish robust guidelines and evaluation criteria for relevant measures while enhancing policy co-ordination to ensure flexibility and responsiveness to environmental scenarios (Russel et al., 2020[23]); (Campos et al., 2018[24]). Capacity building and educational programmes should be developed to inform and involve relevant local stakeholders in the decision-making process (Danish, 1995[25]).

Regulatory frameworks should combine elements of both approaches with their own advantages and disadvantages. Education plays a key role in relying on communities in developing regions for climate change adaptation. Communities often need basic-level education on possible community-led adaptation frameworks, which could be considered a top-down approach. However, as communities start taking measures on their own, bottom-up approaches can be favoured. Supporting effective adaptation strategies depends on the local context. As mentioned before, limiting consideration to only top-down or bottom-up approaches could result in sub-optimal solutions for the communities most affected by, but least resourced to adapt to climate change (Qamar and Archfield, 2022[12]); (Conway et al., 2019[16]). Blending insights from bottom-up and top-down approaches can generate a more holistic understanding of people's and communities' vulnerabilities to climate risks and their potential responses, encompassing physical, social, and economic aspects. While top-down modelling approaches are effective in understanding how impacts are likely to differ at different temperature levels, a more detailed picture and effective adaptation at any level of temperature stabilisation require contributions from bottom-up approaches. Developing hybrid methods and information is likely to be more useful than relying on a single approach, both in the short and long term, for decision-makers and communities alike (Conway et al., 2019[16]).

Finally, revisions of such national policy frameworks need to be aligned with countries' international commitments, taking into consideration to timeframes set for achieving goals and targets, the means of implementation, as well as updates in innovation and technology which can help achieve these.

Recommendation

- **Progressively revise and update national regulatory frameworks**. Consider the benefits and challenges of top-down and bottom-up approaches. Updating national laws and regulations aligned with Nationally Determined Contributions (NDCs) updates, as well as the establishment of National Adaptation Plans (NAPs) and Long-Term Strategies (LTS), are essential to achieving global commitments established in the Sustainable Development Goals (SDGs) and the three UN environmental conventions (climate change, biodiversity, and desertification), while maintaining science-based policy decisions.

Comprehensive planning and strategic environmental assessment

The increased utilisation of Strategic Environmental Assessments (SEAs) is crucial for promoting sustainable decision-making in plans, programmes and policies in LAC. SEAs serve as a valuable environmental management instrument that enables countries to incorporate environmental aspects of sustainable development into policy and planning processes. They facilitate the inclusion of mitigation and adaptation to climate change considerations from an integrated perspective in planning and territorial planning, thereby promoting informed and participatory decision-making involving key stakeholders, including the public, private sector, and civil society (MMA, 2022[26]). SEAs are comprehensive assessments that evaluate the environmental and health effects of policies, plans, and programmes, aiming to shift them towards sustainable outcomes. By integrating environmental and health considerations with economic and social factors, SEAs provide a holistic sustainability assessment and facilitate informed decision-making processes. They are applied at the early stages of decision-making to support the formulation of effective and sustainable policies. SEAs are a logical step that structures the preparation of projects and complements the project-specific focus of Environmental Impact Assessments (EIAs) (OECD, 2006[27]).

Progress has been made towards the adoption and regulation of SEAs in LAC, although further advancements are necessary. In 2019, Chile, Costa Rica and Uruguay, implemented regulations for the environmental analysis of policies, plans, and programmes related to territorial planning. Additionally, Brazil, Cuba, the Dominican Republic, El Salvador, Guatemala and Venezuela issued government agreements or draft legislation regarding the utilisation of SEAs for policy, plan, and programmes analysis (Massuela Calenga, Montes de Oca Risco and Ulloa Carcassés, 2019[28]). SEAs serve as a crucial tool for ensuring the sustainability of policies and programmes. However, the LAC region faces certain challenges in SEA development, including the absence of tailored SEA methodologies for various policy contexts and governance scenarios. Furthermore, there is a need for effective monitoring mechanisms for programs implemented under SEA processes. To advance SEA practices in the region and align them with sustainable criteria, it is crucial to secure the support of decision-makers for the proper adaptation of plans and policies (Rodrigo-Ilarri et al., 2020[29]).

Some countries in the LAC region have adopted different legal instruments for introducing and applying SEAs. Bolivia, Chile, and Peru have general laws that apply nationwide, while Colombia and Mexico have introduced a national development plan encompassing SEA, and specific legislation applicable at the city level, respectively. On the other hand, Brazil does not have a national framework regulating SEAs, but they are regulated at the state level in Bahia, Minas Gerais, and Sao Paulo (Rodrigo-Ilarri et al., 2020[29]).

SEAs in LAC could offer several benefits beyond providing information for better decision-making. Through a step-by-step approach, SEAs enhance transparency and communication regarding environmental and health aspects of development, contributing to the overall well-being of the region. SEAs contribute to a high level of environmental protection by supplying planning authorities with suggestions to mitigate negative effects and explore alternative development opportunities. Additionally, SEAs promote sustainable economic development, facilitate the transition to greener economies, enhance planning and programming processes, improve decision-making efficiency, strengthen governance, build public trust, and serve as a valuable tool for climate change adaptation and mitigation. (UNECE, 2016[30]).

There are challenges in applying SEAs in the LAC region. First, SEAs are not always mandatory, as there might not be political willingness for their wider implementation. Second, there is a lack of institutional and procedural frameworks in applying SEAs, therefore assessments are not always complete on impacts and do not offer alternatives. There is a need for the development of methodologies that offer comprehensible and achievable alternatives, tailored to the regional context. Third, there is a lack of institutional and technical capacity from the side of evaluators. It is crucial for LAC countries to provide training to civil servants, enabling them to develop a system based on strategic thinking rather than solely focusing on legal compliance. This can be achieved through the formulation of detailed guidelines for each stage of the SEA process and by ensuring the disclosure of concepts and legal requirements within each governmental agency (Rodrigo-Ilarri et al., 2020[29]); (Massuela Calenga, Montes de Oca Risco and Ulloa Carcassés, 2019[28]).

Co-ordinated regional action for adopting SEA could ensure a higher level of environmental protection in LAC. Once SEA guidelines are developed, it is essential to focus on the technical implementation procedures of these guidelines. Increasing awareness and understanding among policymakers in the region is also vital to ensure the widespread adoption of SEAs. Countries need to revise their legal frameworks, considering the necessary requirements to align SEAs with development planning. Additionally, they can establish regional agreements for knowledge dissemination and exchange, develop harmonised standards and methods tailored to the region's specific conditions, and advance the creation of regional SEA methodologies that include an analysis of alternatives and incorporate simple criteria for determining the most viable alternative. It is also important to propose regional environmental goals related to SEA that are realistic for each country, considering social and economic factors. Moreover, countries should focus on developing SEA capabilities, strengthening inter-institutional communication mechanisms, and establishing networks among all relevant stakeholders. Effective SEA depends on an adaptive and continuous process that emphasises institutional strengthening, governance, and decision-making, rather than simply relying on a linear, technical approach focused solely on impacts (Box 4.3) (Rodrigo-Ilarri et al., 2020[29]); (OECD, 2006[31]).

Box 4.3. International Support on the development of SEAs in LAC

SEAs in LAC are gaining traction, supported by multilateral economic and social development organisations such as the World Bank, the UN Economic Commission for Latin America and the Caribbean (UN ECLAC), the Central American Commission on Environment and Development (CCAD), and UNEP. The Initiative for the Integration of the South American Regional Infrastructure (IIRSA), a multinational, multisectoral, and multidisciplinary organisation co-ordinating 12 South American governments, along with multilateral financial institutions like the Inter-American Development Bank (IDB) and the Development Bank of Latin America and the Caribbean (CAF), as well as the OECD, in collaboration with the private sector, is developing a joint programme aiming to promote the integration of transport, energy, tourism, and telecommunications infrastructure among South American countries and includes the use of SEA as a complement to EIA for projects financed by these institutions.

Source : (Massuela Calenga, Montes de Oca Risco and Ulloa Carcassés, 2019[28])

Recommendation

- **Agree on long-term strategies, plans and programmes.** Increase the use of SEAs to promote sustainable decision-making in plans, programmes and policies. Transparency and periodic strategic evaluation will also contribute to compliance regarding Measurement, Reporting and Verification (MRV) commitments established in the UNFCCC instruments.

Environmental information and monitoring

Collecting environmental data for better policymaking

The lack of environmental information and data gaps undermines the importance of environmental problems and delays a clear understanding of ecological costs associated with projects (Gligo et al., 2020[32]). This information gap leads to an incomplete comprehension of the nature and scale of climate change issues and the necessary policies for addressing them. Moreover, it affects the assessment of trends and progress in mitigation and adaptation efforts, limiting the capacity to evaluate policies, establish indicators and monitor impacts. In recent years, there has been a growing interest in measuring progress towards sustainable development and improving environmental accounting in developing countries due to the fact that lack of data leads to lost business opportunities, and costly and ineffective public service interventions by governments, especially, for poor and vulnerable households (OECD, 2017[33]).

Being able to gather relevant, timely, disaggregated, and reliable environmental data allows countries to establish priorities, make informed policy choices to address the climate change challenges, and follow progress towards achieving their international and national climate commitments. The data revolution, characterised by a vast increase in the volume of digital data known as "big data" and more specifically earth observation data, offers governments and national statistical offices the possibility to produce and use such data, to complement and strengthen official statistics, without replacing them. New technology allows for easier, faster, and cheaper data production to make informed choices on policies and priorities. National statistical offices can play a crucial role in improving accessibility, transforming and analysing data, while adopting open data policies and fostering evidence-based decision making (OECD, 2017[33]).

There are important methodological and strategic challenges that need to be addressed, such as striking a balance between producing data for global monitoring and for national policy making. Another issue is to expand statistical information and analysis related to environmental conditions and sustainability indicators at both the country-specific and regional levels, as well as to strengthen monitoring and evaluation capacity. It is crucial for LAC countries to strengthen, expand, and equip the production of environmental statistics with human capabilities and allocate a regular budget for statistical activities. Across the region, a lack of national statistical legal frameworks hinders the definition of roles, targets, and budget allocation, which should align with the United Nations Fundamental Principles of Official Statistics. Moreover, funding allocation for national statistical plans and strategies is inadequate, and the available data is often insufficiently disaggregated, making it impossible for policymakers to track or compare the situations of different population groups or communities (OECD, 2017[33]). There are still significant differences in the capabilities of statistical systems among countries in the region. Some countries lack the means and infrastructure to produce high-quality data. Therefore, it is necessary for all LAC countries to enhance, expand, and equip the production of environmental statistics with well-trained human resources and a regular budget (OECD, 2017[33]); (Ocampo, 2021[34]).

National statistical systems in LAC need to increase its institutional capacity, embrace openness, form partnerships, and promote data use to maximise the benefits of the data revolution. Governments may establish clear regulatory frameworks defining the scope, objectives, and requirements for environmental statistics. Establishing national registries on mitigation and adaptation measures in LAC requires different policy approaches to support their development, implementation, and maintenance. Well-funded National Statistical Institutes with specialised units focused on environmental statistics are essential (UN ECLAC, 2017[35]). At the same time, it is important to note that an important amount of information in the region is gathered by non-governmental agencies. These agencies must adopt best practices used by statistical offices. Promoting the use of data for decision-making by engaging with users within and outside the government and leading programmes to increase statistical literacy and use are also vital. Strategic alliances on a regional level, including with international organisations active in the region can be formed to synergise and combine resources from agencies, donors, and countries.

The OECD publication *Environment at a Glance in Latin America and the Caribbean* is a first step in collecting and using available environmental data and information and developing indicators for the region. Information available covers climate mitigation, with data on GHG emissions, air pollution and energy mix. On climate adaptation, information focuses on climate hazards and climate impacts on biodiversity. Other indicators cover selected climate policies, on climate actions taken, environmentally related taxes, carbon pricing and Official Development Assistance (ODA) for climate and biodiversity (OECD, 2023[36]). Various international efforts to collect and organise data exist; however, these usually do not cover all LAC countries. A more comprehensive approach, which supports countries' efforts worldwide towards reaching net-zero GHG emissions and a more resilient economy by 2050, would be equally beneficial for LAC countries.

Data collection can be enhanced in the LAC region through collaboration with other international organisations in the region, and national statistical offices. Support towards national statistical offices and environmental agencies through capacity building and adequate financing can also help countries develop skills to collect data at national and local level and improve capacities in LAC. Such data, combined with other economic statistics, could also promote the System of Environmental Economic Accounting (SEEA) in LAC (Box 4.4). The region still requires detailed and granular environmental data, among others, on matters related to biodiversity inventories, ecosystem mapping, emissions, and air pollution. While SEEA provides a framework for standardising data, the collection of foundational data remains critical and necessary in the region.

Box 4.4. Promoting the System of Environmental Economic Accounting (SEEA) in the LAC region

The SEEA serves as the international statistical standard for natural capital accounting and measuring the relationships between the economy and the environment, recording stocks and flows of environmental assets and their changes. LAC countries are particularly interested in obtaining detailed and effective information on green growth strategies, food security and environmental sustainability, poverty and the environment, climate change, conservation strategies, and environmental planning, among others.

As of 2019, Brazil, Chile, Colombia, Cost Rica, Ecuador, Guatemala, and Mexico had made continuous efforts in developing environmental accounting. Other countries in the region have also made significant progress in environmental accounting, five countries have shown interest, and ten do not have available environmental accounting.

Source: (UN ECLAC, 2019[37]); (Ocampo, 2021[34])

Monitoring and evaluation mechanisms

Expanding MRV and Monitoring, Evaluation, and Learning (MEL) systems are critical for tracking mitigation and adaptation actions in LAC. MRV systems can enhance transparency and accountability, as they help countries demonstrate to stakeholders their efforts to reduce GHG emissions and adapt to climate change. MEL systems help assess the effectiveness of mitigation and adaptation actions and therefore can support countries align their policies with their climate objectives and improve the efficiency of their actions. At the same time, differences in climate risks and uncertainties presented by climate change require countries to adapt their interventions when applying monitoring and evaluation standards (Noltze et al., 2021[38]).

Establishing mechanisms for quality control, verification, and validation of data, and expanding international and regional co-operation for transparent and comparable statistics are also important. The region should aim to expand environmental accounts and comparable information to develop regional environmental accounts. Improving data collection and data quality through a set of commonly used indicators would support further harmonisation which would allow for data validation and transparency (Noltze et al., 2021[38]). Finally, efforts should be made to adopt information technologies, modernise data collection and dissemination methods, and ensure the broad accessibility of environmental statistics (Guevara Sanginés, Mercado García and Lara Pulido, 2020[39]).

Several countries in LAC have implemented MRV and MEL systems, but a gap remains with respect to actual data gathering. Mexico has implemented a National MRV System since 2015, which tracks emissions from forest sources, including deforestation and forest degradation, in line with international efforts to reduce emissions. Additionally, in 2022, Mexico launched a platform for states to evaluate their progress in implementing mitigation and adaptation measures (Government of Mexico, 2022[40]). Colombia has also developed an Environmental Information System (SIAC), an inter-institutional and interdisciplinary system led by the Ministry of Environment. This system gathers diverse environmental information at all levels and across sectors. Moreover, Colombia employs three instruments for environmental data collection: the Forest and Carbon Monitoring System (SMByC), the National Forest Inventory (IFN), and the National Forest Information System (SNIF) (Gómez, 2017[41]); (CODS, 2021[42]). In the Dominican Republic, the National Council for Climate Change and Clean Development Mechanism has developed a National MRV System, which measures, reports, and verifies GHG emissions and climate action at the national level. This system includes the Inventory of Greenhouse Gas Emissions (INGEI) co-ordinated by the Ministry of Environment and Natural Resources, as well as registries and financing systems co-ordinated by relevant ministries (CNCCMDL, 2020[43]). The Dominican Republic's National Adaptation Plan emphasises the strengthening of monitoring and evaluation systems, including the improvement of indicators, particularly those related to vulnerability, to inform decision-making (Presidency of the Dominican Republic, 2016[44]).

Recommendation

- **Collect more and better information for climate change.** Increase standards in non-statistical offices and establish robust co-ordination mechanism to capture existing data. Prioritise the development of new data collection efforts especially in climate change vulnerability and biodiversity. Invest in reliable data collection methods and information technologies while creating accurate indicators to assess the complexity of mitigation and adaptation policies.

Finance for climate action: from international commitments to national measures and private financing

To achieve their emission reduction targets, countries should plan long-term low GHG emission development strategies. Across the LAC region, Argentina, Belize, Chile, Colombia, Costa Rica, Guatemala, Mexico and Uruguay have developed and submitted their national long-term strategies (LTS) to the UNFCCC. Implementing their LTS will require economy-wide transformation, including through infrastructure investments, demand-side adjustments (i.e. energy), as well as appropriate legislation to help reduce emissions and put in place an enabling environment for green investments (Miranda, 2021[45]). LAC countries also often lack the necessary data, tools, or capacity to implement low GHG emission development strategies and therefore complete their emission reduction estimations (UNFCCC, 2021[46]). In addition, and most importantly, many LAC countries only marginally address climate change considerations through their national budgets, nor do they align their fiscal policy with their climate goals. This is especially the case for countries whose budget is allocated to carbon-intensive activities; such as exploration and extraction of hydrocarbons and minerals, and fuel trading, instead of allocating budget towards measures to address climate change and promote sustainable development (i.e. renewable energy and energy efficiency, natural disaster prevention etc) (GFLAC, 2021[47]).

Scaling up finance for climate action, whether international, national, or local, is deemed necessary for countries to reach their international climate commitments, notably the goals of the Paris Agreement. Ramping up of finance is equally important for both mitigation and adaptation action, by reducing GHG emissions and adapt to climate change impacts. LAC countries are especially vulnerable to climate impacts and increased biodiversity loss, and are therefore in need of additional green investments.

To finance the green transition, LAC economies need to increase investment and mobilise resources from both public and private sources. Clean energy and energy efficiency investments will be crucial in achieving a net-zero emissions economy. Mobilising the necessary resources requires implementing the right incentives, phasing out fossil fuel subsidies, and raising additional public revenues through environmental taxes and Emission Trading Systems (ETS). Throughout this process, climate change policies must also ensure a just transition by compensating the most vulnerable. It is important to support sub-national, national, and international development institutions as they play a crucial role in further mobilising public and private resources. Finally, developing regulatory tools such as sustainability and green bonds standards and taxonomies, as already done in a few LAC countries, will be crucial to maintaining transparency and avoiding greenwashing in green investments (OECD et al., 2022[6]).

Reforming government support to fossil fuels: A source of domestic finance

Environmentally sustainable fiscal policies and strategies to mobilise resources from both the public and private sectors can be a source of financing the green transition in the LAC region. It is important for LAC governments to gradually eliminate subsidies for fossil fuels and leverage the potential of sources of revenue that support the green transition. Fossil fuel subsidies strain national budgets, contribute to air pollution (with associated health costs), and send signals to the markets that can decrease the competitiveness of low-carbon alternatives (negatively affecting social and environmental goals) (Rentschler and Bazilian, 2017[48]). Such subsidies often have regressive distributional impacts when not adequately targeted, as they tend to benefit more high-income households with higher fuel and energy consumption. (OECD et al., 2022[6]). Phasing out fossil fuel subsidies, particularly those benefiting wealthier populations, directly frees up financial resources.

In 2020, fossil fuel consumption subsidies in LAC amounted to USD 12 billion (UN ECLAC, 2022[49]), mainly concentrated in eight countries: Argentina, Bolivia, Colombia, Ecuador, El Salvador, Mexico, Trinidad and Tobago, and Venezuela. Phasing out these subsidies, while implementing mitigation or compensation measures for vulnerable sectors, could unlock USD 354 billion in fiscal space over the next decade (UN ECLAC, 2022[49]).

Reforming government support for fossil fuels is a key component of decarbonising the economy and mitigating GHG emissions. Such reforms could free up substantial fiscal resources and improve price signals to expedite the development of lower-carbon alternatives. Since 2016, Argentina, Chile, Colombia, and Mexico have all witnessed an increase in fossil fuel subsidies. In Argentina, Chile, and Colombia, most of the support comes in the form of direct transfers, whereas in Brazil, Costa Rica, and Mexico, support is provided through the tax code in the form of tax expenditures. For many other LAC countries, fossil fuel support is offered through induced transfers, which involve market regulation and price support to maintain lower end-user prices relative to the full cost of supply. The majority of government support is directed towards the production and consumption of petroleum. While LAC countries made progress by reducing government support for fossil fuels by 32% between 2012 and 2019, these subsidies more than doubled in 2021 compared to 2020, primarily due to rising energy prices during the global economic rebound (OECD, 2023[36]).

Generalised fossil fuel subsidies can directly contribute to urban sprawl, reducing the effectiveness of public transport and resulting in higher emissions from increased use of personal vehicles. Achieving a green and just transition in LAC requires a phased elimination of fossil fuel subsidies, establishment or adjustment of environmental taxes, and promotion of productive diversification to expand the tax base. These measures should be implemented within a policy framework that provides support to the firms and households most vulnerable to energy price volatility (UN ECLAC, 2022[49]).

It is crucial for LAC countries to understand the real impact of fossil fuel subsidies and support measures on the most vulnerable populations. Direct conditional and unconditional cash transfers have proven to be a more targeted and cost-efficient approach to assist lower-income households. Countries could also conduct ex-ante assessments of the impacts of subsidy phase-outs on different segments of the population to establish compensatory measures that mitigate any negative effects. Instead of abruptly eliminating subsidies, governments should facilitate a systematic transition that includes inter-ministerial co-ordination, gradual building of trust through socialisation, active government and stakeholder participation, clarity on potential winners and losers through macroeconomic modelling exercises, improved targeting of support, and effective communication of changes to all stakeholders (OECD et al., 2022[6]).

Carbon pricing

Carbon pricing encourages the shift toward low- and zero-carbon options in production and consumption decisions (OECD, 2021[50]). Enhancing carbon pricing could provide an incentive for private actors to make production or consumption decisions consistent with global goals, to limit climate change and mitigate health damage from local pollution. It could also increase revenues used to finance green public-sector investments and ensure a green and just transition. However, carbon pricing is only one of the tools countries use to organise their mitigation efforts. To ensure that any possible negative effects of carbon pricing measures - such as increasing household costs - are mitigated, each country should balance such instruments with governance, innovation, and green budgeting, thus turning risks to opportunities (OECD et al., 2022[6]). In this sense, each country should consider a policy mix and not view carbon pricing as the only approach to mitigate GHG emissions.

Carbon markets and carbon pricing instruments are being acknowledged as part of the mechanisms and tools available for countries to achieve their climate mitigation targets and shift towards a net-zero carbon economy. Setting up a carbon pricing mechanism, such as imposing a carbon tax or fee on emissions could send a clear signal towards more sustainable production and consumption patterns. Depending on how governments design such instruments and how they decide to use revenues collected, carbon pricing could also support aligning other policies to climate mitigation targets towards a green transition and a more sustainable and inclusive development (United Nations, 2021[51])(Box 4.5).

Box 4.5. Costa Rica's Payment for Environmental Services

Costa Rica's Payment for Environmental Services (PES) programme is a pioneering national initiative that compensates landowners for their contributions to carbon storage, hydrological services, and the preservation of biodiversity and landscapes. This programme has received recognition for its remarkable success in reducing deforestation rates in Costa Rica, transforming it from one of the world's highest-deforestation countries to one with net-negative deforestation as of the early 2000s. Between 1997 and 2004, approximately USD 200 million was invested in the PES programme, resulting in the protection of over 460 000 hectares of forests, the establishment of forestry plantations, and the generation of additional income for more than 8 000 forest owners.

Under this programme, landowners receive direct payments for the environmental services their lands provide when they adopt sustainable land-use and forest-management practices. The programme is financed through Costa Rica's fuel tax and water charge, in addition to its own initiatives, such as Certificates of Conservation of Biodiversity, carbon credits, and strategic collaborations with the public and private sectors.

Source : (UNFCCC, 2020[52]); (CBD, n.d.[53])

As of 2022, approximately 23% of global emissions are subject to some form of carbon tax or are regulated by an ETS. In LAC, Argentina, Chile, Colombia, Mexico, and Uruguay have established national carbon taxes. Additionally, five states in Mexico have implemented subnational carbon taxes. Mexico stands out as the sole LAC country with an operational ETS, while Brazil, Chile, and Colombia have announced their intentions to develop similar systems in the future. Moreover, in LAC, Colombia is the only country that has implemented a carbon credit mechanism (World Bank, 2023[54]).

Global revenues from carbon taxes and ETS pricing continued increasing, reaching USD 95 billion in 2023 (World Bank, 2023[54]). OECD's analysis on effective carbon rates (ECRs) for 44 OECD and G20 countries, show that even though there is some improvement in countries' carbon pricing performance when comparing 2015 to 2018 data, less than a fifth of the goal to price all emissions at least at EUR 60 per tonne CO_2 was reached in 2018 (OECD, 2021[50]). Data for OECD member and partner countries in the LAC region indicate that most of them attain an overall score above the 19% average for the 44 countries in the OECD database (Table 4.1). This is rather positive, considering especially that Colombia, Costa Rica, and Mexico mark lowest on CO_2 emissions from energy use (intensities per capita); and Chile marks below OECD average (OECD, 2023[55]).

Table 4.1. LAC countries mostly attain above average carbon pricing scores

2018 data

	Carbon pricing score at EUR 60 per tonne CO_2					
Country	**Road**	**Off-road**	**Industry**	**Agriculture & fisheries**	**Residential & commercial**	**All sectors average**
MEX	97%	4%	0%	4%	1%	30%
ARG	78%	42%	2%	90%	4%	28%
COL	66%	19%	6%	19%	4%	25%
CHL	75%	0%	1%	0%	0%	17%
BRA	4%	0%	0%	0%	0%	1%
All 44 countries average	80%	25%	5%	38%	10%	19%

Note: This table includes emission from the combustion of biomass in the emission base. OECD data on effective carbon rates cover 44 OECD and G20 countries.
Source: (OECD, 2021[50])

Several countries in LAC have established carbon taxes. Chile, with over 17 million hectares of forests, aims to achieve carbon neutrality by 2050. In 2022, the government introduced a carbon tax of approximately USD 5 per metric tonne of CO_2 generated by industries and private drivers, with plans to review the tax rate, potentially reaching USD 35 per metric tonne by 2030. Colombia plans to establish a tax reform that encourages the use of clean energy, reduces pollution, and aims to collect about USD 3.4 billion per year. The country's goal is to reduce its emissions by 51% by 2030.

Voluntary carbon markets raised approximately USD 2 billion in revenues and have evolved to become more sophisticated, featuring new investors, financial products, technological platforms, and service providers, setting the stage for significant growth in the next decade. Carbon credit markets have the potential to support the deployment and scaling up of technological removals of CO_2, but this will largely depend on a significant increase in credit prices (World Bank, 2023[54]).

LAC countries hold enormous potential for the development of carbon credit markets, thanks to their extensive forests and biomes. In 2021, credits generated by the forestry and land-use sector accounted for over 60% of the trading volume and 70% of the market value. Afforestation and reforestation projects represented about 50% of all registered Nature-based Solution (NbS) projects, while avoided deforestation accounted for 19%. Since 2020, LAC has become the second-largest region in terms of volume for carbon credits traded on voluntary markets, trailing only Asia. Additionally, LAC holds the second-largest reserve of unused carbon credits, exceeding 100 million, which could be considered in future negotiations. The volume of credits offered by the region nearly doubled between 2020 and 2021, with more than 80% of LAC credits originating from forestry and land-use projects. Brazil and Peru were the largest producers of carbon credits in the region (CAF, 2022[56]).

In May 2022, the Brazilian government signed a decree regulating the carbon credit market, intending to export credits to countries and companies that need to offset emissions. The carbon market is expected to bring revenues of up to USD 100 billion to Brazil. A study carried out by the International Chamber of Commerce of Brazil has noted that in the next decade, the country has the potential to supply 5% to 37.5% of the global demand for voluntary carbon credits and up to 22% of the global regulated market demand. In 2018, Mexico established a voluntary carbon market without mandatory targets (Maciel, 2022[57]).

Carbon markets present significant environmental integrity risks that countries must address when developing or establishing them. Four key factors influence environmental integrity: accounting for international transfers, the quality of generated units i.e., whether the mechanism ensures that the issuance or transfer of units leads to emission reductions in the transferring country, the ambition and scope of the transferring country's mitigation targets, and incentives or disincentives for future mitigation actions (Schneider and La Hoz Theuer, 2018[58]). Countries in LAC should carefully consider these factors when creating carbon markets to minimise environmental risks, avoid greenwashing, and mobilise sustainable finance. To ensure environmental integrity, countries must establish clear common goals, set time-bound actions, define measurement baselines, gain consensus on scope, and ensure alignment at various levels. Concerns about the integrity of voluntary carbon markets can damage confidence in global carbon credit markets, making it essential for LAC countries to prioritise supply-side integrity, preventing one credit from equating to less than one real tCO_2e avoided, removed, or reduced, and avoiding double counting of resources and CO_2, while preserving social and environmental objectives. Additionally, they should consider market integrity, reducing information asymmetries, and creating interoperable, liquid, and standardised markets. Lastly, demand-side integrity should be a priority, emphasising mitigation over offset use, high-quality uniquely claimed credits, and transparent reporting (Oueslati, 2023[59]).

International climate finance and challenges for LAC countries

The mitigation and adaptation efforts needed to address climate change in LAC will require significant financing. Estimates show that the region needs between USD 90 to USD 100 billion per year to achieve its climate goals (Ivanova et al., 2021[60]). However, many countries in LAC lack the financial capacity to cover these costs, making external financing from both the public and private sectors essential. The Glasgow Pact emphasised the need for developed countries to deliver on the USD 100 billion goal and urged multilateral development banks and other financial institutions to increase both their investments and climate finance effectiveness. Scaling up financial resources requires a clear understanding of each country's vulnerabilities and needs impacted by climate change, as well as simplified and enhanced access to finance (UNFCCC, 2022[61]).

LAC[1] is the third region in terms of climate finance[2] provided and mobilised by developed countries between 2016 and 2020. Only an annual average of USD 1.5 billion was received for SIDS, where the Caribbean is the part of the world with more countries with that status (OECD, 2022[62]). In the Caribbean, per-capita GHG emissions are high, despite the small population size. In this regard, countries like Barbados, Grenada, and Trinidad and Tobago stood out as top emitters in the Caribbean in 2019. When analysing the top 10 countries with the highest total emissions, Argentina, Paraguay and Venezuela feature prominently, reflecting significant per capita emissions levels (OECD et al., 2022[6]).

International climate finance is not enough to cover all financial needs for LAC countries. In parallel to what is provided and mobilised by bilateral and multilateral donors, private finance is vital in achieving LAC countries' climate commitments. Sustainability-linked debt and equity markets can play a crucial role in mobilising private finance that can support climate actions (Ivanova et al., 2021[60]).

To achieve the temperature and adaptation goals of the Paris Agreement, it is crucial for LAC countries to develop robust climate policies accompanied by investment policy reforms that remove barriers to attracting private finance and investment, stimulate market growth, and mitigate regulatory risks to enable the development of bankable projects (OECD/The World Bank/UN Environment, 2018[63]). These efforts should be supported by capacity-building, especially for transformative fiscal policy, and by enhancing LAC countries' advocacy for increased financial support and external resources for their conditional NDCs.

International climate finance provided to and mobilised for LAC

Most of the climate finance provided and mobilised in developing countries by developed countries between 2013 and 2020 was public (bilateral and multilateral), although private finance mobilised by these donors increased by about 30% from 2016 to 2020 globally (OECD, 2022[62]). Considering the trillions needed globally to meet climate and development objectives by 2030 development banks must not only mobilise domestic and foreign private sector capital but also support governments in project planning, development, and deployment (OECD/The World Bank/UN Environment, 2018[63]); (Prasad et al., 2022[64]).

In the LAC region, public climate finance provided between 2016 and 2020 was by a large majority loans (81%) and a smaller part grants (17%), while the share of equity was only at 2% (OECD, 2022[65]). Other analysis shows there is variation in loan access, with the majority of such financing going to Brazil, Mexico, and Colombia (The Dialogue, 2023[66]). LAC countries also benefited from 26% of the total private climate finance mobilised during the period 2016-20 (OECD, 2022[65]).

In LAC, funding is predominantly directed towards mitigation rather than adaptation, even though LAC countries are prioritising and accelerating adaptation projects related to water, agriculture, infrastructure, and NbS. The Caribbean, in particular, requires significant financing for adaptation projects due to vulnerabilities to climate change and extreme weather events. Adaptation and resilience prioritisation could also contribute towards cost-effective emissions abatement, considering the region's vulnerability to climate risks (Miranda, 2021[45]).

Between 2016 and 2020, Small Island Developing States (SIDS) accounted for 2% of the total climate finance provided and mobilised (OECD, 2022[62]). Moreover, during this period, nearly 48% of the climate finance allocated to SIDS was directed towards adaptation efforts. Additionally, 12% of the total climate finance allocated to SIDS was earmarked for cross-cutting objectives. Over these five years, a cumulative total of USD 3.6 billion was allocated and mobilised for adaptation efforts in SIDS, averaging USD 0.7 billion annually (OECD, 2022[65]). The Caribbean region, which hosts the largest number of SIDS, faces significant vulnerability to biodiversity loss and climate change, driven in part by their limited economic alternatives. This vulnerability is further compounded by factors such as small population sizes, remoteness from international markets, high transport costs, susceptibility to external economic shocks, and fragile land and marine ecosystems. Additionally, the slow onset of events like sea-level rise poses an existential threat to these small island communities, necessitating drastic measures like population relocation, with all the associated challenges. These challenges are exacerbated by limited institutional capacity, scarce financial resources, and a high degree of susceptibility to systemic shocks.

Multilateral banks have made ambitious commitments to scale up climate action and are intensifying their efforts to increase green and climate finance activities. CAF announced during COP26 that it will increase financing for green projects from 24% in 2020 to 40% in 2026, allocating USD 25 billion over the next five years to promote green growth (CAF, 2021[67]). The Green Climate Fund (GCF) approved approximately USD 3 billion for 32 climate projects worldwide in 2021, surpassing the previous year's record of USD 2.1 billion. The GCF's portfolio reached USD 10 billion by the end of 2021, with over USD 37 billion in co-financing and 190 projects in 127 countries (GCF, 2021[68]). The Global Environment Facility (GEF) invested a quarter of its portfolio to the LAC region in 2022 (GEF, 2022[69]). The IDB approved nearly USD 4.5 billion for climate-related operations in 2021, accounting for 30% of its total annual approvals (IDB, 2022[70]). The World Bank's International Bank for Reconstruction and Development (IBRD) and the International Development Association (IDA) have provided over USD 5.8 billion in lending to support climate actions in LAC countries (World Bank, 2021[71]).

Mobilising private finance for climate action

Between 2012 and 2021, Argentina, Brazil, Colombia, Ecuador, and Mexico ranked among the top 20 beneficiary countries, collectively receiving over USD 40 billion in mobilised private climate-related development finance. The region received 17% of total mobilised private finance, equivalent to USD 8.5 billion, from 2018 to 2020 (OECD, 2023[72]). LAC countries need to secure significant investments from both public and private sources and innovate their financial instruments and strategies. Implementing environmentally related taxes can generate additional revenues, incentivise sustainable behaviour, and expedite the shift towards green practices. At the same time, the region could scale up the use of debt tools, including green, social, sustainable, and sustainability-linked (GSSS) bonds, explore debt-for-nature swaps, and leverage catastrophe (CAT) bonds and natural disaster clauses.

Many countries in LAC have high levels of external debt, making resources for environmental protection limited. According to the World Bank, Caribbean countries had external debt stocks of approximately 165% of exports of goods and services in 2013, while Mesoamerica had 130% and South America had just over 100%. In this sense, resources targeting environmental protection are usually limited (UNEP, 2017[73]). In terms of Green, Social, and Sustainability (GSS) debt issuance in LAC, the market has more than doubled from USD 13.6 billion in 2019 to USD 30.2 billion in early 2021. Social and sustainability bond issuance reached USD 18.3 billion in 2019. Total GSS issuance in 2020 amounted to USD 16.3 billion, reaching USD 12.5 billion by September 2021. Green bonds represent the largest share in the LAC market, accounting for 62% of GSS issuance. Chile (USD 17.8 billion) and Brazil (USD 11.7 billion) are the largest issuers of GSS bonds, with Mexico in third place at USD 7.8 billion. These top three countries make up 77% of all GSS issuance in the LAC region. The number of green bond issuances in LAC increased from 8 in 2019 to 12, with the addition of Barbados, Bermuda, Ecuador, and Panama (Climate Bonds Initiative, 2021[74]).

Several sustainable finance mechanisms and instruments are incorporating concerns from shareholders, investors, and consumers, such green and sustainability debt and equity products. For example, Panama Stock Exchange introduced voluntary reporting and disclosure guidelines for ESG factors in 2019, while Colombia issued its Green Bonds and Best Practices Guide in 2020 to promote the development of a bond market in the country. The Dominican Republic also released Green Bond Guidelines to standardise good practices for issuers. In the LAC region, sovereign green bonds primarily focus on energy projects, followed by transport, water, and land use (Climate Bonds Initiative, 2021[74]).

Blended finance offers a potential solution to support LAC countries on their way towards a more sustainable transition. Blended finance can help address the risk-return and low bankability of investments by combining public and private financing and structuring various financial instruments (direct investments, credit lines, bonds, grants, etc.). It can facilitate private investments in project financing structures, particularly in cases of high financial or commercial risk, by mitigating the risk of default that often discourages investors (OECD, 2022[75]).

At the same time blended finance has been slow to flow into the LAC region, primarily due to the absence of policies and frameworks guiding the engagement of developing countries, including Least Developed Countries (LDCs) and SIDS, in attracting, deploying, and scaling blended finance. Additionally, implementation and capacity challenges have hindered the scaling of blended finance in developing countries. Blended finance provides an opportunity to align local financing priorities with local development goals, addressing underfunded social sectors in many developing countries, which are structural obstacles to achieving the SDGs. Therefore, it is essential to offer further insights and guidance on various aspects, including macroeconomic fundamentals, governance, regulatory frameworks, infrastructure and market characteristics. At an operational level, addressing contract risks, streamlining pipeline origination and project preparation, reducing high transaction costs resulting from small deal sizes, exploring untested business models, and filling information and data gaps are all critical steps required to scale blended finance, especially in the context of social sectors (OECD, 2022[76]).

In addition to climate finance, the financial sector also needs to support businesses and sectors in adopting cleaner technologies, improving energy efficiency, and transforming the economy. Policymakers have several tools at their disposal to ensure actionable and credible targets, supporting private sector investments with positive environmental impacts. The OECD Guidance on Transition Finance aims to promote the mainstreaming of credible transition planning across public and private entities, as well as the inclusion of meaningful assessment of transition plans in the considerations of financial market participants. By addressing challenges and barriers such as unclear standards and definitions, difficulties in measuring sustainability performance, and the risk of greenwashing, the Guidance proposes elements of credible corporate climate transition plans. These elements can support the growth of the transition finance market while ensuring environmental integrity (OECD, 2022[77]).

Sustainable finance or green taxonomies can support meeting the financial needs necessary to reach climate change commitments and achieve targets. Green taxonomies, which are comprehensive classification systems, also help investors in identifying environmentally sustainable activities and invest in sustainable infrastructure, while preventing greenwashing. Furthermore, by classifying economic activities as green or sustainable, companies may also evaluate the "greenness" of their own business activities and practices.

LAC countries are slowly developing official definitions on sustainable finance linked to Paris Agreement goals; with Colombia being the first country in the region to implement a Green Taxonomy in 2022. The Colombian Green Taxonomy covers two pillars. The first pillar focuses on several sectors, such as energy, construction, transport, manufacturing etc, with an objective to achieve climate mitigation. The second pillar focuses on land use in the livestock, agriculture and forestry sectors. The first pillar is also governed by the "Do No Significant Harm" (DNSH) principle, arguing that any assets to be considered green should not only contribute to climate mitigation, but also avoid harming environmental objectives of climate adaptation. The second pillar, even though it does not follow the DNSH principle, sets adaptation as one of the five environmental objectives. However, implementing the green taxonomies may be hampered by several challenges, such as lack of environmental data and information at the company level, as well as limitations in understanding the scope and reasoning behind implementation (Prada Hernández et al., 2023[78]).

In March 2023 Mexico also presented its Sustainable Taxonomy, which addresses climate change; gender equality; and access to basic services at the local level. Climate adaptation, as well as ecosystems and biodiversity conservation are two of the six environmental objectives set, while the taxonomy also sets social objectives, including access to basic services in municipalities. It covers six sectors: agriculture and forestry; energy; manufacturing; transport; construction; and waste management (Souza and Gasparotto, 2023[79]).

Other LAC countries, such as Chile, are developing their own Green Taxonomies. Chile's objectives are both climate mitigation and adaptation and resilience; and it will cover "brown" sectors such as mining. It is being considered to include minimum social safeguards and later develop social metrics. Adding social objectives when developing Green Taxonomies allows for issues such as social cohesion, local economic development, and local vulnerabilities to be taken into consideration, under the overall target of sustainability (Merle, Gondjian and Gong, 2021[80]). Introducing, also, considerations of local needs and specificities and linking the taxonomies to regional and local adaptation plans, could help educate the local markets and encourage them to develop green products (CBI, 2021[81]).

Developing a common regional framework for taxonomies in the LAC region would further provide clarity and transparency, facilitating the comparability and interoperability between the LAC region and other regions that are introducing their own frameworks. It would also support increasing climate flows in sustainable projects (UNDP, 2022[82]). The recently released Common Framework for Sustainable Finance Taxonomies for LAC countries by UNEP is a guidance document for those countries and stakeholders in the region that are in the process of developing taxonomies. Based on similar principles, taxonomies following this Common Framework would guarantee some level of interoperability, therefore could help pave the way towards the development of a regional taxonomy with clear prioritisation of economic sectors and activities, as well as metrics system to define screening criteria (UNEP, 2023[83]).

Recommendation

- **Adopt green fiscal policies to generate domestic public resources to support climate action and carbon mitigation approaches**. Reform, redirect and progressive eliminate fossil fuel subsidies and establish carbon pricing through taxes and levies, which can also incentivise the net zero transition.
- **Align and mobilise private investment support through innovative financing strategies and instruments**, such as blended finance aligned with Environmental, Social and Governance (ESG) objectives, innovative debt instruments, and by developing regional and national green taxonomies for mitigation and adaptation projects. These should respond to local priorities and concerns and be coherent with public and private investment opportunities.

Technology innovation and transfer to enhance green development.

Technology transfer to developing countries has been a key mandate of the UNFCCC. It encompasses the transfer of both technology and know-how, which includes capacity building. This transfer aims to address technical, legal, and administrative barriers, establish sound economic policies, and promote the implementation of climate-friendly technologies (World Bank, 2007[84]). The term refers to technology deployment for climate change mitigation and adaptation, including infrastructure, operations, manufacturing, and innovation. It also covers the development of institutional and policy capabilities to facilitate technology diffusion and co-operation within and between countries (Garrett and Moarif, 2018[85]). The role of technological innovation and technology transfer in achieving environmental objectives has been widely recognised and emphasised during international climate negotiations (COP UNFCCC). Moreover, it can facilitate productive transformation towards less resource-intensive sectors, by attracting greener investments and by joining higher-value global supply chains with environmental and sustainability criteria (OECD et al., 2022[6]).

Productivity and competitiveness in the LAC region could improve with technology transfer and innovation. Innovative technologies are necessary to support infrastructure's resilience to climate change. This is necessary both for the local communities and population, but also for productive economic sectors which need to adapt to climate change. Globally, countries are introducing policy measures tackling issues such as droughts, rising sea levels, flooding, and soil degradation, which have an effect on water supplies, food availability and security, energy supply, and buildings' resilience. On the other hand, past analysis by the OECD has shown that the main determinants of international climate change mitigation technology transfer, measured by patent activity, include geographic distance and level of trade between countries, existing human capital in recipient countries, stringency or flexibility in national environmental policies, and level of investment for in-house technology development in medium- and large-sized industrial facilities (Haščič et al., 2010[86]). LAC countries grapple with low productivity, economic dependence on low-value-added sectors, and limited economic diversification, hindering competitiveness and overall development. Innovation holds the potential to overcome these challenges and bridge productivity gaps resulting from high informality, low skill levels, and limited technology adoption (OECD/CAF, 2019[87]).

Patents and trademarks often serve as indicators of technological and non-technological innovation, respectively. LAC countries may not be among the major contributors to innovation, but the region's average follows the global trend. In 2019, environment-related patents in LAC countries accounted, on average, for about 15% of total patents, compared to just above 11% globally and an OECD average of about 4.5%. Nevertheless, this figure is driven by a few countries such as Antigua and Barbuda, Guatemala, and Paraguay, which demonstrate a high percentage of environment-related patents in total patents, due to the very low number of total patents (Figure 4.1). On the contrary, the LAC countries with the highest number of environment-related patents in the region are Brazil, Chile, and Mexico (OECD, 2023[55]).

Even though climate change technology innovation and transfer may benefit countries' transformation, not all LAC countries have the same capacity or framework to absorb such technology. Enhancing this capacity requires the implementation of public policies which can accelerate innovation, promote international co-operation, and ensure compliance with environmental and sustainability criteria. Based on comparative analysis by the IDB, examining "Climate Technology Transfer Mechanisms and Networks in Latin America and the Caribbean", the following points could be highlighted to facilitate climate technology transfer:

- R&D national strategies and technological roadmaps for specific technologies must be deployed.
- Increasing the levels of investment in R&D and innovation is necessary to implement R&D strategies.
- Low-price imports jeopardise the development of local innovative products, while a strong local manufacturing sector supports the adoption and diffusion of new green technology products.
- An enabling environment can support the development of local green technology or allow for technology transfer, i.e., a set of support measures such as investment subsidies, subsidised financing, financial guarantees, tax benefits, access and connection to infrastructure networks.

Figure 4.1. Percentage of environment-related patents over all patents

2019 data for LAC countries

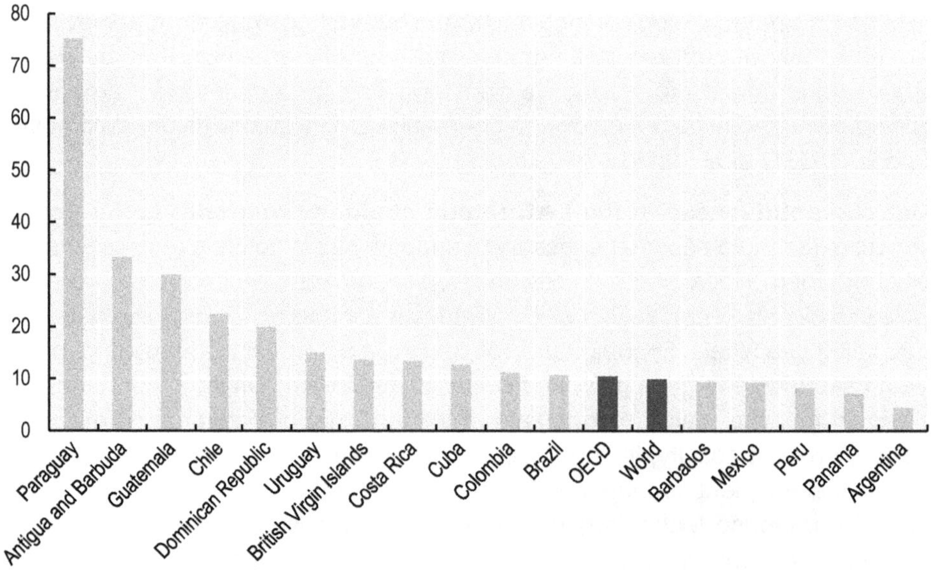

Note: Environmental innovation measured using patent data. Data based on inventor's country of residence.
Source: (OECD, 2023[88])

Countries would need to clearly identify their technology needs. The Technology Needs Assessment (TNA), introduced since COP7, allows countries to both prioritise technologies based on their social, economic and environmental impacts, as well as their climate change mitigation or adaptation potential. Developing countries tend, however, to prioritise technology that is already mature, meaning technology that is low-cost, easily accessible, and often already in the country. On the contrary, technologies that are linked to niche markets, such as electric vehicles, carbon capture, hydrogen fuel cells etc, are very rarely deployed beyond a certain geographical region (UNEP, 2022[89]).

There are various mechanisms and networks that promote climate technology development and transfer from developed to developing countries. International development co-operation provides leverage for addressing the lack of finance, capacity, and policy support in facilitating climate technology transfer (UNEP, 2022[89]). International organisations are also developing mechanisms and instruments to enable technology transfer. The UNEP Climate Technology Centre and Network offer technical assistance to developing countries, aiming to provide access to knowledge on climate technologies and foster collaboration among climate technology stakeholders. In the LAC region, UNEP has launched regional programmes and projects to support countries' responses to climate change. The Regional Getaway for Technology Transfer and Climate Change Action for Latin America and the Caribbean (REGATTA) strengthens capacity and knowledge sharing of climate change technologies for both mitigation and adaptation in the region (REGATTA, n.d.[90]). MOVE is an initiative that supports the transition to electric mobility in the region by preparing local actors to evaluate new technologies and identify funding opportunities (MOVE, n.d.[91]). The OECD Clean Energy Finance and Investment Mobilisation (CEFIM) programme supported Colombia's efforts to attract finance and investment in clean energy, a sector highly dependable on green innovation and technology. Mobilising finance and investment for bioenergy in Colombia should be complemented by building awareness in the national energy market and enabling capacity to implement such projects (OECD, 2022[92]).

Recommendation

- **Support industrial development and promote innovation.** Undertake a green industrialisation pathway by promoting local production of environmentally friendly clean technologies and innovation. This may include manufacturing electric vehicles, wind turbines, batteries, and solar heaters. It could support the region to reduce public debt, boost economic resilience, create job opportunities, and promote more equitable income distribution.

Green jobs supporting the transition to a low-carbon economy

Enhancing the green transition in the LAC region is expected to have several effects in the labour market. The shift to a low-carbon economy will mean changes in economic sectors that score high at emitting GHG, with a possible phasing-out of certain activities; as well as an enforcement of economic activities that are more "green", as renewable energy, sustainable agriculture and tourism. At the same time, climate change phenomena, such as rising temperatures, are expected to impact productivity levels, equivalent to a loss of 2.5 million full-time jobs in the LAC region by 2030 (ILO, 2019[93]).

The green transition in LAC is expected to add over 10% more net jobs in the LAC region. Not all of these will be green jobs, nor will they be jobs in green economic activities (OECD et al., 2022[6]) (Box 4.6). As extensively analysed over the (OECD et al., 2022[6]) Latin America Economic Outlook 2022, to guarantee that the jobs created will be green and will serve in preserving or restoring the environment, some prerequisites need to be met:

- Securing financing and supporting public and private investments towards green innovation, technologies and economic activities, so that new employment will be created.
- Offsetting socioeconomic effects of the transition to a low-carbon economy and the potential job losses, by introducing well-designed active labour market policies, such as training, re-skilling and up-skilling to new or existing workers, respectively; and guaranteeing continuity in social protection coverage.
- Expanding social protection systems to minimise any income losses, attract more workers in the formal economy, and reduce any inequalities that often affect the most vulnerable.

Box 4.6. What are green jobs?

The International Labour Organisation (ILO) defines green jobs as "decent jobs that contribute to preserve or restore the environment, be they in traditional sectors such as manufacturing and construction, or in new, emerging green sectors such as renewable energy and energy efficiency". Green jobs help improve energy and raw materials efficiency; reduce GHG emissions; decrease waste and pollution; protect and restore ecosystems; and support climate change adaptation.

Source: (ILO, n.d.[94])

Fostering job creation in new green technologies through a tailored mix of innovation and employment incentives, training schemes and placement services, could help innovative companies emerging in green industries to create higher-paying formal jobs. By applying well-designed social and labour policies, innovative companies emerging in green industries could create higher-paying formal jobs. Active labour market policies could focus on protecting workers against job losses linked to the green transformation, through designed and co-ordinated social assistance measures, individual unemployment accounts and policies that enable the most vulnerable workers affected by the transition to a green economy. Targeted up-skilling, re-skilling and re-training is necessary to tackle any short- and medium-term effects of the green transition. In parallel, access to such training should also be available for new workers wanting to enter the workforce, such as women (OECD, 2022[95]). It would also be necessary to ensure sustainable financing of these measures, so as to create a minimum threshold of social protection for those with no access to unemployment benefits or assistance; and to guarantee universal access to essential health care and a targeted basic income (OECD et al., 2022[6]).

The transition to a green economy could also affect the levels of informality in the labour market in the LAC region. LAC is one of the regions where informality thrives (OECD/ILO, 2019[96]). The green transition could on the one hand create more formal jobs; especially as new productive companies related to green technologies emerge. On the other hand, informality could also increase in some sectors, such as in retrofitting buildings or in brown supply chains of green sectors (Saget, Vogt-Schilb and Luu, 2020[97]) Training programmes that can help unemployed people gain employment in environmental sectors and green occupations, combined with wage subsidies and the opportunity to gain formal experience is a way of reducing informality during the green transition. Initiatives strengthening self-employment and entrepreneurship programmes through active labour market policies could also help formalise micro-enterprises negatively affected by the transition (OECD et al., 2022[6]).

Finally, policies introduced should also address any environmental health risks deriving from existing or new economic activities, by expanding general health coverage and/or targeting the people most at risk, such as those without adequate sanitation or access to good-quality water or air (OECD et al., 2022[6]).

Recommendation

- **Establish investment and policy frameworks that promote the creation of green jobs**. Ensure the implementation of active labour market policies, relying on effective social dialogue, to facilitate the transition of workers into new, formal, high-quality green jobs and strengthen the social security system to support both workers and entrepreneurs in transitioning to a low-carbon economy.

Waste Management and Circular Economy

Implementing efficient waste management policies and infrastructure in LAC can unlock green development, create jobs, and curb methane emissions. LAC generates almost 1 kg of waste per capita daily, with 85% of the waste being collected in urban areas. Waste collection coverage varies across countries, ranging from 95% in cities in Uruguay and Colombia to 12% in Port au Prince in Haiti. Developing and improving the waste and recycling sector in LAC could promote green development, create approximately 450 000 jobs, and increase the region's GDP by 0.35% if a municipal recycling rate equivalent to that of Germany is achieved (UN ECLAC, 2021[98]). Currently, the region produces 541 000 tonnes of municipal waste per day, with an estimated 25% increase by 2050. Many cities in the region still rely on open dumps, leading to significant methane emissions. Open dumpsites receive 145 000 tonnes of waste daily, including 17 000 tonnes of plastic waste. Approximately 50% of municipal waste in the region is organic, and 90% of waste is not utilised (UN Environment, 2018[99]). LAC countries could implement more effective and efficient waste management policies such as waste separation at source and organic waste treatment, building adequate waste collection and treatment infrastructure, and promotion of waste recycling practices (UN Environment, 2018[99]). These measures can significantly reduce methane emissions and enhance the quality of life in cities.

Addressing plastic pollution is crucial, considering its impact on climate change and the environment. Plastic pollution is a massive source of waste and an accelerator to climate change. Plastics generate GHG emissions throughout their lifecycle, with about 90% of GHG emissions from plastics being attributed to the production and conversion stage (OECD, 2022[100]). Furthermore, LAC's beaches have some of the highest levels of litter density, with almost 90% of plastics mismanaged or sent to landfills, and only 10% being recycled in 2019. The region's plastic waste generation is projected to double by 2060 (Figure 4.2). It is estimated that LAC could almost entirely prevent plastic leakages into its aquatic environments by 2060 at an annual cost of 0.74% of its GDP (OECD et al., 2022[6]). Plastic-specific policies must target different lifecycle stages, these should include fiscal instruments discouraging plastic production and use, product design improvements to enhance durability and promote reuse and repair, measures to increase recycling rates, and investments in waste management infrastructure and litter collection (OECD, 2022[100]).

Figure 4.2. Plastic waste by end-of-life fate in 2019 and projections for 2060

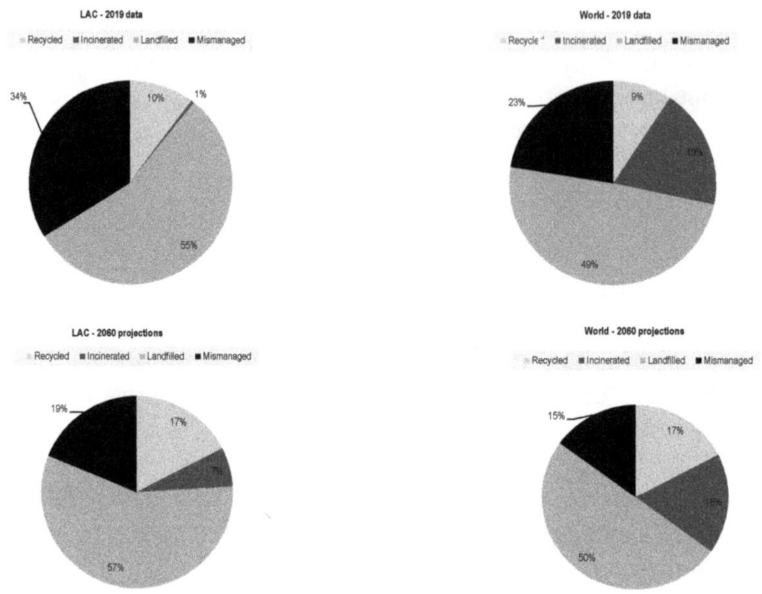

Note: Latin America and the Caribbean (LAC) figure covers both OECD and non-OECD countries in the LAC region.
Source: (OECD, 2023[101]), "Global Plastics Outlook: Plastic waste by end-of-life fate and region - projections", OECD Environment Statistics (database), https://doi.org/10.1787/e4e8c086-en (accessed on 26 September 2023).

LAC countries should design policies considering the entire life cycle of products, including production, consumption, waste management, and recycling. Investments from the public and private sectors will be greatly needed, as well as an increase in capacity building, innovation, and technology transfer. Transitioning to the circular economy also requires co-ordination of LAC countries' national and international efforts. Harmonising standards for circular economy goods, reducing tariffs and non-tariff barriers, and enhancing the granularity of international trade classifications can help firms, countries, and regional actors adopt sustainable practices (OECD et al., 2022[6]).

LAC countries must strengthen their legal frameworks and implement Extended Producer Responsibility (EPR) schemes to effectively manage hazardous waste and promote recycling. EPRs aim to hold producers accountable for the environmental impacts of their products throughout the product chain, promoting pollution reduction and material circularity. EPR schemes, based on the polluter-pays principle, establish collective Producer Responsibility Organisations (PRO) to manage producer contributions, eliminating the need for additional state budgetary resources (UNEP, 2022[102]). Until 2017, 11 LAC countries had developed solid waste management regulations with some form of EPR schemes (Quispe, 2017[103]). However, there is a lack of formal regulations and overall implementation of legal frameworks. Developing robust legal regulations that adopt a whole-life-cycle approach and enhance EPR policies is vital.

Countries like Argentina, Brazil, Chile, Ecuador, Mexico, and Peru have mandated packaging producers and importers to declare material volumes through Pollutant Release and Transfer Registers. For instance, in 2021 Chile published a decree introducing new EPR packaging requirements, including obligatory recycling rates starting in September 2023. Chile is also developing guidelines for the Container and Packaging Management System (SIGENEM) in collaboration with 25 important consumption product companies (Langhill, 2021[104]). In 2020, Colombia approved a law establishing EPR for glass, metal, aluminium, paper, and cardboard packaging. Packers, fillers, and importers of packaged products are required to submit waste management plans, and since 2021, producers must meet reuse targets for waste packaging, with geographic coverage targets starting in 2022 (Langhill, 2021[104]). Brazil has a Sectorial Agreement on Reverse Logistics for General Packaging that requires information provision to consumers about suitable ways to return packaging materials and facilitate their recycling, invest in waste management co-operatives, and legal agreements with retailers and waste management systems to establish voluntary collection points (Langhill, 2021[104]).

The transition towards a resource efficient, circular economy can help improve material use, and environmental, economic and social outcomes. Overcoming challenges related to resource management and promoting the sustainable use of materials are necessary steps towards the transition from a linear to a circular economy. In parallel, introducing circular economy policies requires a transformation of existing policies and sectors, to guarantee that synergies and trade-offs are taken into consideration (Box 4.7).

Box 4.7. Synergies and trade-offs when applying circular economy policies.

Countries around the globe are introducing resource-efficient and circular economy (RE-CE) policies, which include economic, environmental and social objectives, which may create synergies or carry trade-offs, affecting the implementation of the policies.

The OECD has grouped these synergies and trade-offs in four key objectives:

1. **Reducing primary material extraction and increasing resource efficiency**, through taxation on primary materials use, and subsidies to support the secondary materials sector.
2. **Strengthening markets for secondary materials and promoting materials circularity**, through the implementation of coherent policies that lead to proper incentive mechanisms, as well as the presence of well-functioning markets for secondary materials.
3. **Managing waste to minimise associated environmental impacts**, by aligning waste management policies with incentives to primarily reduce, re-use and recycle materials, before turning to incineration or landfilling.
4. **Building economic resilience and reducing geopolitical supply risks through materials circularity**, strong domestic recycling and secondary sectors, in line with trade agreements.

Source: (Livingstone et al., 2022[105])

Costa Rica has one of the lowest levels of municipal waste generated per capita, among the OECD members. Nevertheless, municipal waste generation has gradually increased since 2016, and the country's landfills still receive 80% of all municipal waste. While the country has made progress in closing illegal dumpsites, waste disposal in inappropriate sites remains considerable, especially in rural regions. There has been progress in waste management but local governments face difficulties in guaranteeing selective, accessible, regular and efficient waste collection and treatment services. Costa Rica needs to increase waste collection and recovery, improve sorting at source, and invest in modern waste treatment infrastructure to divert waste from landfills, curbing GHG emissions from the waste sector, which make for 15% of national emissions. Waste collection fees could be better designed to cover the costs of the service and encourage waste sorting. Costa Rica should also include major waste streams – such as organic, packaging and construction and demolition waste – into EPR schemes and set mandatory recovery targets. Incentives for the use of recovered and recycled materials as inputs into production processes are needed to develop a domestic market, as well as an integrated and publicly accessible digital platform to provide data on waste collection and treatment, as well as quantities of materials disposed and viable for recycling. Currently, the government has been updating the National Waste Management Plan and developing the National Circular Economy Strategy, as well as promoting the principles of the circular economy in local governments and businesses through technical guidelines, organisational standards, and training. In 2022, more than 40 municipalities were trained on facilitating the transition to a circular economy for local governments (OECD, 2023[106]).

The circular economy is a fundamental step towards achieving climate targets as it offers a systemic approach to reducing emissions and increasing resilience to the effects of climate change. It also promotes the creation of more liveable cities, the distribution of value throughout the economy, and stimulates innovation. The circular economy is built on three important principles: i) designing out waste and pollution, ii) keeping products and materials in use, and iii) regenerating natural systems (Ellen Macarthur Foundation, 2019[107]). These models provide an opportunity to restore and maintain the usefulness of products, components, and materials, preserving their value through changes in production models, redesigned processes and products, as well as the creation of new business models and added value. LAC countries can take several actions to support the circular economy. These include formalising recyclers, applying EPR criteria, and improving collection, treatment, and final disposal systems. Promotion of reuse should be central, as currently, only 4% of urban waste is recycled on average in LAC, which contrasts with the approximately 20% recycling rate in developed countries (UN ECLAC, 2021[98]). At the same time, it is essential for countries to develop national strategies or roadmaps that define guidelines and targets with short, medium, and long-term visions. In LAC, eight countries have already revised their circular economy roadmaps, namely Argentina, Brazil, Chile, Colombia, Costa Rica, Ecuador, Uruguay, and Peru (Samaniego et al., 2022[108]).

Recommendation

- **Advance with sectoral roadmaps.** Achieving a circular economy requires a state policy on Extended Producer Responsibility (EPR) and modification of unsustainable consumption practices. Productive sectors, commerce, and society at large should assume their role in the efficient use of materials and resources through their entire lifecycle, waste minimisation, recycling and re-use must be intrinsic to market rules.

Sustainable Ocean Economy

Healthy and productive oceans offer multiple benefits, including economic opportunities, food security, resilient coastal ecosystems, and climate change adaptation. The blue economy - which encompasses the sustainable use of ocean resources for economic growth, improved livelihoods and jobs, and ocean ecosystem health - spans over various ocean sectors, including renewable energy, fisheries, maritime transport, climate, tourism, disaster risk management, and waste management and wastewater treatment (World Bank, 2023[109]). Given the essential role of the ocean in human well-being and economic activities, protecting marine and coastal ecosystems is crucial for fostering sustainable growth in LAC while protecting marine and coastal ecosystems (OECD et al., 2022[6]).

A sustainable ocean economy has the potential to significantly contribute to the development of the LAC region. Ocean services alone estimated to have contributed USD 25 billion to the total GDP of LAC in 2018, and USD 7 billion to the Caribbean's GDP (OECD et al., 2022[6]); (World Bank, 2023[109]). Over one-fourth of the population in LAC live in coastal areas, and almost all population in the Caribbean. The fishery and aquaculture sectors employ over 2.3 million people in the region. The region's ocean areas, particularly in Chile, Ecuador, and Peru, are known for their productivity, accounting for up to 20%

of the world's catch in some fisheries and capturing blue carbon. Moreover, the Eastern Caribbean and the Galapagos archipelagos, known for their marine biodiversity, attract substantial international tourism, with tourism contributing up to 50% of GDP in some Eastern Caribbean countries. Implementing blue policies can foster sustainable economic opportunities in the fishery and aquaculture sectors, sustainable tourism, and renewable energy generation. Taking steps towards sustainable fisheries, including the protection of marine and river ecosystems, can increase employment, enhance food security, and promote exports.

The protection, conservation, and restoration of coastal, river and marine ecosystems directly contributes to climate change mitigation. The LAC region is globally recognised for its unique marine biodiversity and being home to the second largest barrier reef in the world. With 47 out of 258 marine eco-regions, it holds the highest concentration of marine eco-regions worldwide (Tambutti and Gómez, 2020[110]). Blue carbon coastal ecosystems, such as seagrass meadows, tidal marshes, and mangroves uptake and store carbon for the atmosphere in the ocean. Mangroves, in particular, can store three to four times more carbon than most forests on the planet. Conserving and restoring these ecosystems is essential to maximise their sequestration potential.

Despite some progress, the pace of policy actions is not keeping up with the pressures on oceans. The international agreement reached at Convention on Biological Diversity (CBD) COP15 on the Kunming-Montreal Global Biodiversity Framework (GBF) includes targets to protect the ocean, to scale up positive incentives for the conservation and sustainable use of biodiversity, among others. These commitments, however, need to turn to action, including in LAC. Policies that regulate harmful activities such as deep-sea mining and oil drilling, and promote sustainable tourism could help safeguard marine ecosystems and species. Governments have a key role to play in putting in place and effective and coherent policy mix in the LAC region to ensure the conservation and sustainable use of oceans, seas and marine resources (OECD, 2017[111]).

Policies such as marine spatial planning and marine protected areas can help reconcile ecological, economic, and social objectives. As of 2021, over 45 countries were either implementing or approving marine spatial plans. With respect to marine protected areas, the six countries that have led the increase in marine protected areas in the region in recent years are Argentina, Brazil, Chile, Colombia, Mexico and Panama, to help reach the 30% global target. Of the LAC countries, Chile has already met the 2030 marine protected area target of the GBF, while other four territories (part of France) have also met the target (Figure 4.3) (OECD, 2023[36]).

Figure 4.3. Marine Protected Areas in the LAC region

Percentage of Economic Exclusive Zones

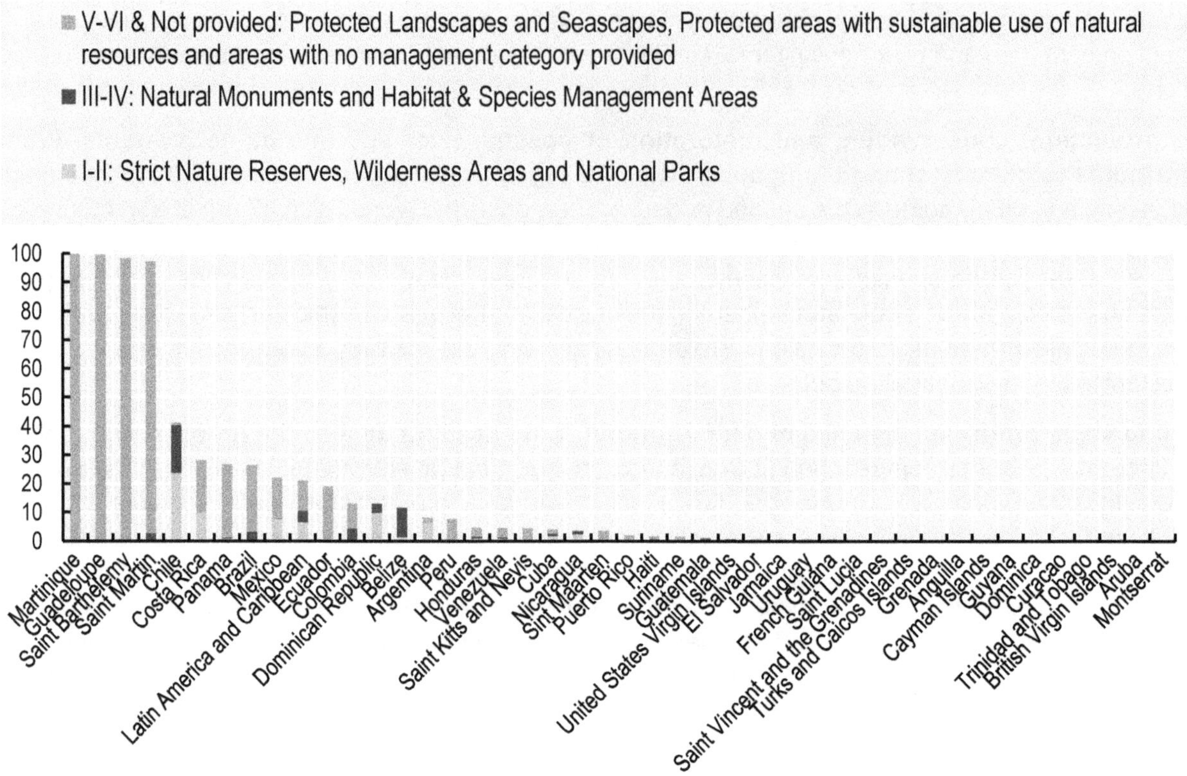

Note: The Global Biodiversity Framework establishes the "30x30" conservation target, calling for 30% of the earth's land and sea to be conserved through the establishment of protected areas and other area-based conservation measures.
Source: (OECD, 2023[112])

At the same time, LAC countries must improve ocean governance and planning to alleviate the increase marine and coastal pollution. Plastic pollution in particular is a critical issue, especially in vulnerable sub-regions such as the Caribbean, as it can be an imminent threat to habitats and natural processes, reducing ecosystems' ability to adapt to climate change, and directly affecting environmental health. Countries in the region can develop integrated coastal zone management (ICZM) as an integrated ecosystem-based approach that considers trade-offs and pays particular attention to fisheries and aquaculture, sustainable tourism, renewable energy generation, integrated management of river basins and lakes, and marine ecosystems protection (OECD et al., 2022[6]).

LAC countries should develop plans to restore fish stocks, establish regional and international policy frameworks, eliminate subsidies contributing to overfishing, and address illegal, unreported, and unregulated (IUU) fishing. It is important to maintain the levels of fish stocks in good health high (Figure 4.4). Investing in science-based stock assessments can help LAC countries better manage fish stocks, to avoid stocks falling below sustainability standards. Collective action against IUU fishing at the regional level can also reinforce monitoring, control and transparency along the fishing value chain. In parallel, action against IUU fishing at the national level would also require a review of national budgets, to guarantee that resources are directed towards sustainable fisheries management and practices, while direct or indirect support to unsustainable fishing is eliminated (OECD, 2022[113]).

Additionally, the ocean presents renewable energy options such as offshore wind, wave and tidal power, and the utilisation of temperature and salinity gradients for energy production (OECD et al., 2022[6]).

Figure 4.4. Status with respect to biological sustainability standards of fish stocks assessed (and total number of stocks assessed) by LAC country, 2021

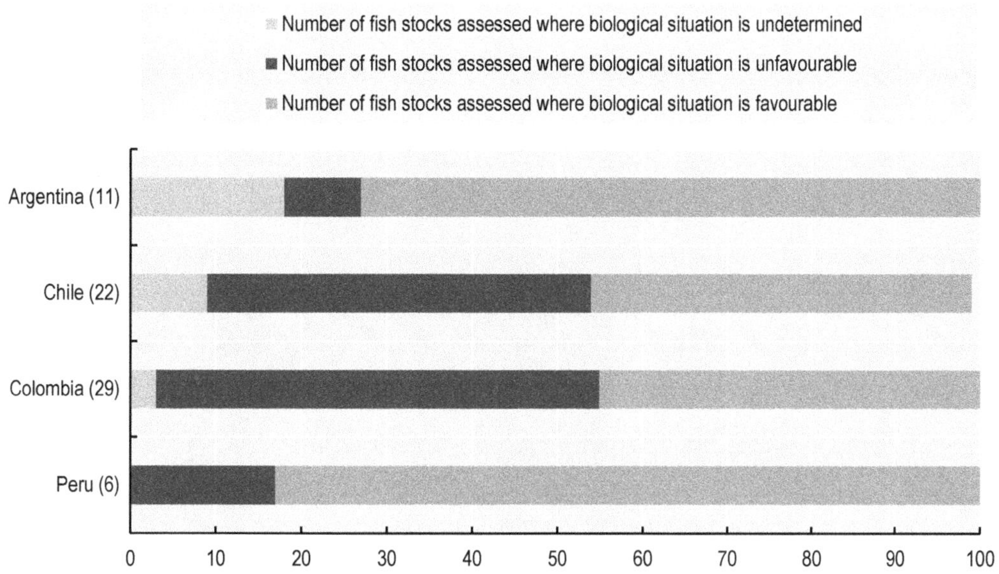

Note: Number next to country indicates the number of stocks assessed per country.
Source: (OECD, 2022[113]), OECD Review of Fisheries 2022, OECD Publishing, Paris.

Incorporating blue carbon into climate change mitigation strategies is crucial for LAC countries. The warming of oceans, acidification, plastic pollution, and overfishing pose significant threats to the blue economy and ocean sustainability (World Bank, 2023[109]). Ocean warming and acidification damage marine ecosystems and comprises the ability of the ocean to provide food, livelihoods and safe coastal living. Climate change effects include increased coastal erosion, coral bleaching, and ecosystem flooding. A blue carbon approach can support countries in meeting their NDCs by mainstreaming blue carbon solutions.

Ocean sustainability should also be included as a target in market-based instruments in the LAC region. The number of countries with economic (market-based) instruments targeted at ocean sustainability in LAC countries has increased over time. By 2022, Argentina, Brazil, Chile, Costa Rica, Ecuador, Mexico, Panama and Peru had introduced ocean-related instruments, up from four countries in 1994[3] (Figure 4.5) (OECD, 2023[114]). These countries have introduced ocean-related taxes (such as taxes on fisheries, maritime transport or marine pollution) except for Argentina, Mexico, and Peru. Even though most ocean-related instruments are taxes, the share of tradable permit systems is highest in the ocean domain (more than in any other environmental domain). Ocean-related tradable permit systems include, for example, individual fishing quotas (Argentina, Chile, Ecuador and Peru), and territorial user rights (Chile and Mexico) (OECD, 2023[114]).

Figure 4.5. Sustainable ocean-related policy instruments in Latin America and the Caribbean

2021 data

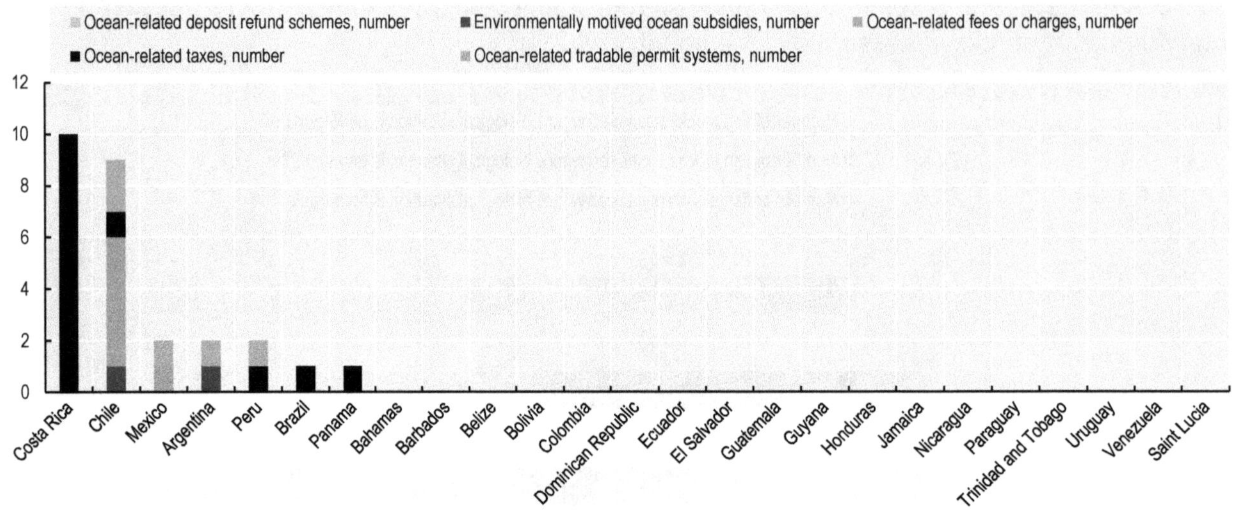

Note: Countries with zero ocean-related policy instruments do have other policy instruments in their toolbox.
Source: (OECD, 2023[114])

Moreover, ocean-sustainability-related taxes raised USD 1.1 billion in 2021, a level which declined over the last decade (despite the growing number of such taxes implemented). The share of ocean-related tax revenue in total Environmentally Related Tax Revenue (ERTR) has also decreased to 1.5% half its value a decade earlier, and at about 0.01% of GDP on average (Figure 4.6).

Figure 4.6. Ocean-related tax revenue

2021 data

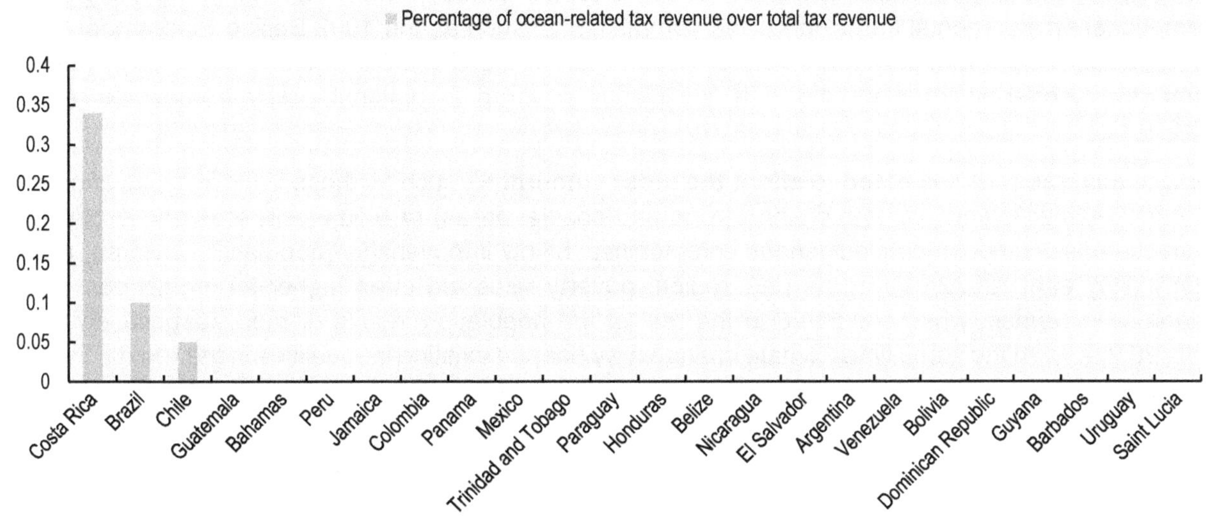

Note: Revenue raised from taxes directed at ocean sustainability. Ocean sustainability-related taxes include taxes on energy products for maritime transport, use or ownership of maritime transport vessels, taxes on resource extraction from oceans, fishing licences, revenue from auctioning individual transferable quotas for fisheries, taxes directed at containing ocean pollution etc. Total environmentally related tax revenue corresponds to the revenue raised by all tax bases for the total environment.
Source: (OECD, 2023[114])

Recommendation

- **Implement policies promoting marine spatial planning and expanding marine protected areas**. These measures can help reconcile ecological, economic, and social objectives. Reach the 2030 marine protected area target of the Global Biodiversity Framework (GBF).
- **Promote sustainable fishing**. Introduce or further improve sustainable fisheries management and practices to combat illegal fishing activities. Include ocean sustainability as a target in market-based instruments.

Gender equality and climate change

Gender equality and social inclusion are important factors to consider when addressing climate change. Women and men face differentiated impacts from environmental degradation, climate hazards, and environmental policies, due to existing inequalities, socio-economic characteristics, as well as cultural and other barriers. In emerging economies, women are often the ones responsible for food production and water collection, while they also need to manage energy use at the household level. Worldwide, an increasing incidence and intensity of natural hazards such as droughts, landslides, floods and hurricanes tend to affect women more due to their greater economic vulnerability. Traditional gender roles dictate that women become the primary caregivers for those affected by disasters, such as children, elderly, and others in need. At the same time, women's empowerment could help deliver positive impacts on environment and climate change, as often women have more "green" preferences and behaviours. The gender-environment nexus can help policymakers develop an integrated policy framework where both environmental sustainability and gender equality are brought to the forefront (OECD, 2021[115]).

While the gender equality and environmental sustainability agendas have progressed in the last years, this has largely been done in silos. Despite gender mainstreaming being integrated in international environmental frameworks and commitments, such as the 1992 Beijing Platform for Action, the 2015 Paris Agreement, and the Gender Action Plan of the UNFCCC, there is still a long way to go before the gender-environment nexus is sufficiently covered in national policy frameworks (OECD, 2021[115]).

Climate adaptation is expected to affect the most vulnerable, such as those living in areas affected by extreme weather events, climate change (rural and coastal areas) or biodiversity loss and ecosystems' destruction (island countries); indigenous communities; highly impoverished population; children, and the elderly (Roy et al., 2022[116]). In the LAC region, poverty rates are often higher for indigenous groups, children and women, when compared to the rest of the population, adults or men, respectively (Reyer et al., 2015[117]). At the same time, climate change may deepen existing inequalities in the region, including those based on gender, due to its social and economic impacts.

UNDP analysis on NDCs inclusion of gender equality actions and targets, shows that from the LAC region, only nine NDCs submitted initially (1st generation) included a gender perspective. However, the number increased to 22 NDCs in the 2nd generation submissions. Despite the rising presence of gender equality references in LAC countries' NDCs, and the acknowledgment of women's roles in different environmental sectors, such as energy, agriculture, and waste management, some gaps still remain, making it clear that further work is needed to implement policies and to guarantee that an integrated approach is introduced in policymaking. These gaps, in the LAC region, are mainly including and securing finance for gender mainstreaming in environmental policies, collecting information and data, and applying Measurement, Reporting and Verification MRV of climate change actions (Table 4.2).

The recent COVID-19 health crisis offered an opportunity to governments worldwide to introduce recovery measures that support both environmental sustainability and social inclusion, with a special focus on gender equality. However, recent analysis shows that neither a green nor a gender-responsive recovery were sufficiently promoted, while the gender-environment nexus was almost absent in the measures introduced. In the LAC region specifically, from the 2 025 recovery policy measures evaluated, only 7 measures from countries, where considered as falling under the gender-environment nexus, that is being both green and gender-sensitive. The majority of these measures focuses particularly on supporting women's economic empowerment in environment-related economic sectors such as agriculture, water, energy or tourism. The support is provided usually via small grants or credit (UNDP; UN Women; OECD, n.d.[118]).

Table 4.2. Inclusion of gender equality in different policy areas of NDCs

Data available for Nationally Determined Contributions submitted by LAC countries

LAC country	Vision	Policy	Governance	Capacity Building	Planning Instruments	Finance	Information & Data	MRV	Actions, Measures & Indicators	Women's recognition and empowerment
Antigua and Barbuda										
Argentina										
Bahamas										
Belize										
Bolivia										
Chile										
Colombia										
Costa Rica	x									
Dominica										
Dominican Republic										
Ecuador										
El Salvador										
Grenada										
Guatemala										
Haiti										
Honduras										
Mexico										
Panama										
Paraguay										
Peru		x			x					x
Suriname										
Uruguay										

Note: Data presentation by authors. Light grey (with x) indicates inclusion in 1st generation NDCs. Dark grey indicates inclusion in 2nd generation NDCs. Black indicates inclusion in both NDCs. White indicates no inclusion in NDCs.
Source: (UNDP, n.d.[119])

LAC countries need to prioritise women's participation in environmental policy- and decision-making, gender mainstreaming in climate change policies, and gender-responsive implementing measures which address gender inequalities at the local level, especially in regions affected by climate change. Including women in the different stages of decision-making, in the public and private sectors, can help enhance environmental action, as well as guarantee a level of gender-responsiveness of the decisions taken (Strumskyte, Ramos Magaña and Bendig, 2022[120]). Moreover, considering women's increased burden of unpaid care work, as well as strong presence in informal employment in LAC countries (OECD/ILO, 2019[96]), and the shift towards a green economy, women's role in sectors such as agriculture, tourism, and renewable energy, needs to be taken into consideration when developing sectoral policies. Supporting such efforts with a set of gender-environment indicators and gender-sensitive data collection, could allow for the development, implementation and monitoring of unbiased environmental policies, that take into consideration the differentiated needs of women and men.

Mexico acknowledges the differentiated impact of climate change to women and men, often linked to societal criteria and vulnerabilities. A special mention is made in the country's NDC with special focus on gender-responsive and gender-transformative cross-cutting actions, however concrete results are needed at the local level. Mexico's climate change adaptation policy includes a four-step approach to include gender equality: (i) providing gender analysis and analysis on vulnerability, to recognise the specificities and differentiated access women and men have to natural resources; (ii) identifying gender gaps and lack of sectoral information at the local level; (iii) implementing measures, taking into consideration local women's experiences in the community, their traditional knowledge, and engagement with the measures introduced to guarantee ownership; and (iv) guaranteeing monitoring and evaluation mechanisms, by introducing gender-sensitive indicators, to measure the gender-responsive effects of policy measures introduced. Projects introduced in the state of Oaxaca, for example, were developed with a bottom-up approach, with full engagement of stakeholders. Local women highlighted the lack of spaces for temporary shelter after severe climate-related events, as well as the lack of planning which takes into consideration the differentiated needs of various groups. Secure financial resources are also highlighted as an important parameter in introducing and implementing gender-responsive actions (OECD, 2023[121]).

Costa Rica's National Adaptation Plan 2022-26 applies horizontally a gender perspective, focusing on the participation and inclusion of women and vulnerable groups in initiatives such as knowledge management, resilience for human systems and planning, biodiversity and ecosystems management, resilient infrastructure, productive and eco-competitive systems, and green investments and finance. The project "Adapting to Climate Change", financially supported by the UN Adaptation Fund, aims at reducing community vulnerability to climate change and improving resilience in critical sectors such as agriculture, water resources management, and coastal areas. It promotes capacity building for women working in agriculture, at the local level. Over 5 000 women have benefited directly, and over 68 000 indirectly. About 590 women have received training; and USD 500 000 have been disbursed as credit for women. The project develops skills and proposes favourable financing with flexibility over collaterals. The project "Plus Women Plus Nature", supported by UNDP, focuses on gender equality and women's empowerment in biodiversity management and preservation. aims at improving women's economic autonomy and creating jobs which contribute to protecting Costa Rica's natural capital. About USD 1.4 million are provided to women for business activities linked to NbS. Some challenges still remain, and are being examined by Costa Rica: access to finance for women and women-led organisation, capacity building and knowledge transfer; quantifying the impact and benefits of the project to women; increasing women's participation in decision-making; advancing with gender-sensitive indicators; and building alliances and partnerships between different stakeholders in order to close the gender gap (OECD, 2023[121]).

The Dominican Republic includes an intergovernmental Gender and Climate Change Panel in its NDC. The Panel is to prioritise enhancing knowledge on the interlinkages between environment and gender equality, increasing women's participation in decision-making mechanisms for adaptation and mitigation, and risk management. The Panel will also provide support in implementing the measures identified in a National Gender and Climate Change Action Plan, as well as tackle key challenges such as access to financing and stakeholder participation in advancing with the set actions (OECD, 2023[121]).

Recommendation

- **Pursue green growth through gender equality**. Acknowledging the differentiated impact of climate change on women and men and adopting an integrated policy framework to reach gender equality and empower women, can support achieving a just and green economic transition. Gender equality and women's economic empowerment can be achieved through gender-sensitive and gender-responsive climate policies, instruments and measures, as well as gender-disaggregated environmental information.

Environmental education for climate action

Environmental education plays a crucial role in promoting climate action. Article 4 of the UNFCCC calls upon parties to promote and co-operate in education, training, and public awareness related to climate change. It also emphasises the importance of encouraging broad participation in this process, including non-governmental organisations (UN, 1992[122]). By providing people with a comprehensive understanding of the climate crisis and equipping them with knowledge, skills, and values, it enables individuals to become agents of change, shaping attitudes and behaviours that lead to both individual and collective action (OECD, 2021[123]). Furthermore, environmental education fosters awareness and understanding of the environment and its natural resources. Schools can serve as spaces to create and implement environmental solutions, fostering more sustainable lifestyles and strengthening resilience to climate change. Through education, children can actively contribute to all aspects of climate change policymaking, mitigation, and adaptation (Ogando, 2022[124]).

Expanding environmental education in LAC remains a significant challenge. Environmental studies are complex and difficult to teach and comprehend, which demands resources and support from institutional agencies to address. Lack of access to training opportunities, necessary infrastructure, resources, and reference materials pose barriers to expanding environmental education in the region. It is crucial to invest in environmental education programmes, training, and adaptable resources for teachers and trainers to provide reference materials on integrating environmental themes and concepts into formal and non-formal educational systems. As of 2023, 26 countries in LAC have included an environmental focus at some level in their primary school curricula (UNEP, 2023[125]). Moreover, implementing environmental education programmes in rural areas presents a challenge that can be addressed through alliances and partnerships with assistance organisations.

Pedagogy, procurement, and partnerships are three key areas of action to support climate change mitigation and adaptation across all levels of education. Pedagogy assumes that increased scientific and technical knowledge raises environmental awareness and concern, leading to improved environmental behaviours. Procurement allows educational institutions to build resilience and reduce safety risks by selecting goods, services, and works with reduced environmental impacts. This can be achieved by designing energy- and water-efficient facilities, addressing food waste, promoting clean school transport and green public transport, incorporating cycling in urban planning, and procuring energy-efficient equipment such as lighting and Information and Communications Technology (ICT), while also limiting e-waste. Lastly, education can enhance synergies between educational institutions, public administration, businesses, and civil society, reinforcing learning practices, procurement policies, and strengthening social ties within communities, all for the benefit of the environment (OECD, 2021[123]).

Policymakers should aim to build a flexible, adaptable, and resilient workforce that is sensitive to changes in the economy due to new environmental standards and regulations. Policies need to be developed to ensure the responsiveness of training systems to evolving skill demands. Assessing the information on the supply and demand of skills is essential to align qualifications and programmes, prevent skills gaps and shortages, and support individuals in adapting to the changes created by the green economy. Achieving this requires inclusive training systems that address gender gaps (OECD, 2021[123]). Research has also shown that support for climate policies is influenced by three important factors: i) the perceived effectiveness of the policies in reducing emissions, ii) their perceived distributional impacts on lower-income households (inequality concerns), and iii) individuals' own household gains and losses. Education plays a significant role in shaping policy views and overall reasoning and beliefs about climate policies (Dechezleprêtre et al., 2022[126]). At the same time, policies in the region should be developed aiming to foster job creation in new green technologies through a mix of innovation and employment incentives, skills development, and employment services. Countries should promote additional public and private investments that contribute to increasing the necessary added value of the green sectors to boost the creation of formal jobs, as well as develop policies aiming to establish an environmental perspective on their vocational educational and training systems.

Recommendation

- **Promote equitable and green education.** Establish an active environmental education strategy, formal and informal, to induce a behavioural change in society creating awareness, sensitivity and responsibility towards environmental-sustainability and climate change. Education systems, from early childhood, must ensure that future generations shift individual behaviours and preferences away from the current unsustainable methods of production and consumption. Environmental knowledge, green skills should be part of the curricula across all components of the educational systems.

References

all., M. (2014), *Environmental Impact Assessment Systems in Latin America and the Caribbean*, International Association for Impact Assessment, https://conferences.iaia.org/2014/IAIA14-final-papers/Acerbi,%20Marcelo.%20%20EIA%20systems%20in%20Latin%20America%20and%20the%20Caribbean.pdf. [127]

Boteler, B. et al. (2015), *Experiences in bottom-up adaptation approaches in Europe and elsewhere*, https://www.ecologic.eu/sites/default/files/publication/2017/2716-d-4-2-experiences-of-bottom-up-adaptation-approaches.pdf. [18]

CAF (2022), *Assessment of the Carbon Credit Market in Latin America and the Caribbean*, https://scioteca.caf.com/bitstream/handle/123456789/1949/assessment%20of%20the%20CM%20in%20LAaC.pdf?sequence=4&isAllowed=y. [56]

CAF (2021), *CAF to allocate USD 25 billion over the next five years to promote green growth*, https://www.caf.com/en/currently/news/2021/11/caf-to-allocate-usd-25-billion-over-the-next-five-years-to-promote-green-growth/ (accessed on 11 October 2022). [67]

CBD (n.d.), *https://www.cbd.int/ - Costa Rica*, https://www.cbd.int/financial/pes/costarica-pestechnical.pdf (accessed on 2023). [53]

CBI (2021), *Taxonomy Roadmap for Chile: One more step towards consolidating the local Green Finance Agenda*, https://www.climatebonds.net/files/reports/taxonomy_chile_report_a4_en.pdf. [81]

Climate Bonds Initiative (2021), *Latin America & the Caribbean Sustainable Finance State of the Market 2021*, Climate Bonds Initiative, https://www.climatebonds.net/files/reports/cbi_lac_2020_04e.pdf. [74]

CNCCMDL (2020), *Experiencia dominicana en el diseño de un isystema de monitoreo, reporte y verificación (MRV) de gases de efecto invernadero*, https://mepyd.gob.do/wp-content/uploads/drive/VIMICI/Convocatorias/Conovocatoria/Sistematizacion/7.%20Disen%CC%83o%20sistema%20MRVde%20gases%20de%20efecto%20invernadero%20%281%29.pdf. [43]

CODS (2021), *Sistemas MRV y Financiamiento Climático en Colombia*, Centro de los Objectivos de Desarrollo Sostenible para América Latina, https://cods.uniandes.edu.co/sistemas-mrv-y-financiamiento-climatico-en-colombia/. [42]

Cognuck González, S. and E. Numer (2020), *What is climate governance?*, https://www.unicef.org/lac/media/19651/file/what-is-climate-governance.pdf. [4]

Conway, D. et al. (2019), "The need for bottom-up assessments of climate risks and adaptation in climate-sensitive regions", *Nature Climate Change*, Vol. 9/7, pp. 503-511, https://doi.org/10.1038/s41558-019-0502-0. [16]

Danish, K. (1995), "International Environmental Law and the "Bottom-Up" Approach: A Review of the Desertification Convention", *Indiana Journal of Global Legal Studies*, Vol. 3/1, http://www.repository.law.indiana.edu/ijgls/vol3/iss1/9. [25]

Dechezleprêtre, A. et al. (2022), "Fighting climate change: International attitudes toward climate policies", *OECD Economics Department Working Papers*, No. 1714, OECD Publishing, Paris, https://doi.org/10.1787/3406f29a-en. [126]

Ellen Macarthur Foundation (2019), *Completing the Picture: How the circular economy tackles climate change*, https://circulareconomy.europa.eu/platform/sites/default/files/emf_completing_the_picture.pdf. [107]

EU (2022), *EU-LAC Partnership*, https://www.eeas.europa.eu/sites/default/files/documents/Factsheet%20EU_LAC_en_2022_2510fin.pdf. [131]

EUROCLIMA+ (n.d.), *EUROCLIMA+*, https://www.euroclima.org/ (accessed on 10 October 2022). [130]

Funaro, R. (ed.) (2021), *Climate Policies in Latin America and the Caribbean: Success Stories and Challenges in the Fight against Climate Change*, Inter-American Development Bank, https://doi.org/10.18235/0003239. [2]

Garrett, J. and S. Moarif (2018), "Reporting on capacity-building and technology support under the Paris Agreement: Issues and options for guidance", *OECD/IEA Climate Change Expert Group Papers*, No. 2018/01, OECD Publishing, Paris, https://doi.org/10.1787/f5330a47-en. [85]

GCF (2021), *Annual Results Report*, https://www.greenclimate.fund/sites/default/files/document/20220412-arr2021.pdf. [68]

GEF (2022), *The GEF Monitoring Report*, https://www.thegef.org/sites/default/files/documents/2022-11/EN_GEF.C.63.03_The%20GEF%20Monitoring%20Report%202022.pdf. [69]

GFLAC (2021), *Sustainable Finance Index - Results report for Latin America and the Caribbean, 2020*, https://fd31067a-8e9b-4ab4-a7be-d30689ad3aa1.filesusr.com/ugd/32948d_45d5502a4fe4467cb159f60f03255347.pdf?index=true. [47]

Gligo, N. et al. (2020), *La tragedia ambiental de América Latina y el Caribe*, https://repositorio.cepal.org/bitstream/handle/11362/46101/1/S2000555_es.pdf. [32]

Gómez, X. (2017), *Colombia: Integrando la métrica de la mitigación y adaptación ante el cambio climático*, https://ledslac.org/wp-content/uploads/2017/06/05-Colombia.-Integrando-la-m%C3%A9trica-de-la-mitigaci%C3%B3n-y-adaptaci%C3%B3n.pdf. [41]

Government of Belize (2022), *Government and Conservation Partners Sign Protected Areas Co-Management Agreements*, https://www.pressoffice.gov.bz/government-and-conservation-partners-sign-protected-areas-co-management-agreements/. [22]

Government of Brazil (2023), *United for Our Forests: Joint Communiqué of Developing Forest Countries in Belém*, https://www.gov.br/mre/en/contact-us/press-area/press-releases/united-for-our-forests-joint-communique-of-developing-forest-countries-in-belem (accessed on 29 August 2023). [5]

Government of Costa Rica, G. (2018), *cambioclimatico.org - Plan Nacional de Descarbonización - Gobierno de Costa Rica 2018-2050*, https://cambioclimatico.go.cr/wp-content/uploads/2019/02/PLAN.pdf (accessed on August 2023). [13]

Government of Mexico (2022), *Lanza México herramienta que ayudará a monitorear acciones de mitigación y adaptación en las entidades del país*, https://www.gob.mx/semarnat/prensa/lanza-mexico-herramienta-que-ayudara-a-monitorear-acciones-de-mitigacion-y-adaptacion-en-las-entidades-del-pais (accessed on 1 August 2023). [40]

Guevara Sanginés, A., A. Mercado García and J. Lara Pulido (2020), "Disponibilidad de estadísticas ambientales en nueve países latinoamericanos. An Assessment of the Availability of Environmental Statistics in Nine Latin American Countries", *Realidada, Datos U Espacio Revista Internacional de Estadistica y Geografía*, Vol. 11/2, https://rde.inegi.org.mx/index.php/2020/08/06/disponibilidad-de-estadisticas-ambientales-en-nueve-paises-latinoamericanos/. [39]

Haščič, I. et al. (2010), "Climate Policy and Technological Innovation and Transfer: An Overview of Trends and Recent Empirical Results", *OECD Environment Working Papers*, No. 30, OECD Publishing, Paris, https://doi.org/10.1787/5km33bnggcd0-en. [86]

Hermansen, E. and G. Sundqvist (2022), "Top-down or bottom-up? Norwegian climate mitigation policy as a contested hybrid of policy approaches", *Climatic Change*, Vol. 171/3-4, https://doi.org/10.1007/s10584-022-03309-y. [11]

IDB (2022), *Inter-American Development Bank Sustainability Report 2021*, https://publications.iadb.org/publications/english/document/Inter-American-Development-Bank-Sustainability-Report-2021.pdf. [70]

IEA (2020), *Implementing Effective Emissions Trading Systems: Lessons from international experiences*, https://iea.blob.core.windows.net/assets/2551e81a-a401-43a4-bebd-a52e5a8fc853/Implementing_Effective_Emissions_Trading_Systems.pdf (accessed on September 2023). [10]

ILO (2019), *Working on a warmer planet: The impact of heat stress on labour productivity and decent work*, https://www.ilo.org/wcmsp5/groups/public/---dgreports/---dcomm/---publ/documents/publication/wcms_711919.pdf. [93]

ILO (n.d.), *What is a green job?*, https://www.ilo.org/global/topics/green-jobs/news/WCMS_220248/lang--en/index.htm (accessed on 22 August 2023). [94]

IPCC (2022), *Sixth Assessment Report - Mitigation of Climate Change: Summary for Policymakers*, https://www.ipcc.ch/report/sixth-assessment-report-working-group-3/. [133]

Ivanova, A. et al. (2021), *Climate Change in Latin America and the Caribbean Challenges and Opportunities*, https://www.imf.org/en/Blogs/Articles/2021/10/28/blog-climate-change-latin-america-the-caribbean-challenges-and-opportunities (accessed on 31 July 2023). [60]

Langhill, R. (2021), *EPR in Latin America - Progress toward implementation*, https://www.loraxcompliance.com/blog/env/2021/07/26/EPR_in_Latin_America_-_Progress_toward_implementation.html#. [104]

Lemos, M. and A. Agrawal (2006), "Environmental Governance", *Annual Review of Environment and Resources*, Vol. 31/1, pp. 297-325, https://doi.org/10.1146/annurev.energy.31.042605.135621. [3]

Livingstone, L. et al. (2022), "Synergies and trade-offs in the transition to a resource-efficient and circular economy", *OECD Environment Policy Papers*, No. 34, OECD Publishing, Paris, https://doi.org/10.1787/e8bb5c6e-en. [105]

Maciel, E. (2022), *Carbon pricing in Latin America: How is this market growing?*, https://www.developmentaid.org/news-stream/post/145275/carbon-pricing-in-latin-america-how-is-this-market-growing (accessed on 1 August 2023). [57]

Marr, M., D. Marett and N. Wohlgemuth (2018), *"MRV in Practice" - Connecting bottom-up and top-down approaches for developing National MRV systems for NDCs*, https://transparency-partnership.net/system/files/document/GH_New%20Climate_MRV%20in%20Practice_2018.pdf (accessed on 2023). [9]

Massuela Calenga, D., A. Montes de Oca Risco and M. Ulloa Carcassés (2019), "LA EVALUACIÓN AMBIENTAL ESTRATÉGICA: DESDE EL ENFOQUE DE SU DESARROLLO HISTÓRICO HASTA SU APLICABILIDAD EN LA ACTUALIDAD.", *HOLOS*, Vol. 6, pp. 1-22, https://doi.org/10.15628/holos.2019.8704. [28]

Merle, C., G. Gondjian and Y. Gong (2021), *The New Geography of Taxnomies: A Global Standard-setting Race*, https://gsh.cib.natixis.com/api-website-feature/files/download/12087/the_new_geography_of_taxonomies_final_version_november_2021_natixis_gsh.pdf (accessed on 13 July 2023). [80]

MINAM (2022), *Aprendizajes sobre el proceso de consulta a las cominidades indígenas para la elaboración del Reglamento de la Ley Marco sobre Cambio Climático del Perú*, https://cdn.www.gob.pe/uploads/document/file/2827915/Libro_Sistematizaci%C3%B3n%20del%20Proceso%20de%20Consulta%20Previa.pdf.pdf?v=1675798796. [19]

Ministry of Environment Peru (n.d.), *Comisión de Alto Nivel de Cambio Climático*, https://www.gob.pe/institucion/minam/campa%C3%B1as/7744-comision-de-alto-nivel-de-cambio-climatico. [14]

Miranda, T. (2021), *Nationally Determined Contributions across the Americas - A Comparative Hemispheric Analysis*, https://iamericas.org/NDC-Report-2021/. [45]

MMA (2022), *Guida de Evaluación Ambiental Estratégica para incorporar el Cambio Climático en Instrumentos de Ordenamiento y Planificación Territorial*, https://mma.gob.cl/wp-content/uploads/2022/08/Guia-de-Evaluacion-Ambiental-Estrategica-para-incorporar-el-Cambio-Climatico-en-Instrumentos-de-Ordenamiento-y-Planificacion-Territorial.pdf. [26]

MOVE (n.d.), *Movilidad Eléctrica Latinoamérica y el Caribe*, https://movelatam.org/ (accessed on 10 October 2022). [91]

Noltze, M. et al. (2021), "Monitoring, evaluation and learning for climate risk management", *OECD Development Co-operation Working Papers*, No. 92, OECD Publishing, Paris, https://doi.org/10.1787/58665de0-en. [38]

Ocampo, R. (2021), *Impementación de las cuentas ambientales en América Latina y el Caribe*, https://seea.un.org/sites/seea.un.org/files/2._situacion_regional_cuentas_ecosistemicas_rolando_ocampo.pdf (accessed on 31 July 2023). [34]

OECD (2023), *3rd LAC Regional Policy Dialogue on Environmental Sustainability: Addressing Climate Change Adaptation in Latin America & the Caribbean*, https://www.oecd.org/greengrowth/3rd-lac-policy-dialogue.htm. [121]

OECD (2023), "Biodiversity: Protected areas", *OECD Environment Statistics* (database), https://doi.org/10.1787/5fa661ce-en (accessed on 18 August 2023). [112]

OECD (2023), *Environment at a Glance in Latin America and the Caribbean: Spotlight on Climate Change*, OECD Publishing, Paris, https://doi.org/10.1787/2431bd6c-en. [36]

OECD (2023), "Global Plastics Outlook: Plastic waste by end-of-life fate and region - projections", *OECD Environment Statistics* (database), https://doi.org/10.1787/e4e8c086-en (accessed on 23 August 2023). [101]

OECD (2023), "Green growth indicators", *OECD Environment Statistics* (database), https://doi.org/10.1787/data-00665-en (accessed on 1 August 2023). [55]

OECD (2023), *OECD Environmental Performance Reviews: Costa Rica 2023*, OECD Environmental Performance Reviews, OECD Publishing, Paris, https://doi.org/10.1787/ec94fd4e-en. [106]

OECD (2023), "Patents in environment-related technologies: Technology indicators", *OECD Environment Statistics* (database), https://doi.org/10.1787/e478bcd5-en (accessed on 17 August 2023). [88]

OECD (2023), *Private Finance Mobilised by Official Development Finance Interventions. Opportunities and challenges to increase its contribution towards the SDGs in developing countries*, https://www.oecd.org/dac/2023-private-finance-odfi.pdf. [72]

OECD (2023), "Sustainable Ocean Economy", *OECD Environment Statistics* (database), https://doi.org/10.1787/4c44ff65-en (accessed on 28 September 2023). [114]

OECD (2022), *Aggregate Trends of Climate Finance Provided and Mobilised by Developed Countries in 2013-2020*, Climate Finance and the USD 100 Billion Goal, OECD Publishing, Paris, https://doi.org/10.1787/d28f963c-en. [62]

OECD (2022), *Climate Finance Provided and Mobilised by Developed Countries in 2016-2020: Insights from Disaggregated Analysis*, Climate Finance and the USD 100 Billion Goal, OECD Publishing, Paris, https://doi.org/10.1787/286dae5d-en. [65]

OECD (2022), *Empowering Women in the Transition Towards Green Growth in Greece*, OECD Publishing, Paris, https://doi.org/10.1787/a9eacee6-en. [95]

OECD (2022), *Enabling Conditions for Bioenergy Finance and Investment in Colombia*, Green Finance and Investment, OECD Publishing, Paris, https://doi.org/10.1787/20f760d6-en. [92]

OECD (2022), *Global Plastics Outlook: Policy Scenarios to 2060*, OECD Publishing, Paris, https://doi.org/10.1787/aa1edf33-en. [100]

OECD (2022), *International Programme for Action on Climate*, https://www.oecd.org/climate-action/ipac/ (accessed on 2023). [128]

OECD (2022), "OECD blended finance guidance for clean energy", *OECD Environment Policy Papers*, No. 31, OECD Publishing, Paris, https://doi.org/10.1787/596e2436-en. [75]

OECD (2022), *OECD Guidance on Transition Finance: Ensuring Credibility of Corporate Climate Transition Plans*, Green Finance and Investment, OECD Publishing, Paris, https://doi.org/10.1787/7c68a1ee-en. [77]

OECD (2022), *OECD Review of Fisheries 2022*, OECD Publishing, Paris, https://doi.org/10.1787/9c3ad238-en. [113]

OECD (2022), *Scaling up blended finance in developing countries*, https://www.oecd.org/dac/scaling_up_blended_finance_in_developing_countries.pdf (accessed on September 2023). [76]

OECD (2022), "Subnational government climate expenditure and revenue tracking in OECD and EU Countries", *OECD Regional Development Papers*, No. 32, OECD Publishing, Paris, https://doi.org/10.1787/1e8016d4-en. [17]

OECD (2021), *Effective Carbon Rates 2021: Pricing Carbon Emissions through Taxes and Emissions Trading*, OECD Series on Carbon Pricing and Energy Taxation, OECD Publishing, Paris, https://doi.org/10.1787/0e8e24f5-en. [50]

OECD (2021), *Gender and the Environment: Building Evidence and Policies to Achieve the SDGs*, OECD Publishing, Paris, https://doi.org/10.1787/3d32ca39-en. [115]

OECD (2021), *Implementing the OECD Recommendation on Policy Coherence for Sustainable Development: Guidance Note*, https://www.oecd.org/gov/pcsd/pcsd-guidance-note-publication.pdf. [8]

OECD (2021), "Think green: Education and climate change", *Trends Shaping Education Spotlights*, No. 24, OECD Publishing, Paris, https://doi.org/10.1787/2a9a1cdd-en. [123]

OECD (2018), "Blended finance instruments and mechanisms", in *Making Blended Finance Work for the Sustainable Development Goals*, OECD Publishing, Paris, https://doi.org/10.1787/9789264288768-9-en. [132]

OECD (2017), *Development Co-operation Report 2017: Data for Development*, OECD Publishing, Paris, https://doi.org/10.1787/dcr-2017-en. [33]

OECD (2017), *Marine Protected Areas: Economics, Management and Effective Policy Mixes*, OECD Publishing, Paris, https://doi.org/10.1787/9789264276208-en. [111]

OECD (2015), *Aligning Policies for a Low-carbon Economy*, OECD Publishing, Paris, https://doi.org/10.1787/9789264233294-en. [1]

OECD (2006), *Applying Strategic Environmental Assessment*, https://www.oecd.org/environment/environment-development/37353858.pdf (accessed on April 2023). [27]

OECD (2006), *Applying Strategic Environmental Assessment. Good Practice Guidance for Development Co-operation*, https://www.oecd.org/environment/environment-development/37353858.pdf. [31]

OECD/CAF (2019), "Innovation and technology (Dimension 5)", in *Latin America and the Caribbean 2019: Policies for Competitive SMEs in the Pacific Alliance and Participating South American countries*, OECD Publishing, Paris, https://doi.org/10.1787/ef1c27ba-en. [87]

OECD et al. (2022), *Latin American Economic Outlook 2022: Towards a Green and Just Transition*, OECD Publishing, Paris, https://doi.org/10.1787/3d5554fc-en. [6]

OECD/ILO (2019), *Tackling Vulnerability in the Informal Economy*, Development Centre Studies, OECD Publishing, Paris, https://doi.org/10.1787/939b7bcd-en. [96]

OECD/The World Bank/UN Environment (2018), *Financing Climate Futures: Rethinking Infrastructure*, OECD Publishing, Paris, https://doi.org/10.1787/9789264308114-en. [63]

Ogando, P. (2022), *A pending task: 5 reasons why we need environmental education*, https://www.unicef.org/lac/en/stories/a-pending-task-5-reasons-why-we-need-environmental-education (accessed on 6 June 2023). [124]

Oueslati, W. (2023), *OECD'S contribution to G7: Climate change and environment*, https://www.iges.or.jp/sites/default/files/inline-files/3_G7%20OECD%20Symposium_Walid%20Oueslati.pdf (accessed on September 2023). [59]

Prada Hernández, A. et al. (2023), *Overcoming the Babel tower challenge! A taxonomy to create a common language for sustainable finance in the Latin American & Caribbean region*, https://wwfint.awsassets.panda.org/downloads/wwf_taxonomies_latin_america_eng_16jan202.pdf. [78]

Prasad, A. et al. (2022), "Mobilizing Private Climate Financing in Emerging Market and Developing Economies", *IMF Staff Climate Note 2022/007*, https://www.imf.org/en/Publications/staff-climate-notes/Issues/2022/07/26/Mobilizing-Private-Climate-Financing-in-Emerging-Market-and-Developing-Economies-520585. [64]

Presidéncia de la República Dominicana (n.d.), *Consejo Nacional para el Cambio Climático y Mecanismo de Desarrollo Limpio (CNCCMDL)*, https://cambioclimatico.gob.do/index.php/sobre-nosotros/historia. [15]

Presidency of the Dominican Republic (2016), *Plan Nacional de Adaptación para el Cambio Climático en la República Dominicana 2015-2030 (PNACC RD)*, https://bvearmb.do/bitstream/handle/123456789/164/Plan-Nacional-Adaptacion-Cambio-Climatico-2015-2030-PNACC-RD.pdf?sequence=1&isAllowed=y. [44]

Qamar, M. and S. Archfield (2022), "Consider the risks of bottom-up approaches for climate change adaptation", *Nature Climate Change*, Vol. 13/1, pp. 2-3, https://doi.org/10.1038/s41558-022-01572-6. [12]

Quispe, C. (2017), *http://cairplas.org.ar/ - Responsabilidad Extendida del Productor en América Latina*, http://cairplas.org.ar/news/49/Responsabilidad-Extendida-del-Productor-en-America-Latina.pdf (accessed on 2023). [103]

REGATTA (n.d.), *REGATTA Communities of Practice*, https://cambioclimatico-regatta.org/index.php/en (accessed on 10 October 2022). [90]

Rentschler, J. and M. Bazilian (2017), "Policy Monitor—Principles for Designing Effective Fossil Fuel Subsidy Reforms", *Review of Environmental Economics and Policy*, Vol. 11/1, pp. 138-155, https://doi.org/10.1093/reep/rew016. [48]

Reyer, C. et al. (2015), "Climate change impacts in Latin America and the Caribbean and their implications for development", *Regional Environmental Change*, Vol. 17/6, pp. 1601-1621, https://doi.org/10.1007/s10113-015-0854-6. [117]

Rodrigo-Ilarri, J. et al. (2020), "Advances in Implementing Strategic Environmental Assessment (SEA) Techniques in Central America and the Caribbean", *Sustainability*, Vol. 12/10, p. 4039, https://doi.org/10.3390/su12104039. [29]

Roy, J. et al. (2022), "2018: Sustainable Development, Poverty Eradication and Reducing Inequalities", in *Global Warming of 1.5°C*, Cambridge University Press, https://doi.org/10.1017/9781009157940.007. [116]

Russel, D. et al. (2020), "Policy Coordination for National Climate Change Adaptation in Europe: All Process, but Little Power", *Sustainability*, Vol. 12/13, p. 5393, https://doi.org/10.3390/su12135393. [23]

Saget, C., A. Vogt-Schilb and T. Luu (2020), *Jobs in a net-zero emissions future in Latin America and the Caribbean*, https://www.ilo.org/wcmsp5/groups/public/---americas/---ro-lima/documents/publication/wcms_752069.pdf. [97]

Samaniego, J. et al. (2022), *Panorama de las hojas de ruta de economía circular en América Latina y el Caribe*, https://repositorio.cepal.org/bitstream/handle/11362/48632/1/S2201064_es.pdf. [108]

Sanderson, H. et al. (eds.) (2018), *The Diversity of Adaptation in a Multilevel Governance Setting*, Elsevier, https://doi.org/10.1016/c2016-0-02106-x. [24]

Schneider, L. and S. La Hoz Theuer (2018), "Environmental integrity of international carbon market mechanisms under the Paris Agreement", *Climate Policy*, Vol. 19/3, pp. 386-400, https://doi.org/10.1080/14693062.2018.1521332. [58]

SGP (n.d.), *ICCA-GSI PHASE 1*, https://sgp.undp.org/index.php?option=com_content&view=article&id=414&Itemid=524#.WOPDI0UrIdU. [21]

Souza, L. and T. Gasparotto (2023), *A new Taxonomy is born: insights on the Mexican Sustainable Taxonomy*, https://gsh.cib.natixis.com/our-center-of-expertise/articles/a-new-taxonomy-is-born-insights-on-the-mexican-sustainable-taxonomy (accessed on 13 July 2023). [79]

Strumskyte, S., S. Ramos Magaña and H. Bendig (2022), "Women's leadership in environmental action", *OECD Environment Working Papers*, No. 193, OECD Publishing, Paris, https://doi.org/10.1787/f0038d22-en. [120]

Tambutti, M. and J. Gómez (eds.) (2020), *The outlook for oceans, seas and marine resources in Latin America and the Caribbean: Conservation, sustainable development and climate change mitigation*, Economic Commission for Latin America and the Caribbean (ECLAC). [110]

The Dialogue (2023), *A Roadmap to Unlock New Climate Finance in LAC*, https://www.thedialogue.org/analysis/a-roadmap-to-unlock-new-climate-finance-in-lac/#:~:text=Of%20these%20investments%2C%20around%2080,overshadow%20those%20of%20sustainable%20activities. (accessed on 13 July 2023). [66]

UN (1992), *United Nations Framework Convention of Climate Change*, https://unfccc.int/resource/docs/convkp/conveng.pdf. [122]

UN ECLAC (2022), *How to finance sustainable development. Recovery from the effects of COVID-19 in Latin America and the Caribbean*, http:///repositorio (accessed on 1 August 2023). [49]

UN ECLAC (2021), *Avances hacia una economía circular en América Latina y el Caribe: Desafíos y oportunidades para lograr un estilo de desarrollo más sostenible y bajo en carbono*, https://www.cepal.org/es/eventos/avances-economia-circular-america-latina-caribe-desafios-oportunidades-lograr-un-estilo. [98]

UN ECLAC (2019), *https://comunidades.cepal.org/ - Avances y desafíos de las cuentas ambientales y ecosistémicas en América Latina y el Caribe*, https://comunidades.cepal.org/estadisticas-ambientales/es/grupos/discusion/avances-y-desafios-de-las-cuentas-ambientales-y-ecosistemicas-en-america-latina-y (accessed on 2023). [37]

UN ECLAC (2017), *La sitación de las estadísticas, indicadores y cuentas ambientales en América Latina y el Caribe*, https://repositorio.cepal.org/bitstream/handle/11362/43139/1/S1701237_es.pdf. [35]

UN Environment (2018), *Waste Management Outlook for Latin America and the Caribbean*, https://www.unep.org/ietc/resources/publication/waste-management-outlook-latin-america-and-caribbean. [99]

UNDP (2022), *Building a common framework of sustainable finance taxonomies in Latin America and the Caribbean*, https://www.undp.org/latin-america/press-releases/building-common-framework-sustainable-finance-taxonomies-latin-america-and-caribbean (accessed on 13 October 2022). [82]

UNDP (n.d.), *Advancing gender equality in NDCs: progress and higher ambitions*, https://data.undp.org/content/gender-and-ndc/ (accessed on 7 July 2023). [119]

UNDP; UN Women; OECD (n.d.), *Gender Response Tracker with a Green Lens*, https://data.undp.org/gendertracker/ (accessed on 1 August 2023). [118]

UNECE (2016), *Protocol on Strategic Environmental Assessment - Facts and Benefits*, https://unece.org/DAM/env/eia/Publications/2016/Protocol_on_SEA/1609217_UNECE_HR.pdf. [30]

UNEP (2023), *Common Framework of Sustainable Finance Taxonomies for Latin America and the Caribbean*, https://www.undp.org/latin-america/publications/common-framework-sustainable-finance-taxonomies-latin-america-and-caribbean (accessed on 13 July 2023). [83]

UNEP (2023), *New environmental education guide for Latin America and the Caribbean*, https://www.unep.org/news-and-stories/press-release/new-environmental-education-guide-latin-america-caribbean-region (accessed on 6 June 2023). [125]

UNEP (2022), *Integrate Extended Producer Responsibility within the International plastics Treaty*, https://apps1.unep.org/resolutions/uploads/integrate_epr_within_the_international_treaty_on_plastics_pollution_1.pdf. [102]

UNEP (2022), *Technology Transfer for Climate Mitigation and Adaptation: Analysing needs and development assistance support in technology transfer processes*, UNEP Copenhagen Climate Centre, https://unepccc.org/wp-content/uploads/2023/06/tech-transfer-policy-brief-oecd.pdf. [89]

UNEP (2017), *GEO-6: Global Environmental Outlook: Regional assessment for Latin America and the Caribbean*, https://www.unep.org/resources/report/geo-6-global-environment-outlook-regional-assessment-latin-america-and-caribbean. [73]

UNFCCC (2023), *Long-term strategies portal*, https://unfccc.int/process/the-paris-agreement/long-term-strategies (accessed on 2023). [135]

UNFCCC (2023), *NDC Registry*, https://unfccc.int/NDCREG (accessed on 2023). [134]

UNFCCC (2022), *Glasgow Climate Pact*, https://unfccc.int/sites/default/files/resource/cma2021_10_add1_adv.pdf (accessed on 20 September 2022). [61]

UNFCCC (2021), *Report of the Standing Committee on Finance*. [46]

UNFCCC (2020), *https://unfccc.int/ - Payments for Environmental Services Program | Costa Rica*, https://unfccc.int/climate-action/momentum-for-change/financing-for-climate-friendly-investment/payments-for-environmental-services-program (accessed on 2023). [52]

UNFCCC (2019), *Climate action and support trends 2019. Based on national reports submitted to the UNFCCC secreatriat under the current reporting framework*, https://unfccc.int/sites/default/files/resource/Climate_Action_Support_Trends_2019.pdf. [7]

UNFCCC (n.d.), *About Carbon Pricing*, https://unfccc.int/about-us/regional-collaboration-centres/the-ciaca/about-carbon-pricing#Which-types-of-carbon-pricing-exist?- (accessed on 1 August 2023). [129]

United Nations (2021), *United Nations Handbook on Carbon Taxation for developing countries*, https://desapublications.un.org/file/918/download. [51]

Williams, K. and H. Tai (2016), "A Multi-Tier Social-Ecological System Analysis of Protected Areas Co-Management in Belize", *Sustainability*, Vol. 8/2, p. 104, https://doi.org/10.3390/su8020104. [20]

World Bank (2023), *Blue Economy in Latin America and the Caribbean*, https://www.worldbank.org/en/news/infographic/2023/06/07/oceans-blue-economy-in-latin-america-and-the-caribbean (accessed on 18 August 2023). [109]

World Bank (2023), *State and Trends of Carbon Pricing 2023*, https://doi.org/10.1596/978-1-4648-2006-9. [54]

World Bank (2021), *Promoting Climate Change Action in Latin America and the Caribbean*, https://www.worldbank.org/en/results/2021/04/14/promoting-climate-change-action-in-latin-america-and-the-caribbean (accessed on 3 October 2022). [71]

World Bank (2007), *International Trade and Climate Change*, The World Bank, https://doi.org/10.1596/978-0-8213-7225-8. [84]

Notes

[1] The countries covered in this report were: Antigua and Barbuda, Argentina, Bahamas, Barbados, Belize, Bolivia, Brazil, Chile, Colombia, Costa Rica, Cuba, Dominica, Dominican Republic, Ecuador, El Salvador, Grenada, Guatemala, Guyana, Haiti, Honduras, Jamaica, Mexico, Montserrat, Nicaragua, Panama, Paraguay, Peru, Saint Kitts and Nevis, Saint Lucia, Saint Vincent and the Grenadines, Suriname, Trinidad and Tobago, Uruguay, and Venezuela (OECD, 2022[62])

[2] According to the United Nations Framework Convention on Climate Change (UNFCCC) Standing Committee on Finance, climate finance "*aims at reducing emissions and enhancing sinks of greenhouse gases and aims at reducing vulnerability of, and maintaining and increasing the resilience of, human and ecological systems to negative climate change impacts*". The OECD provides analysis and tracks progress on the developed countries' collective goal of mobilising USD 100 billion per year for climate action in developing countries, as was presented in COP15 and reiterated and extended in COP21.

[3] These were Chile, Costa Rica, Mexico and Panama.

Annex A. Climate adaptation in LAC countries' policy frameworks

Table A.1. Climate adaptation in national policy frameworks in LAC countries

Country	National Adaptation Plan	Sectoral NAPs and other outputs	Adaptation within NDCs	National Adaptation Legislation and Policies (general framework)	Adaptation in other national plans and strategies
Antigua and Barbuda	No	No	Yes (conditional targets on buildings, renewable energy, water, gender, finance,)	Antigua & Barbuda's 2015-2020 National Action Plan: Combatting Desertification, Land Degradation & Drought	
Argentina	No	No	Yes (as reflected in Adaptation Communication of Argentina)	Law 27520/2019 on Minimum Budgets for Adaptation and Mitigation to Global Climate Change	National Action Plan for Energy and Climate Change 2017; National Plan for the Restoration of Native Forests (PNRBN) 2018
Bahamas	No	No	Yes (target on reducing vulnerability, with components on preparedness, funding, food and water security, ecosystems' management, energy, education, information and monitoring)	2005 National Policy for the Adaptation to Climate Change	Climate Change and Carbon Market Initiatives Act 2022
Barbados	No	No	Yes (though no explicit targets)	Proclamation of the Planning and Development Act (2021); 2021 Physical Development Plan (PDP)	Barbados Comprehensive Disaster Management (CDM) Country Work Programme (CWP) 2019-2023; other policies on tourism, coastal zone management, storm water management, other sectoral plans (agriculture, fisheries, water and health)
Belize	No	No	Yes (with sectoral targets on coastal zone and marine resources, agriculture, fisheries and aquaculture, human health, tourism, forestry and biodiversity, land use, human settlements and infrastructure, water resources)	2014 National Climate Change Policy, Strategy and Action Plan (with focus on priority sectors including agriculture, tourism, energy, forestry and fisheries)	
Bolivia	No	No	Yes (targets for water, forestry and agriculture)	The Mother Earth Law and Integral Development to Live Well (Law No 300/2012); Economic and Social	2016 Supreme Decree No. 2.914 on Deforestation monitoring and control

				Development Plan - PDES 2021-2025	
Brazil	12-May-16	Yes	Yes (reference to country's NAP)		
Chile	07-Sep-17	Yes (Agriculture, Biodiversity, Fisheries and Aquaculture)	Yes (special attention to water)	National Climate Change Strategy 2006; Framework Law on Climate Change 21455/2022	National Policy of Land Management (PNOT) 2021
Colombia	27-Feb-18	No	Yes	National Climate Change Decree (SISCLIMA); Law no 1931/2018 establishing guidelines for the management of climate change	Resolution no. 126/2022 adopting Policy Guidelines for Sustainable Cattle Farming 2022-2050
Costa Rica	05-May-22	No	reference to co-benefits and NAP	National Adaptation Policy 2018-2030 (Decree 41091-MINAE); National Plan of adaptation to Climate Change 2022-2026	Decree No. 41127/2018 creating the National Measuring System for Climate Change
Cuba	No	No	Yes	State Plan for confronting climate change (Tarea Vida) 2017	
Dominica	No	No	Yes (ecosystems, coastal and marine resources, health, agriculture)	Climate Resilience Act 2018; National Resilience Development Strategy 2018-2030; Climate Resilience and Recovery Plan 2020-2030	National Forest Policy 2022
Dominican Republic	No	No	Yes	Law 1-12: National Development Strategy 2030	National Adaptation Strategy for the Agricultural Sector 2014-2020; Climate Change and Gender Action Plan (PAGCC-RD) 2018;
Ecuador	No	No	Yes (energy, agriculture, forestry, water, ecosystems, risk management)	Executive Decree 1815/2009; Executive Decree 495/2010 on Interinstitutional Committee on Climate Change; National Climate Change Strategy 2012-2025; National Climate Change Mitigation Plan (Planmicc)	National Forestry Restoration Program
El Salvador	No	No	Yes (agriculture, ecosystems, cities, electricity, infrastructure, water resources, waste management, health, transport)	National Plan for Climate Change	Action Plan for the restoration of ecosystems and landscapes in El Salvador with an adaptation-based mitigation approach: 2018-2022 project; Environmental strategy for adaptation and mitigation to climate change in the agricultural, forestry and aquaculture sectors 2018; National plan for integrated management of water resources 2018
Grenada	06-Nov-19	Yes (National	only reference to co-	National Climate	

		Climate Change Policy)	benefits and NAP	Change Policy; National Sustainable Development Plan 2020-2035	
Guatemala	02-Aug-19	No	Yes (agriculture, marine coastal zones, forestry and ecosystems, water resources, health, infrastructure)	Framework law to regulate reduction of vulnerability, mandatory adaptation to the effects of climate change, and the mitigation of greenhouse gas effects (Decree of the Congress 7-2013)	National Plan for Innovation and Development 2020-2024 (PLANID)
Guyana	No	No	Yes (agriculture, water)		
Haiti	No	No	Yes (agriculture, fishing, water resources, road infrastructure, coastal zones, health and habitat)		
Honduras	No	No	Yes (water resources, ecosystems, agriculture, infrastructure)	Decree no.297/2013 (Law on Climate Change); National Plan for Adaptation to Climate Change 2018-2030	
Jamaica	No	No	Yes (co-benefits)		
Mexico	No	No	Yes (agriculture)	General Law on Climate Change 2012; Law of General Ecological Balance and Protection of the Environment;	General Law for Sustainable Forest Development 2018;
Nicaragua	No	No	Yes	Presidential Decree 7/2019 establishing the national policy of climate change mitigation and adaptation and creating the national response system to climate change	
Panama	No	No	Yes	National Strategy for Climate Change 2050 (Executive Decree 34/2019)	National plan on climate change for agriculture (PNCCSA) 2018
Paraguay	03-May-20	No	Yes	National Law on Climate Change no. 5875/2017	National Forest Strategy for Sustainable Growth (ENBCS) 2019
Peru	22-Jul-21	No	Yes	Framework Law no 30754/2018 on Climate Change; Supreme Decree 003-2022-MINAM declaring the climate emergency of national interest	Mechanisms of Compensation for Services to Ecosystems (Law No. 30215/2014); National Strategy for the Restoration of Ecosystems and Degraded Forest Lands (ProRest 2021-2030)
Saint Kitts and Nevis	No	No	Yes	National Climate Change Adaptation Strategy 2018	Food and Nutrition Security Policy and Plan of Action 2019
Saint Lucia	21-Sep-18	Yes (Agriculture, Fisheries, Water, Communication Strategy, Monitoring and Evaluation	Yes (link to NAP)	National Environment Policy (NEP) and National Environmental Management Strategy (2004; Revised 2014)	

		Strategy)			
Saint Vincent and the Grenadines	14-Nov-19	No	Yes (coastal zones, water resources, health, agriculture)		
Suriname	02-Jun-20	No	Yes (agriculture)	Policy Development Plan 2017-2021; Multi-Annual Development Plan 2022-2026	Suriname National REDD+ Strategy
Trinidad and Tobago	No	No	Yes (co-benefits)		
Uruguay	03-Dec-19	Yes (Agriculture, Cities, Coastal)	Yes	National Policy for Climate Change 2017; National Action Strategy for Climate Empowerment 2022;	National Adaptation Plan to Climate Variability and Change for Cities and Infrastructures 2018; Law No. 19.772/2019 on Land-use Planning and Sustainable Development of the Coastal Area of the Atlantic Ocean and the Rio de la Plata; National Adaptation Plan to Climate Variability and Change for the Agriculture Sector 2019; Gender and Climate Change Action Plan 2021; National Waste Management Plan 2021
Venezuela	No	No	Yes (agriculture, water resources, mining, health, risk reduction, ecosystems)		

Note: The table is not exhaustive. Other legislation or plans may also exist. Authors examined the main legislative texts available.

Annex B. NDCs and LTS in LAC

Table B.1. General overview of NDCs and LTS in the LAC region

			Fundamentals		Scope and Coverage			Carbon Removal
Country	NDC Submission date	LTS	Relevant Targets	Conditionality	Covers all sectors	Gases coverage	Covers all categories of the IPCC (emissions inventory methodology)	Does it include Carbon Capture and Storage Technologies?
Antigua and Barbuda	Sep-21	No	Net zero by 2040	Conditional	Yes	GHG		No
			·86% renewable energy generation from local resources in the electricity sector by 2030			(CO_2, CH_4, N_2O)		
			·100% all new vehicle sales to be electric vehicles by 2030					
Argentina	Nov-21	Yes 06/11/2022	Climate neutrality by 2050	Absolut unconditional target	Yes	GHG	Yes	No
			-349 MtCO2e by 2030			(CO_2, CH_4, N_2O, HFCs, PFCs)		
Bahamas	Nov-22	No	-30% GHG_{BAU} by 2030	Conditional	Yes	GHG		No
						(CO_2, CH_4, N_2O)		
Barbados	Jul-21	No	Carbon neutrality by 2030		Yes			No
			-35%GHG_{BAU} by 2030 (unconditional)	Unconditional				
			-70% GHG_{BAU} by 2030 (conditional)	Conditional				
Belize	Sep-21	Yes 03/05/2023	Promise of net zero by 2050	Unconditional	Yes	GHG		No
			Sectoral targets			(CO_2, CH_4, N_2O)		
Bolivia	Apr-22	No	Sectoral targets non GHG targets	Conditional and unconditional	Yes	GHG + Black Carbon		No
						(CO_2, CH_4, N_2O, HFCs, PFCs, SF_6, NF_3)		
Brazil	Apr-22	No	Climate neutrality by		Yes	GHG	Yes	No

			2050 -50% GHG_{2005} by 2030	Relative unconditional target		(CO_2, CH_4, N_2O, HFCs, PFCs, SF_6)		
Chile	Apr-20	Yes 03/11/2021	Climate neutrality by 2050 95 MtCO2e by 2030	Absolut unconditional target	Yes	GHG + Black Carbon (CO_2, CH_4, N_2O, HFCs, PFCs, SF_6, NF_3)	Yes	No
Costa Rica	Dec-20	Yes 12/12/2019	Climate neutrality by 2050 9.11 MtCO2e by 2030	Absolut unconditional target	Yes	GHG + BC +Criteria gases (CO_2, CH_4, N_2O, HFCs, PFCs, SF_6), CO, NOx, NMVOC, SO_2 and black carbon	Yes	No
Colombia	Dec-20	Yes 12/11/2021	Climate neutrality by 2050 169.44 MtCO2e by 2030 -51% GHG_{BAU} by 2030 -40% BC_{2014} by 2030	Absolut unconditional target	Yes	GHG + Black Carbon (CO_2, CH_4, N_2O, HFCs, PFCs, SF_6)	Yes	No
Cuba	Dec-20	No	Sectoral targets non GHG targets	Conditional	No	(CO_2, CH_4, N_2O)	No	No
Dominica	July – 2022	No	-45% GHG_{2014} by 2030	Conditional	Yes	(CO_2, CH_4, N_2O, HFCs, NMVOC, SO_2)	Yes	No
Dominican Republic	Dec-20	No	Carbon neutrality by 2050 -27% GHG_{BAU} by 2030 -7% GHG_{BAU} by 2030 -6% BC_{BAU} by 2030	 Conditional Unconditional	Yes	GHG + Black Carbon (CO_2, CH_4, N_2O)	Yes	No
Ecuador	Mar-19	No	-9% GHG_{BAU} by 2025 -21% GHG_{BAU} by 2025	Unconditional Conditional	Yes	GHG + BC +Criteria gases (CO_2, CH_4, N_2O, HFCs, PFCs, SF_6), CO, NOx, NMVOC, SO_2 and black carbon	Yes	No
El Salvador	Dec-21	No	AFOLU climate neutrality by 2050	n/d	Yes	GHG (CO_2, CH_4, N_2O)	Yes	No
Grenada	Nov-20	No	CO2 neutrality	Conditional	Yes	GHG	Yes	No

			only by 2050					
			-40 GHG_{2010} by 2030			(CO_2, CH_4, N_2O, HFCs, PFCs, SF_6)		
Guatemala	May-22	No	-22.6% GHG_{BAU} by 2030	Conditional	Yes	GHG	Yes	No
			-11.2% $GHGI_{BAU}$ by 2030	Unconditional		(CO_2, CH_4, N_2O)		
Guyana	May-16	No	Already CO2 neutral	Conditional	No	CO_2		No
			Sectoral targets	Unconditional				
Haiti	Jun-22	No	-31.8% GHG_{BAU} by 2030	Conditional		GHG		No
			-6.32% GHG_{BAU} by 2030	Unconditional		(CO_2, CH_4, N_2O)		
Honduras	May-21	No	-16% GHG_{BAU} by 2030	Conditional		GHG (CO_2, CH_4, N_2O, HFCs)		No
Jamaica	Jul-22	No	Net zero by 2050	Conditional	No	GHG		No
			-28.5% GHG_{BAU} by 2030					
			-25.4% GHG_{BAU} by 2030	Unconditional		(CO_2, CH_4, N_2O, HFCs)		
Mexico	Nov-22	Yes 16/11/2016	-30% GHG_{BAU} by 2030	Conditional	Yes	GHG + Black Carbon	Yes	No
			-40% GHG_{BAU} by 2030	Unconditional		(CO_2, CH_4, N_2O, HFCs, PFCs, SF_6)		
Nicaragua	Dec-20	No	Sectoral targets	Conditional		GHG (CO_2, CH_4, N_2O, HFCs, PFCs)		No
Panama	Dec-20	No	Climate neutrality by 2050	n/d	Yes	GHG		No
			Sectoral targets			(CO_2, CH_4, N_2O)		
Paraguay	Jul-21	No	Carbon neutral by 2050	Conditional	Yes	GHG + Black Carbon		No
			-20% GHG_{BAU} by 2030					
			-10% GHG_{BAU} by 2030	Unconditional		(CO_2, CH_4, N_2O, HFCs, PFCs, SF_6)		
Peru	Dec-20	No	Climate neutrality by 2050		Yes	GHG	Yes	No
			GHG emissions of 179 $MtCO_2e_{max}$ by 2030	Conditional		(CO_2, CH_4, N_2O, HFCs, PFCs, SF_6)		
			GHG emissions of 208.8 $MtCO_2e_{max}$ by 2030	Unconditional				
Saint Kitts and Nevis	Oct-21	No	Net zero by 2050	Conditional	Yes	CO_2		No
			-61% GHG_{2010} by 2030					

Saint Lucía	Jan-21	No	-7% GHG_{2010} by 2030	Conditional	Energy	GHG + criteria pollutants (CO_2, CH_4, N_2O)		No
Saint Vincent and the Grenadines	Feb-16	No	-22% GHG_{BAU} by 2025	Unconditional	Yes	GHG (CO_2, CH_4, N_2O, HFCs)		No
Surinam	Dec-19	No	Already CO_2 neutral Sectoral targets	Conditional	Yes	GHG (CO_2, CH_4, N_2O)		Yes
Trinidad and Tobago	Feb-18	No	-15% GHG_{BAU} by 2030	Conditional	Energy	GHG (CO_2, CH_4, N_2O		No
Uruguay	Dec-22	Yes 12/12/2021	CO_2 neutrality only by 2050 Sectoral targets	Conditional and unconditional		GHG (CO_2, CH_4, N_2O, HFCs)		No
Venezuela	Nov-21	No	-20% GHG_{BAU} by 2030	Conditional	No	No		No

1. 11 $MtCO_2e$ by 2030
2. 44 $MtCO_2e$ by 2030
Note: Climate neutrality refers to net-zero emissions on all GHGs (or at least CO_2, CH_4 and N_2O); both "net zero" and "carbon neutrality" are considered to be ambiguous terms since it is not clear which gases the countries aim to cover, and therefore their GHG scope should be considered as unclear. Brazil and Mexico allow higher emissions levels than the targets established in their 2016 NDCs.
Source: (UNFCCC, 2023[1]); (UNFCCC, 2023[2]).

References

UNFCCC (2023), *Long-term strategies portal*, https://unfccc.int/process/the-paris-agreement/long-term-strategies (accessed on 2023). [2]

UNFCCC (2023), *NDC Registry*, https://unfccc.int/NDCREG (accessed on 2023). [1]

www.ingramcontent.com/pod-product-compliance
Lightning Source LLC
Chambersburg PA
CBHW061216240926
51846CB00006B/1241